Benev

Benevolent Barons

*American Worker-Centered
Industrialists, 1850–1910*

QUENTIN R. SKRABEC, JR.

McFarland & Company, Inc., Publishers

Jefferson, North Carolina

LIBRARY OF CONGRESS CATALOGUING-IN-PUBLICATION DATA

Skrabec, Quentin R.
    Benevolent barons : American worker-centered industrialists,
1850–1910 / Quentin R. Skrabec, Jr.
        p.   cm.
    Includes bibliographical references and index.

    ISBN 978-0-7864-9494-1 (softcover : acid free paper) ∞
    ISBN 978-1-4766-2029-9 (ebook)

    1. Industrialists—United States—Case studies.   2. Capitalists and
financiers—United States—Case studies.   3. Capitalism—United
States—History.   4. Industrial relations—United States—History.
5. Labor—United States—History.   6. United States—Economic
conditions.   I. Title.

HC102.5.A2S5547 2015
338.097309'034—dc23   2015019342

BRITISH LIBRARY CATALOGUING DATA ARE AVAILABLE

On the cover: view of the blast furnaces, Steel Works, Homestead, PA,
1907 (Library of Congress)

Printed in the United States of America

*McFarland & Company, Inc., Publishers
    Box 611, Jefferson, North Carolina 28640
    www.mcfarlandpub.com*

Our Lady of Montligeon and
souls and hearts of
Pittsburghers past and future

Acknowledgments

I would like to especially thank Alesha Shumar, archivist at University of Michigan. Once again I would like to thank the outstanding help of the staff of the Benson Research Center at The Henry Ford. In particular, Peter Kalinski was invaluable in my research. They have been at the core of building my literary pantheon, which contains many names honored in Greenfield Village such as H.J. Heinz, Edward Drummond Libbey, William McKinley, George Westinghouse, and William McGuffey. Furthermore, Greenfield Village and The Henry Ford gave endless hours of inspiration. Also the University of Pittsburgh librarians, especially Wendy Pfleg, plus Barry Ched and Gil Pietrzak of the Carnegie Library of Oakland. This library, the philanthropic gift of Andrew Carnegie, was the first library I ever entered, and it remains my first stop for any research. Thanks also to Julie Ludwig, associate archivist of the Frick Collection (New York), and Greg Langel of the Frick Center in Pittsburgh. Thanks, of course, to the Library of Congress and its staff. The Heinz History Center was a true treasure both for its archives and inspiration for this effort. I would also like to thank the many supportive associates at the University of Findlay.

Table of Contents

Preface

I am a product of industrial paternalism. Braddock Hospital in Pittsburgh, where my father, mother, and I were born, was a gift from the area's great industrialists. My family worshipped at St. Thomas Catholic Church, a gift of steel baron Charles Schwab. I found wonder in the Carnegie Library of Swissvale. As I grew older, a streetcar ride opened up more than ten Carnegie libraries in nearby burghs. The main Carnegie Library and Museum in Oakland revealed the world to me, offering an array of courses for young students. The Carnegie system made education and opportunity available to thousands of steel workers' children. The huge Frick Park, where I spent my childhood in play and nature study, was a gift of the great capitalist Henry Clay Frick. In grade school, industrial philanthropy offered me a scholarship to study engineering at Pittsburgh's Buhl Planetarium. My full academic scholarship at the University of Michigan also came from industrial philanthropy, as did my master's degree at Ohio State. I had no inside edge other than my academic performance and prayer. Today such opportunities have disappeared with deindustrialization and the growth of government.

It is not *en vogue* to honor famous American industrialists and capitalists these days. Most are remembered as robber barons or capitalist pigs. They are best known for their extremes, but more often they were just like us except with endless amounts of money. They suffered from the same sins and held to the same virtues as most of us. They could be mean, ruthless, and vindictive as well as openhearted and giving. Their lives were often contradictory. They were no more saints or devils than most of us. We can all be greedy; it is often only the scale that we see. Reading their letters,

1

you come to see that it was only money (with all its problems and blessings) that separated them from us.

A pantheon of great industrialists is not one of saints and angels. These were men of complexities and contradictions, like Henry Ford, who advanced black workers in industry and built plants to employ the handicapped at full wages, yet showed racism and hatred towards the Jews. There was Frick, who was blinded by his hatred of unions and bloody strikes, yet anonymously gave $80 million to hospitals, schools, families, and the poor. Andrew Carnegie earned over $300 million on the backs of immigrant workers, only to give it all away.

They made American capitalism work without the social revolution of Europe. They often spent money in a wasteful manner, while giving millions to the community. Critics often cried they should have given more in direct wages, but most often the beneficiaries were not the workers of the time, but their sons, daughters, and grandchildren. Yet it is in gratitude that I have done over forty years of research into these men. My grandfather Skrabec, a steelworker, was proud to have worked for these capitalists who were often considered evil. He passed on that pride with endless stories and trips to industrial sites. These American industrialists were tough businessmen, but not the lions of Wall Street. They were builders of industry and community. Some gave all their money back, while others balanced their own luxurious living with giving back. Some, at the ends of their lives, regretted not paying or treating their workers better. Some of them, like George Westinghouse and H.J. Heinz, tried to create industrial utopias. Even the worst of them built hospitals, schools, poorhouses, parks, museums, and community programs.

Westinghouse deserves a special place in any pantheon of great American capitalists. He embodies the best of American capitalism. The Westinghouse Memorial, dedicated on October 6, 1930, in Pittsburgh, reflects that. The memorial was the result of voluntary donations from over sixty thousand employees of the many companies he founded. An employee built memorial is a rarity. It was meant to be a reflection of the man they knew. Today it is a quiet spot surrounded by key roads for that section of Pittsburgh, but any visitor can feel the spirit of a great man.

The Westinghouse Memorial is not easy to locate since highway bypasses have been added, and traffic in Pittsburgh's Schenley Park area has increased. However, there is no better place to start learning about paternalism in capitalism than at the Westinghouse Memorial. The memorial features a bronze statue of a young man looking at three wall panels of granite and bronze. At first glance, I must admit I didn't get it. I assumed the statue was a youthful George Westinghouse, which it is not. It is a youth looking with inspiration at Westinghouse's accomplishments, and that is the real message of the memorial.

The Whig Party politically created the environment for employee-based capitalism in the early nineteenth century. I consider myself a Whig in search of a party. Employee-driven capitalism required a blend of nationalism, a love of democracy, and capitalism. Capitalism, like its root democracy, contains the full range of humanity. Like democracy, capitalism has no inherent moral requirements. Still, like democracy, its long-term sustainability depends on a concern for one's fellow man. Capitalism is based on the personal freedom of democracy. The paternal capitalism was a voluntary arrangement and an ideal. In the long run, because of man's own weakness, it cannot replace the need for government regulation. Still, there are American capitalists who can be examples for our youth. The great paternal capitalists such as George Westinghouse, H.J. Heinz, Peter Cooper, and others depended on Whig and McKinley Republicanism to protect wages and industrial growth in America. The golden years of paternalism and community philanthropy were the result of a unified political and manufacturing philosophy. It was a national focus versus an international capitalism. I believe that America is not lacking in Westinghouses and Coopers, but in politicians such as Henry Clay and William McKinley.

Introduction

Capitalists and industrialists are often characterized as Scrooge, but American capitalism has a far different history from that of European capitalism. Capitalists come in all stripes, morally reflecting the human population and its culture. In different times, American capitalists were the only sources of funds for hospitals, libraries, welfare money, and other community needs. American capitalism arose naturally from our frontier experience, not from political philosophers. In its earliest form, it was an evolving way of life. American capitalism grew out of the needs of the community, not the individual. It was tempered by moral and religious standards. It was the "city on the hill," but it still had all the fallen nature of human systems. Capitalism, like any economic system, can be abused. Unrestrained capitalism can overlook the needs of the less fortunate or accumulate wealth at the expense of the worker. As abuses rose, the government was forced to regulate. However, it is not government regulation alone but moral values that are needed. In fact, government and capitalism can join in corruption (crony capitalism). From Pope Leo XIII to Pope Francis, all have opposed state socialism, while noting the inherent dangers in unregulated capitalism. Corruption comes from men and not from any economic system; therefore, culture, morals, and values are key to the proper functioning of capitalism. Unfortunately, the moral integrity of capitalism is a reflection of society and the education offered by society. Still, capitalism has the potential to bring out the best of men also. The state of capitalism is truly a reflection of the culture in which it operates, and therefore, the responsibility of all of us.

Today capitalism is called an economic system, but national capitalism of earlier times in America was a natural extension of our political freedom and moral values. Paul Litchfield, president of Goodyear Tire in the 1920s, summarized the concept of capitalism: "Strictly speaking, it is not a system at all. It is merely the right of an individual to earn his living in any way he chooses (except force or fraud), using the gifts God gave him—and to keep what he makes. Freedom is the essence of it, and the incentives it offers. Men of accomplishment are the thing that gives it life and vitality."[1] It is the role of society to develop the virtues that lead these successful individuals to give back. Americans have never asked for income equality, but they have always demanded equal opportunity. Americans have also demonstrated a concern for the less fortunate in society.

Our forefathers rejected the idea that one was born into a permanent position in life. They didn't ask to be born rich but demanded equal opportunity such as education and training. Property was to be earned, not a birthright. This was far different from the world they left. Wealth and education were limited to aristocracy. The poor depended on the benevolence of the aristocracy and the charity of the church. Inability to pay debts resulted in prison. America was built on self-reliance, freedom, and access of all to education. The care of the poor and the disabled was the responsibility of all.

The wealthy did have a social responsibility for the less fortunate on the American frontier. This responsibility was derived from their Christian belief system, not from their state in life. Freedom cut both ways in America. The problems of the poor were seen as an individual problem for all of us, not a system or government problem. Yet America was paternal in its nature. All Americans were called by their Judeo-Christian principles to care for the less fortunate. Unlike Europe paternalism, it was not systematic in America, but cultural. In Europe, paternalism was part of feudal economic arrangement. The Puritans saw ethics and moral values as the heart of successful business and community. Charity was the jewel in the crown of their Christianity.

Charity and giving were part of the American educational system begun by the pilgrims. For over a century, schools made use of schoolbooks such as the *Webster Reader* and *McGuffey Reader*. These readers portray Christian charity as part of justice. Story after story teaches giving generously to the poor; and there are more stories on helping the poor than any other theme. McGuffey put such charity ahead of work and industry. And McGuffey took charity beyond virtue to the level of kindness. He saw charity as a duty for all. McGuffey, in particular, argued it was an individual obligation, not a government one. The poor were not only to be fed, but just as important was the duty to educate them. Charity was the virtue that was linked to the stewardship as a responsibility of the rich. McGuffey's type of capitalism was morally based. Many great philanthropists such as George Westinghouse, George Pullman, Henry Clay Frick, Henry Ford, Andrew Carnegie, Edward Libbey, Michael Owens, and H.J. Heinz were trained on the *McGuffey Reader* and attributed their views to it. One historian noted that "the 'Gospel of Wealth' in its essentials, was simply a reaffirmation of the Christian doctrine of the stewardship of great riches owing less to Herbert Spencer [exponent of Social Darwinism] than to William Holmes McGuffey and Horatio Alger [author of Rags-to-Riches books]."[2] Even the worst of the robber barons felt compelled by their training and society to give back to the community.

McGuffey's foundational principle, that it was the responsibility of the wealthy to help the poor, had an impact on the Gilded Age. The *Oxford Guide to United States History* noted: "The years from 1870 to 1900 saw an unprecedented burst of economic growth in the United States that generated vast wealth for new captains of industry, and in turn, opened a fresh chapter in the history of American philanthropy."[3] No single issue dominated the *McGuffey Readers* more than individual charity and giving. As early as Lesson VII in the *First Reader*, a young reader is told to be kind to a beggar, and the first premise of the Golden Rule is introduced: "We should be kind to the poor. We may be as poor as this old man, and need as much as he." A lesson later in the story of "Little Henry" is an even more powerful example of sharing: "John gave some of his cake to each of his school mates, and then took a piece for himself. He gave the rest to an old blind man." These are extremely powerful lessons for the young mind. These lessons continued as the student's reading progressed. In the *Second Reader*: "They did not ask for it, but she saw that they were in great need, which reminded her to share with them." In the *Third Reader*'s story, "The Way to Be Happy," another plea: "I will give you an infallible rule. Do all in your power to make others happy. Be willing to make sacrifices of your own convenience to promote the happiness of others."[4]

These early moralistic principles found in American education set the foundation for philanthropy as well as employee oriented companies. Some capitalists of the Gilded Age such as Andrew Carnegie saw philanthropy to the community as employee-focused; others, such as Peter Cooper, believed that supporting free education for worker families was employee-focused, while others such as George Westinghouse believed in improving the workers' life at the plant and home as employee focused. These early industrialists believed government was not part of the workplace. Many believed government regulation could help prevent abuses, but it did not foster management's employee concern. History would show the importance of government and unions to assure long-term employee protection; but in the end, the best protection is an employee-focused management.

Capitalism is often challenged today as a system, as it was in its earliest days. It is based on self-improvement, or for the critic, greed. Without a moral guide (or government regulation), it has a propensity for abuse. The failure of the leaders of capitalism can hurt many in society. The success of society and capitalists is entrusted to the industrialists themselves. Government cannot replace moral values in its effort to prevent abuses. Unethical persons often succeed in the freedom of our democratic and capitalistic nation. Too often ethics, moral values, and religious beliefs are viewed as roadblocks to profits. Great ethical capitalists of our past such as George Westinghouse and H.J. Heinz, however, not only applied ethics in their business, but showed that ethics and moral behavior can lead to more profits. Industrialists like Robert Owen showed that the better the treatment of employees, the better the profits.

The history of American capitalism's success can be found in its prudent regulation. Initially, the bounds were set by a moralistic culture of our forefathers such as the pilgrims. Later government regulation was needed to patch holes in the declining morality of society. Finally, the union movement of leaders such as Samuel Gompers enforced better treatment for the worker into the governance of the workplace. Today capitalism is harnessed by unions and government, but a better control is the moral code of an owner. Governance is reactive by nature, but moralistic education is preventive. It is the unique history of capitalism in America that is far different from that of Europe. Still, even with all the protective bounds, the success of capitalism remains dependent on the morals of society. There is no substitute for a moral and caring owner or a paternal manager. No government or union protection can contain the misguided greed of men. It is the society of men that sets the foundational rules of moral behavior.

This is the story of those accomplished Americans who balanced the natural wealth accumulation of capitalism with community and employees. It is not hagiography but a look at some capitalists who represented the best approaches. Industrialists like George Westinghouse were employee-centered, believing their own destiny was tied to their employees and communities. Other "paternal" capitalists, such as Andrew Carnegie, approached paternalism in the manner of an economic plantation owner. Others such as Vanderbilt and Morgan saw capitalism as pure wealth accumulation without any communal responsibility. Still, America was blessed with many capitalists who gave back to the community in some form. Some like Marshall Fields were reluctant philanthropists pressured by society. However, America stood apart from Europe in its brand of paternalism. The community workplace relationship had deep roots in America going back to the Puritans. The idea of paternal capitalism is not fully dead; it still exists in small-town America. Small businesses still see themselves as part of the community and have personal relationships with their employees and give freely to community projects.

One

The Puritan Experiment

While short-lived, the Plymouth Colony (1620–1691) has a special place in American business history and formed a pillar for work in America. By necessity, it was a working community, part economic slavery, part colony, and part commune at its beginnings. The Puritans (Pilgrims) were looking for religious freedom through an economic contract with investors. They were indentured to the trading company. Still, this system of indenture would differ much from the feudal system of Europe. The indentured servant could expect to become a property owner at some point, while the feudal system was a life sentence of serfdom. Distribution of food and wealth was at the discretion of the lord or aristocrat in the feudal system, and land ownership was restricted to the upper class. Even the choice of religion was at the discretion of the king or lord.

The Plymouth colony was founded in November of 1620 by a group of Christian Separatists from the Anglican Church of England. Known in Europe as the Puritans, the group first moved to Holland, but found little freedom for their religious practices. These American Pilgrim colonists were a radical fraction of Puritans who left Holland to obtain freedom of religion as well as to escape the hard times of the early 1600s. They felt called by the Gospel of Matthew to establish the "Kingdom of God," and were financed by a group of wealthy investors who hoped to profit in the New World. These venture capitalists formed a joint stock company known as the Virginia Company of London, having a royal charter issued in 1606. The Virginia Company had been behind the failed Jamestown Colony, which by 1620, was paying some small dividends with a cash tobacco crop. They hoped for a similar profit in New England with furs,

11

fish, and crops. The Pilgrims were considered indentured servants by the company, with all property having communal ownership. The investors of the company supplied the managers or overseers. They initially argued against communal ownership but were left with no choice. The Pilgrims, for their part, never viewed themselves as indentured servants but as paying taxes to the company. It was an unclear and disputed vision, but all property was under communal ownership. Even the houses they built were considered communal property and could be reassigned. Wealth was redistributed by government to the poor. Work requirements were also defined by the investment company. This initial model of communal ownership has been called both exploitative capitalism and communism. Contrary to views held by some, the communal pact was not based on their religious beliefs but forced on the Pilgrims by the management company. Privatization of property would prove to be evolutionary in the colonies.

The Pilgrims came to New England on the *Mayflower* and on the *Speedwell* in 1620. It was on the *Mayflower* that John Winthrop, in a fiery sermon, proclaimed the mission of the new colony as: "We must consider that we will be a city on the hill, and the eyes of all upon us."[1] Winthrop further defined that city as based on the Christian principles of every citizen, put-

Landing of Pilgrims in 1620, published by Currier and Ives in 1876 (Library of Congress).

ting the needs of the community above the individual desires. The sermon is now known as "A Model for Christian Charity." The idea of a holy commonwealth went back to John Calvin.[2] It was an idea exploited by chartered investors of Plymouth. Still, the Puritans were far from socialists or communists. They merely believed the less fortunate in a community were the responsibility of the whole community and the responsibility of each individual. They strongly believed in class and economic divides as part of God's plan, arguing that all should be happy with their lot in life. What was different was the communal responsibility to the less fortunate. However, they made a distinction between the "worthy poor" and the "idle poor." They were intolerant of the "idle poor," who refused to do at least communal work. The idea of work as central to human existence was at the core of Puritan beliefs.

The Puritans believed that charity would further corrupt the idle poor. They believed that charity could foster a class of beggars. The idle poor were encouraged to leave the Puritan community. The definition and differences between the idle poor and the "worthy" remains a matter of debate to this day. Many Americans draw such a distinction when they approach a beggar. From its roots, America has been able to find a middle ground in its approach, evolving from the Puritan view of the Pilgrims and incorporating Catholic concepts of social justice of the nineteenth-century immigrants. The evolution of American religious thought saw charity as part of social justice, but one to be left to the individual versus government. The original American Puritans, the Pilgrims, did set the basis for our nation's view of work and the dignity of the worker. They preferred giving jobs to the poor instead of handouts. Many view the Puritans' approach to the poor as harsh.

The American approach evolved based on Christian ideas in a new environment. The Pilgrims faced something new in the exodus from Europe. They were leaving civilization with its social infrastructure and safety nets. They would depend on themselves, each other, and God to survive and prosper. There would be no king, lords, or government. A cry for help would take years for any response. In such an environment, God becomes critical to survival. The Puritans had to deal with human nature as well as a harsh physical environment. There was no manual or guide for what they were about to face. Their idealism would be challenged and needed to be modified to fit the problems. The "city on the hill" would have to be built with human shortcomings.

In total, there were 120 Pilgrims on the journey, with a smaller group known as the "strangers." The "strangers" were hired as managers of the company, which included Miles Standish as the colony's military leader and Christopher Martin as Royal Governor. The first year proved the most difficult, with the ships arriving in late fall with no growing season left. Nearly half the colonists died the first winter. It was only by the aid of the local Indians who allowed for a solid planting of corn in the spring that the colonists survived. They managed to construct a common house for living quarters. The harsh environment soon changed the idealistic concept of forming a holy commonwealth.

Reform Governor William Bradford kept a diary of the plantation (*Of Plymouth Plantation*), detailing social breakdown under the communal ownership system. Initially, the Pilgrims were forced to beg and steal from the Indians, but even the first planting and building of houses proved disastrous. Bradford described a culture of "free-riding." Elderly, sick, young, and women soon excluded themselves from communal labor. Others tended not to pull their weight under the communal economic model. Even the most able men were soon angered by having to support free-riding and reduced their effort. William Bradford decried the communal system as the root of the problem. Bradford noted in his diary: "For the young men, that were the most able and fit for labor and service, did repine that they should spend their time and strength to work for other's men's wives and children without any recompense. The strong, or man of parts, had no more division of victuals and clothes than that of the weak and not able to do a quarter the other could; this was thought an injustice."[3] Bradford's solution was to give a plot of land to the colonists for their own use.

The Pilgrims were surely aware of the limited success at Jamestown when the colonists were given a small plot of land to work as their own while maintaining a communal framework. Jamestown had really taken the first step towards an American system. By 1621, the Jamestown colony had limited private property, but the communal system still required a tax on private earnings and a requirement for communal work of several months a year. Jamestown's approach (while limited) offered a new possibility of management for the struggling Plymouth Colony. The approach at Plymouth Plantation put private ownership ahead of communal requirements by necessity.

The Pilgrims' initial immigration to Holland had given them knowledge of the emerging system of capitalism. The Dutch trading companies and automated manufacture of the 1600s led Holland to be considered the birthplace of capitalism. The Pilgrims had seen both the creation of great wealth and the rise of unemployment in Holland. Puritans had the first opportunity to apply paternal capitalism in a new world and a new system.

Bradford and Plymouth faced a crisis point in the spring of 1623. The colony was down to four adult women and was dependent on the Indians for daily survival. The Plymouth Plantation was a failure, from the perspective of its investors, with little hope of any return on their investment. A visit of Tom Weston, a wealthy investor and iron manufacturer disguised as a blacksmith, helped change things. Weston was charged with saving the investment. It was clear to him that poor morale was the root of the colony's failure.

Based on Weston's analysis, Governor Bradford made the decision to fully convert to private property. Bradford reported the amazing success: "For it made all hands industrious.... The women now went willingly into the field, and took their little ones with them to set corn; which before would allege weakness and inability."[4] The new system made the colony profitable and would be the new model for future settlements. The system also proved compatible with their religious beliefs, as the colonists gave freely of their surplus to help the less fortunate. Still, the model of their giving was modified. It would augur the American system of capitalism and philanthropy. The Puritan methodology for charitable giving was changed by this experience to giving to those who could not help themselves or were totally incapable of productive work. Later, American capitalists such as John Rockefeller and Andrew Carnegie would subscribe to this approach. The taxation model of the colony would also be a model for a government role in communal needs. Home ownership strengthened and motivated house building in the colony. The collapse of the Puritan collective experiment would also augur the failure of collectivized agriculture by twentieth-century communist nations. It served as a case study for Adam Smith's premise of individual effort and self-interest as an economic force. Adam Smith's principles would argue against the economic waste of slavery and colonization.

The economic success and freedom soon became a beacon for the Puritans of Europe. In 1640, there were 18,000 Puritans in New England; and by 1700, there were over 100,000. New England's approach was oriented to colonization via families. While the wealthy families were still favored, individuals were not granted land. Groups of families were given a land grant for a town. The town then distributed lots for private homes. The town was designed with a common or communal center (also known as a "green") for the grazing of livestock. The necessary grain mill for producing flour was a communal operation as well. The entire town constructed the grain mill as well as a meetinghouse for governance, plus roads and bridges. Firefighting was a communal function, as was defense. As the

New England towns grew and prospered (like those in the South), New England experienced a servant and general laborer shortage. Unlike the South, they resisted slavery. New England found a communal solution. The biggest source of servants were community-assigned orphans and widowed mothers. Another source was labor from those being punished for crimes. Young boys were often "indentured" to craftsmen to learn a trade. The community elders would often require wealthy craftsmen to take on orphans or children from struggling families. The boy apprentices received room and board for their work.

In addition, within the family, Puritan children were put to work early in farm work and household work. The labor shortage also created a communal effort for individual families. House raisings and barn raisings were common in these efforts. Farmers often shared efforts during the harvest. Sharing of food in hard times was considered a virtue. The Puritan model promoted communal help while believing in a class structure. Private property was a fundamental right. The wealthy were not to be envied, but to be accepted as part of God's plan. For their part, the wealthy were expected to contribute to the overall good of the community. There was a type of communal tax that was taken in food or goods. This allowed for a communal fund for those in need that was overseen by the town elders and the town meeting. Wealthy citizens were expected to give more in communal help and charity, but it was an individual's responsibility not enforced by government. They were sensitive to the earlier failures of their initial communal government to enforce and mandate a redistribution of wealth. This responsibility of the wealthy was reinforced in the early education of their youth.

The Puritans' success required the development of cottage industries to support their farming communities. Like all early immigrants, the Puritans moved west to find prosperity. One of the earliest of these movements was to the Connecticut River Valley in 1636. The Connecticut River starts in the mountains of New Hampshire and cuts through Vermont, Massachusetts, and Connecticut into Long Island Sound. In the early 1600s, some Pilgrims and Dutch had fur trading operations instead of farming. It was an extremely fertile valley, which drew immigrants from New York and Pennsylvania. More importantly, the Connecticut River was a huge energy source. The river's fall over its length is estimated to generate an energy potential greater than that of Niagara Falls. The river could support power for gristmills and iron furnaces, making farming more economically successful. The power of the Connecticut River caused a mixing of nationalities and the emergence of American manufacturing. The Valley would birth manufacturers such as Eli Whitney, Samuel Colt, Francis Lowell, Cyrus Buckland, Thomas Blanchard, Alexander Holly, and George Westinghouse. The ethnic mixing retained the Protestant work ethic and economic drive of the Puritans. The Connecticut Valley would launch the Machine Age in America.

It would be in the Connecticut Valley that Puritans applied their communal system to manufacturing organizations. The valley offered all that was needed for iron production which was ideal for community manufacture. The remoteness of valley iron production required the building of a town or community. John Winthrop, Jr., son of the governor, went to London to raise capital to build an ironworks. Winthrop, trained in metallurgy and chemistry at Trinity College, is truly America's first industrialist. The colony and England in 1641 were both short on iron and, in particular, iron nails. England had lumbered out most of its hardwood needed to fuel iron furnaces, and thus was open to colonial production. Without colonial iron, England itself would be dependent on Sweden, which was a political enemy. Winthrop got some capital but opened the investment up for colonists as well. A number of Puritan ministers invested. Saugus Works became very successful at producing iron products, but it struggled for capital throughout its existence. Saugus was America's first large industrial complex, having an iron furnace, rolling mill, and slitting mill. The operation supplied housing and community resources for the workers.

Labor, however, would be the downfall. New England was extremely short on labor for manufacturing efforts; as a result, indentured servants from England were used. These men and families got passage to America and the ironworks supplied board, food, and necessities. The indentured servant was committed to five to seven years of service. This model of getting European workers would continue into the 1900s. The early iron plantation system required hundreds of workers to run the furnace, grow crops, and make necessities. The Puritans wanted Puritans to form the iron-working towns, but the minority of the investors had no interest in a theocracy. The problem was these workers were not Puritans but often criminals or prisoners. British investors tried to help England by eliminating "undesirables." In 1651, more than 60 Scottish prisoners of war captured by Cromwell at Dunbar were brought to Saugus Iron Works. Workers resented the Puritans' religious mode of living. The problem appeared to be their system of communal property and the status of many colonists as indentured servants. Since they had no property rights and their production went into communal stores, the indentured servants lacked motivation and upward mobility. Puritans believed unskilled workers should be happy with their lot in life, and all work honored God. Non-Puritan indentured servants, however, wanted the ability to move up in society. In many ways, but for different reasons, Puritan iron plantations lacked upward mobility of the type found in Europe. It was difficult to build a community, and much time was wasted in punishment of the workers for not meeting Puritan social standards. Workers gained skills but moved on after indentured service.

This propensity of American capitalists to treat workers well while imposing social standards would become a paradigm. The fusion of religious standards and work can be seen throughout American history in manufacturing communities as well as in private industry. As late as the 1940s, industrialists like Henry Ford had sociological departments to impose moral standards on workers. The Puritans, however, took things to extremes trying to impose their rigid religious views.

Industrialists of other colonies took advantage of the unhappy workers. The path to extinction for the Puritan communal manufacture was rooted in the American Protestant inherent tendency to branch off religiously. The Puritan focus on individual autonomy of congregations further fostered that Protestant heritage. While the Puritans allowed congregational freedom, there were dogma restrictions that required the government and Christianity to be tied together. Puritans in Massachusetts and Connecticut operated a theocracy. Roger Williams of Massachusetts, a strict Puritan, saw things differently. He believed in separation of church and state. In 1634, he was banished from Massachusetts and started the colony of Rhode Island. Rhode Island, like Pennsylvania, was based on religious tolerance. Jews, Catholics, atheists, and freethinkers were actually encouraged to come to Rhode Island. The Dutch and the Quakers came on their own. Rhode Island quickly became a mixing bowl and the most secular of the early colonies. The tolerance was even greater than that of the Quakers. Communal iron manufacturing started to prosper in these new colonies.

The Puritans, however, left their mark on the American industrial worker, manager, and society. The "protestant work ethic" would become part of the culture. The need to build community in the workplace was a core principle of the Puritans. In 1831 when Alex de Tocqueville came to America, he said of the influence of the Puritans: "Among them was the proliferation of associations he found in each state, city, town, and village addressing the various needs of the citizenry. In Europe, only the state and its agencies [this included the church], he argued, provided such services."[5] The idea of the wealthy giving back to the community was another core principle. The Puritans' almost unbridled approach to capitalism could only be justified to their religious beliefs by the belief in charity as the highest virtue and a requirement of their faith. This virtue was directed at individuals, not the government. Puritan communities supported the less fortunate through individual charity and communal funds. They had no tolerance for those able-bodied members who tried to avoid work.

Centuries later, the famous German sociologist Max Weber (1864–1920) credited the Puritans with the foundation of American capitalism in his book, *The Protestant Ethic and the Spirit of Capitalism,* Weber particularly emphasized the Puritan approach, promoting hard work versus unfettered charity. Weber correctly identified the Puritan root of capitalism but overlooked the Christian virtue of charity, which was essential to American capitalism. Unlike the unrestrained early capitalism, the Puritans added a paternal element of community. Weber also missed the modifications made later by integrating Catholic social justice into the approach. American capitalism was far from heartless but reflected the melting pot of many religions and paternal views.

The Puritans fostered a paternal, communal, class-rigid, theocratic style of business. The labor shortage, unfortunately, required the use of indentured servants for unskilled labor to maintain economic growth. Indentured servants were treated well, but had no future. Puritans, to their credit, had rejected chattel slavery as an alternative, even though slavery was legal in the colony. Unskilled labor was needed in all of the Puritans' industrial enterprises. America had become a nation of craftsmen, skilled workers, traders, and merchants with an extreme shortage of unskilled labor. For centuries, industrialists would have to recruit unskilled laborers from Europe. As late as 1910, American industrialists were recruiting in Europe for unskilled laborers in exchange for passage and room and board. The need to take care of these new unskilled labors became the responsibility of the manufacturer. The Puritans offered training and education to the indentured servants and their families.

One of the most important legacies of the Puritans to business was their moral and cultural ideals. American education would, for centuries, reflect the importance of giving back and taking care of the poor. The Puritans infused religion and work into a new type of capitalism. Puritan moral capitalism was reflected in the dominance of textbooks such as *McGuffey* and *Webster Readers*. These school texts brought Christian moral values to daily living. It was this moral view of wealth that built a moral foundation for American capitalism. William McGuffey was not a Puritan, but a Scotch-Irish Pennsylvanian. McGuffey, however, was himself a product of Puritan education. McGuffey's legacy was his ability to blend the strict biblical approach of the Puritans into a moralistic nondenominational approach of the Scotch-Irish and the Germans. This Puritan based moral approach favored hard work as well as charity to those who could not help themselves, or the incapable of society. Most importantly, *McGuffey Readers* incorporated the Scotch-Irish belief that the wealthy have a moral responsibility to help the least of society, which was also consistent with the Puritan experiment. The focus was on every individual, not government rules or taxes, to redistribute to the poor.

William McGuffey and Daniel Webster can be credited with much of the success of the Gilded Age by transforming the religious strictness of the Puritans into a pragmatic, moralistic, and individualistic approach to business. Abraham Lincoln called William McGuffey "Schoolmaster of the Nation." McGuffey was not a politician, but many believe that his Hamilton-Federalist-Whig stream of thinking led to the progressive republicanism of Lincoln, McKinley, and Teddy Roosevelt (all of whom were trained on *McGuffey Readers*). Teddy Roosevelt would often relate to McGuffey characters, realizing all in the nation recognized them. The love of the *McGuffey Readers* also cut across party lines. William Jennings Bryan, McKinley's Democratic opponent in 1896 and 1900, also attributed his belief system to the *McGuffey Readers*. The progressive Robert Lafollette was another political liberal of the Gilded Age who said he owed a debt to McGuffey. Even post–World War presidents such as Harry Truman praised the *McGuffey Readers*. President Truman often praised the books for "educating for ethics as well as intellect, building character along with vocabulary."[6]

The texts were the source of knowledge and motivation for American industrialists such as Henry Ford, Andrew Carnegie, H.J. Heinz, George Westinghouse, Henry Clay Frick, Thomas Edison, and John D. Rockefeller, as well as the founder of Kroger Company, A.H. Morrill. Maybe just as important was McGuffey, who inspired generations of hard-working and moralistic workers. McGuffey and his *Readers* laid the foundation for American capitalism.

Two

Genesis of an Industrial Race

The rise of American capitalism came from a confluence of ideas from the Puritans, Scotch-Irish, and Germans. America became a magnet for the unskilled and skilled workers of Europe in search of an economic future. For the Irish, British, and Scotch-Irish, it was partly a quest for political and religious freedom. For Germans and French, religious freedom was the chief motivator. But for all Europeans, it was the hope of owning property someday and a brighter economic future. The feudal village of Europe had developed into a landlord-tenant system. In this system, the landlord owned everything, and the peasant worked the fields paying rent in crop harvest. Free laborers did evolve, but failure to pay bills usually meant jail. Free laborers soon became the working or imprisoned poor. The guild craftsmen were being rapidly eliminated as well, and automation was reducing the need for skilled laborers.

On the other side of the Atlantic, the labor shortage was the main roadblock for economic growth. Skilled and unskilled labor were badly needed. The colonists formed associations to have indentured servants shipped to the colonies. There were common agreements committing the crown, owners, and associations to supply 50 acres of land to the servant at the end of his servitude.[1] The colonies enacted laws to promote the shipping of indentured servants. For Europe, it was a pressure valve release for the social unrest of the unemployed.

The indentured servant system was incapable of fulfilling the needs of the American nation. The South required massive amounts of cheap labor. The indentured servant was too costly and unstable to run the crown-controlled plantation system. Slavery was the other option in labor-short

21

America. The North often restricted the use of slaves via religious opposition. To fill the need for skilled and unskilled labor in the North, further enticements were needed to attract laborers.

The destruction of the guilds put tens of thousands of guild workers into the unskilled ranks, and unemployment became common in Europe. The problem of unemployed workers and free laborers soon became the problem of government to assure political stability throughout Europe. In America, the general labor shortage allowed the guilds to be much more open to all. Master European craftsmen started to emigrate to America. The ambitious youth of America found new opportunity in the crafts not available in Europe. America's craft communities and working industrial plantations offered opportunity for unskilled laborers to learn a craft. This type of opportunity was unheard of in Europe.

The rise of American industry in the western colonies starting in the 1700s would be the engine of immigration. In the 1700s there were a number of rising western manufacturing centers, such as Cincinnati in hog processing, St. Louis in fur trading, New Orleans in trade, and Lexington and Pittsburgh in manufacturing. Outside of New England and eastern Pennsylvania, a vast manufacturing area started to rise on the Allegheny plateau west of the mountains. It was referred to early on as the "Ohio Frontier" or "Ohio Country," but today it includes western Pennsylvania, all of eastern and southern Ohio, the panhandle of West Virginia, and parts of Maryland and Kentucky. The plateau was rich in wood, coal, iron ore, oil, limestone, rye for whiskey, quality industrial clay, and water transportation networks. Since the early 1700s, the Scotch-Irish had created a vast trading network from the American frontier to Europe in furs, whiskey, and ginseng. The Scotch-Irish people were independent and freedom-loving. They were constantly moving west to avoid British taxes and restrictions. The Scotch-Irish established trading posts and then moved west. They were natural capitalists seeking land and money. The Germans took over the posts and established towns and manufacturing centers to supply the frontier.

The American frontier in the 1700s was roughly 40 percent Scotch-Irish, 30 percent to 35 percent English, 10 percent Scotch and Welsh, and 10 percent German. This area was dominated by the Scotch-Irish, who tended to form informal clans. Where possible, the Scotch-Irish used these "clans" to run frontier iron-making operations. The "capital" of the industrial plateau was Pittsburgh, and its main transportation routes were the Ohio River to the west, and the Cumberland Gap to the east. The Scotch-Irish had a deep hatred of the British and their taxes, and thus kept moving their whiskey-making, glass manufacture, and iron-making farther west to avoid British interference.

American manufacturing would become a mixture of German, British, and Scotch-Irish enterprises, but it was the Scotch-Irish who dominated the industry and business. The Scotch-Irish capitalism would also be the seed of American capitalism. The colonial Scotch-Irish iron-makers started on the frontier to avoid the eyes and taxes of the British. They forged a blend of religion and capitalism that made them the most productive of the colonial iron-makers. The Scotch-Irish used the plantation system of the Puritans, but without the religious restrictions. To retain laborers, the Scotch-Irish added a bonus for tons of iron produced. The settlers also dominated the iron hills of Pennsylvania, Maryland, Ohio, and Virginia. They combined whiskey stills and iron-making with fur trading. They had ties to a vast trading network that could export pig iron with shipments of tobacco and furs. As the Scotch-Irish pushed west, Germans immigrants followed, building a supply of much-needed crafts. Lancaster in central Pennsylvania became a supply center for the west.

The German and Scotch-Irish network strengthened through the 1730s as wagons ventured west. Trade brought manufacture to Lancaster such as saddle-making and gunsmithing, to supply the frontier. Lancaster, a growing center for manufacturers, started to attract not only German gunsmiths but also Swiss and Scotch-Irish. In the 1730s, Swiss gunsmith Peter Leman started to develop the "Pennsylvania rifle" at his Lancaster shop. European smoothbore muskets were not suited for hunting in the American backwoods. Leman's new rifle had a longer barrel, improved sights, reduced bore, and better balance. It quickly became popular on the American frontier. By 1740, Lancaster was the capital of American gun manufacture and the home of our greatest gunsmiths. In 1752, General Braddock made a Lancaster Scotch-Irish gunsmith master armorer to his army during the French and Indian War. In the 1770s, Lancaster was critical in supplying the continental army with guns. It became the supply center for the western movement.

Lancaster's population passed 10,000, with leather and clothing trades growing as well. Manufacturing was set up on the guild system of masters-journeymen-apprentices. Apprentices worked for room and board. For diverse products, guilds would cooperate with each other. The city in 1773 had fifteen master weavers, nine master stocking weavers, thirty shoemakers, ten tanners, seven saddlers, five skinners, and two bootmakers. Lancaster was a strong community of independent craftsmen, far different from the feudal towns of Europe or the newly created cities of the Industrial Revolution. The city became a fusion of various fractions of European capitalism. Its manufacturing efforts would also start the evolution of the crafts and guild system into the American factory system. Lancaster would stand in stark contrast to the industrial slums of European manufacturing such as Manchester, England.

German craftsmen in Lancaster, at the western terminus of the Philadelphia turnpike road, developed the "Conestoga wagon," also called the prairie schooner, to move freight. These giant freight wagons were named after Conestoga Creek at Lancaster. The wagons were watertight and used iron belts around the wooden wheels. Six- to eight-horse teams pulled these freight wagons. They moved in convoys of up to one hundred wagons. The wagons were built through cooperative guilds of woodworkers, wheel makers, blacksmiths, and others. By the 1740s, there were around ten thousand Conestoga wagons in use. German Lancaster employed thirteen blacksmiths, five wheelwrights, twenty joiners, and seven turners in the production of these manufactured wagons. The craftsmen's apprentices did the hard labor. The production of the Conestoga wagons by guild cooperation and planning was a new approach to what would be the earliest example of mass production. Such a corporate approach by guilds was not possible in Europe. The Germans even went into breeding "Conestoga" horses to further improve the overall transportation system of the Conestoga. Goods could be moved to Pittsburgh in two weeks at about $120 per wagonload. Lancaster was a manufacturing village of craftsmen, but it required supplies of iron and glass. The city soon became the center of supplier villages to supply glass, lumber, iron, food, and leather.

The Germans established their own variation of the iron plantation system to supply iron to Lancaster. The German ironmasters lived in fine mansions and often set up a feudal type of system for the care of the unskilled laborers. The wealthy ironmasters held festivals and concerts for the workers. Often the iron plantation resembled a castle-and-town type arrangement. The ironmaster was a feudal "suzerain" supplying all needs but owning all resources. Ironmaster and glassmaker Baron Stiegel laid out the Pennsylvania town around his manufacturing operation. He used indentured servants mainly from Germany. The baron built schools and hired teachers for the children of his workers. He built tenant homes in his town for his workers. Gardens and farms were needed to produce food. Glass manufacture was required to create storage containers. It was a benevolent arrangement. Still, for the most part, the operations had skilled workers, but work at the plantation allowed unskilled workers upward mobility. The baron cared for their training and social formation, and even held his own Sunday services for the workers in his mansion house. The ironmasters lived as feudal lords. Baron Stiegel was known for his carriage driven by six white horses.[2] Stiegel lived in a castle above his manufacturing plants. Still, in Pennsylvania, these manufacturing plantations were private enterprises. The chartered royal colonies looked to establish state-owned manufactories.

The need for glassworks and the shortage of glass makers created "state"-owned plantations in many of the colonies. The royal governors of Virginia and New Jersey brought in indentured servants as well as skilled glassmakers to produce glass products. During the Revolutionary War, captured Hessian soldiers were pressed into service on iron and glass plantations. Most of these Hessians learned the skills and remained in the country after the war. These early industrial plantations helped America develop a skilled workforce. Even the unskilled laborers learned skills and earned money to become future landholders. The plantation system (private or state-owned), with all its shortcomings, offered the opportunity for social mobility that was lacking in the feudal system of Europe. The German and New England paternal plantation system, however, would prove too costly for industrial production. Baron Stiegel, for example, would end up bankrupt. Even the slave tobacco plantations of Virginia needed to be subsidized by the mother country of England.

This modified German feudal system was similar to the Connecticut system of the Puritans, but German indentured servants were known as redemptioners. Redemptioners were indentured by the shipping company to pay for their passage by a set number of years of required service. German redemptioners usually brought their whole families and had stability in building a new home. Housing was rented to the families. While German immigrants adapted well to the plantation system, the Scotch-Irish, Scotch, and British immigrants hated its aristocratic embellishment. The Scotch-Irish, however, did respect the paternal elements of the German plantation system.

The German labor arrangement supplied stability and allowed for the normal development of towns. The focus was on keeping what precious unskilled labor was available; still, they failed to use the production or profit sharing of the Scotch-Irish frontier iron-making operations. Without some form of profit sharing, the system was economic slavery. The downfall of the German feudal system in America was its high inherent costs associated with town maintenance and city building. Another drawback was its failure to attract the independent, property focused American free laborer. The Scotch-Irish, in particular, hated the feudal and any aristocratic type system. The Scotch-Irish were natural capitalists, preferring to make a living on the frontier hunting furs or making whiskey on their own plot of land. They soon realized the frontier demanded some community. Community, however, was developed independent of the factory. The Presbyterian Scotch-Irish, like the Puritans, believed in the pursuit of wealth as well as the responsibility of the wealthy to take care of the poor.

Another communal responsibility was the education of the youth. The Scotch-Irish saw education for all as the root of freedom. Like the Puritans, the Scotch-Irish believed the world was made up of a distribution from wealthy to poor. The European system was a class system. It was reinforced by the ignorance of the people. Education was restricted to only the upper class, since many upper-class Europeans saw education of the masses as a threat to the existence of a permanent aristocracy. The great Scottish Enlightenment brought education to all classes with the Education Act of 1616 and the Schools Act of 1696, not out of a love for education, but as a means to change the class culture. The Acts required that every Presbyterian parish establish a school and pay for the services of a schoolteacher. These acts led to the education of even the poor and took the level of general education in Scotland beyond any other country in the world. The Scottish Enlightenment of the 1700s had given Scotland the world's highest literacy rate. The Scottish-Irish believed there would always be wealthy and poor, but all had the right to the advantages given by education. The Scotch-Irish brought their belief in education for all to the American frontier. Scotch-Irish communities required all to help in the building of schools and the hiring of a schoolteacher. Not surprising was that over a century later a Scotch-Irishman, Andrew Carnegie, would give the nation a chain of free libraries.

The Scotch-Irish, much like the Puritans, preferred the freedom of living on the edge of civilization. While the Puritans moved to the frontier for freedom from religious mandates of government, the Scotch-Irish moved to the frontier to avoid the regulations and taxes of government. Most importantly, the Scotch-Irish established schools on the frontier. The Scotch-Irish believed in property rights, thrift, common schools, moralistic education, political free education, hatred of taxes, and charity. They had a fear of government being involved in community building. While they believed in communal responsibility of the individual, they rejected any church or government mandates regarding that responsibility. While the Scotch-Irish were Presbyterian, they feared government-controlled education and believed in nondenominational education based on the basic Christian principles shared by all. Thus the Scotch-Irish, like Quaker communities, were welcoming to Germans, British, and others.

The Scotch-Irish objected to any government regulation on money-making. Iron and whiskey making, in particular, had been under the control of the British government in the colonies. The Scotch-Irish loved the economic freedom of the frontier. Of course, lack of government meant the added responsibility for the development of communities. The Scotch-Irish, like the Puritans, were also bounded by their religious beliefs, and realized that frontier living required community and an individual responsibility for the less fortunate. They started the communal building of poorhouses, hospitals, and mental institutions. American industrial philanthropy would evolve out of the great Scotch-Irish industrialists of the 1800s.

The Scotch-Irish unskilled laborers often stayed long enough at the German and British plantations to learn the business and then moved west to start their own iron operations. They were quick to utilize freed indentured servants of the British and Germans to build manufacturing operations. The Scotch-Irish iron making operations soon dominated because of their productivity bonus arrangements which attracted the independent unskilled laborer. This was something new for the unskilled laborers of America. The Scotch-Irish also combined whiskey distilleries with their iron-making operations, very popular with workers. The Scotch-Irish combined self-reliance with paternal practices, preferring that the workers build their own cabins and hunt and garden for food; however, they did build communal systems when necessary. Workers were free to drink their fill and had no religious views pushed on them. They eventually learned to foster communities but allowed the villages to evolve independently of the industrial operations. The arrangement would prove the ideal blend of labor, management, and capitalism. They used the clan system to maintain an informal type of ownership. The Scotch-Irish pushed their heavy industry operations further west to western Pennsylvania and Ohio with much success. Unskilled laborers preferred the Scotch-Irish labor system to the theocratic system of the Puritans and the aristocratic and feudal system of the Germans.

Unskilled laborers (indentured and free) became a working class making up as much as 20 percent of the population by 1740. In the New England Puritan colonies, indentured servants took one of two paths after their five to seven years of servitude. Puritan servants were often given land after servitude as freedom dues. Non-Puritan servants in New England often became free laborers and moved to the coastal cities. In the cities, they found work in shipbuilding, breweries, construction, and other civic labor jobs. In New

England, they often signed as indentured servants on whaling ships. This created a working poor propertyless class. In Philadelphia, the Quaker "almshouses" helped these working poor with food, shelter, and medical help.[3] Ethnic and religious groups also formed associations to help the poor and working poor. Free laborers also moved west to work for room and board in frontier manufacturing in iron furnace operations, river shipbuilding, and glass factories.

Skilled and unskilled labor poured into this area of manufactories. A 1790 survey of western Pennsylvania, including the five western counties of Allegheny, Washington, Fayette, Westmoreland, and Bedford, support the assumption of much intermixture of blood. The survey of 12,955 families showed 37 percent English, with the "Scotch-Irish" making up 36 percent. Of the 36 percent Scotch-Irish, there were 17 percent Scotch; "Scotch-Irish" were 7.5 percent, 2.7 percent were Ulster Irish, 4.7 percent were English-Irish, and 4.6 percent were southern (Catholic) Irish.[4] This area was dominated by the Scotch-Irish, which tended to form informal clans.

The "capital" of the industrial plateau was Pittsburgh, and its main transportation routes were the Ohio River for the west, and the Cumberland Gap to the east. The plateau had an array of fuel types such as hard wood and coal. The surrounding mountains had abundant iron ore. Manufacturing done earlier in Lancaster now moved closer to the west to Pittsburgh on a rich river plateau. Pittsburgh became a staging point for western migration as iron implements, river boats, and wagons were produced. Glass production blossomed as eastern glass products could not easily be transported over the mountains.

This rich plateau's potential caught the attention of George Washington in his pre–Revolutionary visits to the area. He was one of the earliest to note outcroppings of coal that could be used for heating. Many of the British generals of the Revolutionary War had planned to divide up the area after their victory. Many of the victorious colonial officers did come to "Ohio Country." Most of these early Pittsburgh settlers had been Revolutionary War officers (and Scotch-Irish). These officers found land and trading connections including military supply contracts for Fort Pitt. The military supply connection continued into the 1830s and was clearly a large part of the area's industrial rise. Almost all of these founding citizens became part of the Pittsburgh's manufacturing elite known as the "Pig Iron Aristocracy," which was really part of the first military-industrial complex of the nation. The first of America's industrialists and paternal capitalists was James O'Hara (1754–1819).

O'Hara invested in shipbuilding, which may be considered Pittsburgh's oldest industry. During the Revolutionary War, Pittsburgh had been designated a government boatyard. O'Hara expanded into keelboats in the 1790s. Keelboats moved massive amounts of trade between Pittsburgh, St. Louis, Louisville, and New Orleans. Lewis and Clark had their famous keelboat built in Pittsburgh by O'Hara. O'Hara used the corporate approach to boat and ship building. Using managers, he coordinated the work of skilled craftsmen and unskilled labor to assemble a finished product. Unskilled low-paid laborers would learn the trade and advance in pay. On the frontier, the rules of the guilds and apprenticeship were loosely held to, if at all. This allowed O'Hara to develop the factory system for the manufacture of boats.

O'Hara built a trading empire, moving goods between Pittsburgh, New Orleans, and English ports. He even built seagoing ships in his Pittsburgh shipyards, including the famous *President Adams*, *Pittsburgh*, and *Senator Ross*, which saw action against France in the Quasi-War in 1799. The boat launches were major social events in Pittsburgh featuring great dinners with imported wine. These events were the social events for Pittsburgh elite. O'Hara put his old deputy quartermaster, Isaac Craig, in charge of his shipyards, and set up another soldier friend, Devereux Smith, in grocery distribution. In 1811, they launched the steamboat *New Orleans* for Mississippi River travel. Monongahela rye whiskey was shipped to Europe via O'Hara's Pittsburgh-to-New Orleans connection.

Many blacksmiths were needed to support the operations, which helped give the area its manufacturing start. Boatbuilding also required thousands of buckets of nails, which needed to be produced in mass quantities. By 1802, iron products accounted for $56,548 of Pittsburgh's total value of products and was the largest industry, accounting for 16 percent of the total value. By 1810, iron product manufacture had doubled and accounted for 24 percent of Pittsburgh's production. The industry produced nails and iron implements needed in the West.

O'Hara profited from the trade and built one of Pittsburgh's first mansions. This amazing plantation and mansion ("King's Orchard") was built on the outskirts of old Fort Pitt known as the "King's Artillery Garden" on the Allegheny River side of the point.

O'Hara was a Scotch-Irishman with trading ties in Liverpool, England. In Scotland he had developed ties with the vast Scotch-Irish trading network in America. Trade capitalism became the teacher of young O'Hara. In the 1700s, most of America's tobacco, furs, whiskey, and iron first passed through the trading warehouses of Scotland. It was through the study of this vast Scottish trading system that Adam Smith conceived the basic principles of capitalism with the publication of his book, *The Wealth of Nations*, in 1776. Like Adam Smith, James O'Hara learned the principles of capitalism. James O'Hara may well have been America's first true capitalist.[5] His endeavors used capital for making more money from real estate, iron making, shipbuilding, salt production, shipping, retailing, glass making, banking, and brick making. Like the great Scottish traders of the 1700s, he had no real specialty other than the application of capital to make money. O'Hara would be the ideal for the future quintessential American capitalist. Henry Clay Frick and Andrew Carnegie would emulate O'Hara by making money in a wide range of endeavors including iron, steel, banking, coal, real estate, and transportation.

O'Hara built his career with trade, military, and government ties. He migrated in the 1770s to work as a trader. He also worked with several of the Scotch-Irish fur trading companies such as James Campbell's trading firm of Philadelphia, using to great advantage his ties back in Liverpool and Glasgow. O'Hara built strong ties as an Indian trader for the Ohio Company of Virginia, which operated in Pittsburgh and the Ohio Valley. After military service in the Revolutionary War, he was appointed a presidential elector in 1788 and cast his vote for George Washington. From 1792 to 1794, O'Hara served as quartermaster general; he was responsible for supplying the army of Anthony Wayne and General Arthur St. Clair's western campaign against the Indians from Fort Pitt. O'Hara made his fortune early on, supplying the army of the United States on the western frontier. As a key officer in the 1790s Indian wars, he was a signer of the Treaty of Greenville in 1795. He started a business in salt trade for western military posts and founded a distillery business in the 1790s in Pittsburgh. He is also considered the founder of the First Presbyterian Church in Pittsburgh, which became known as the "cathedral of capitalism." O'Hara's 1800 land holdings cover most of today's downtown Pittsburgh and the north side. In 1800, O'Hara was one of America's wealthy men, with land holdings and manufacturing in several states. Politically, he was a Federalist and supporter of Washington; and during the Whiskey Rebellion, he was called on to lead the Pittsburgh militia against the whiskey rebels, creating a split among the local Scotch-Irish.

One of O'Hara's earliest projects was the building of a transportation network to bring salt from New York to Pittsburgh. O'Hara used vertical integration to tie manufacturing, shipping, and distribution. The network included river transportation companies and wagon trains to potage between rivers.

The sheer volume of nails required in shipbuilding could not be supported by the crafts system of blacksmiths. Prior to 1800, nails were made by painstakingly long operations of blacksmiths on anvils. As volume increased, blacksmith shops grew into small factories and then into naileries. Automation was needed, and O'Hara invested in the necessary machines. Nail production turned blacksmith shops into nail factories in a few short years, breaking down the crafts shop model. O'Hara himself built a glassworks and was the first to use fuel in his glass making with coal.

O'Hara's Pittsburgh businesses included a retail store, brewery, sawmill, gristmill, glassworks, brick making plant, and shipyard. O'Hara developed housing and real estate throughout the area as well. O'Hara developed rows of clapboard houses at reasonable rents for workers. He knew the major constraint to his manufacturing empire was the labor shortage in unskilled, skilled, and managerial workers. He brought in the best managerial talent and expertise from Europe by developing rich neighborhoods of mansions. He poured profits back into community development. O'Hara's community was free market, and he imposed no social or religious standards on his workers. For his time, O'Hara was more dominant than Andrew Carnegie would be many decades later. He would also be the model for paternal capitalists like Andrew Carnegie, giving much to the community.

O'Hara was a strong Federalist and follower of Alexander Hamilton, who believed in the federal use of currency to build manufacturing and transportation. O'Hara's capitalist empire was a monument to Hamilton's vision of America. As a Federalist, O'Hara was a major supporter of a national banking system to stimulate industry. He would be a director of the First United States Bank, establishing a Pittsburgh branch. O'Hara truly used capital, natural resources, and innovation, and not the backs of workers, to succeed. He created prosperity that allowed for good wages. American manufacturing wages were much higher than in Europe at the time, and O'Hara was exporting his product to all of Europe. With innovations such as the use of coal as a fuel, he cut costs below those of Europe while increasing wages. O'Hara proved to be a master and a model for the development of American industrial towns. He provided a perfect blend of democracy, capital, labor, and freedom. His model was more democratic and urban than the Puritan communities and the plantation system. It would be the basis for the nineteenth-century industrial growth of America.

O'Hara used his many ties and networks to build Pittsburgh into an industrial center. He saw philanthropy as a necessity and a part of doing business in America. Only labor limited the growth of Pittsburgh and the O'Hara empire. He realized earlier on that building community and civic attractions was necessary to attract free laborers to the area. He built churches, schools, and housing. Instead of directly supplying room and board for the workers, O'Hara focused on the free market, paying good wages to his workers. He often hired some of Europe's best craftsmen to run his operations, supplying them free houses or even mansions. O'Hara was the first to use massive numbers of free laborers in large major manufacturing operations, but he offered them opportunity to advance to the skilled trades. O'Hara set the example for high wages as a tool for high productivity in Pittsburgh iron and glass industries. It was noted that Pittsburgh nail makers were paid ten times as much as those in Great Britain and the nails produced cost half as much.[6] More than any other product, nails were needed for the western advance of civilization.

O'Hara used the Scotch-Irish network for capital and investment. Besides skilled workers, he bred a generation of capitalists. In 1784, deputy quartermaster-general Isaac Craig worked for General O'Hara at Fort Pitt and became an early partner. They utilized the old Scotch-Irish trading network to become the main supplier to the United States government. Isaac Craig had been born in Ireland and immigrated to Philadelphia as a carpenter in 1741. In 1775 he joined the United States Marines and was severely wounded at the Battle of Brandywine in 1777. After the war, he became the quartermaster at Fort Pitt and married the daughter of the area's most prominent resident, Scotch-Irish General John Neville. Isaac Craig partnered with James O'Hara to build the first glassworks west of the Alleghenies in 1795, which is considered the beginning of the great industrial empire of Pittsburgh. In 1795 he reported: "Today we made the first bottle at a cost of $30,000!"[7] Pittsburgh's rich coal seams made it a natural for glassworks, and O'Hara was one of the first to exploit it. Coal is a much better fuel than wood, which was used by most eastern glassworks. By 1802, the establishment was producing glass bottles, window glass, and decanters. Craig, however, would move into the background as O'Hara's manufacturing base grew.

O'Hara proved that a manufacturing community with trade ties to New Orleans, St. Louis, and even London, could sustain a middle-class community. Pittsburgh's growth was all the faster because of its internal funding. It would be hailed as a worker republic. One historian noted, "Most of the money invested in Pittsburgh came from the town itself with little supplied from the East."[8] Often the investment was generated by the high wages of its workers. Unlike Lancaster works or the early iron plantations, Pittsburgh was built with free laborers. The key, however, was to make the area attractive to workers and their families. A community had to be built with the aid of the wealthy industrialists such as O'Hara and Craig. O'Hara became the model for the next generation of capitalists. This would be a democratic community of free workers, not the feudal system of Europe, or the theocracies of New England. It would be a worker republic of a type not seen before, yet it would have the paternal elements of the earlier models.

O'Hara would also set the ideal of the industrialist giving back to the community through industrial philanthropy. He was the first area philanthropist donating to church-building funds of all dominations. O'Hara, a strict Scotch-Irish Presbyterian, built churches, not for his own faith, but that of his Lutheran and Catholic workers. Having churches of their own faith and an established ethnic community was the perfect enticement for free laborers. O'Hara also helped with the building of schools, which was also a major enticement for workers and their families. While corporate ownership and capital were tightly controlled by the local Scotch-Irish clan, O'Hara did open the management ranks to all nationalities. He allowed workers to rise quickly based on their ability. He offered a bridge for workers to move from the unskilled ranks to the skilled.

Prior to O'Hara, no industrialist in America had ever amassed such a fortune. He would set a lasting example of industrial philanthropy and community giving. O'Hara became so wealthy, he had no place to put his money except into the community he had built. He appeared to be a feudal lord without the slavery of serfs. He was a new type of American "feudal lord" whose position was based on industrial free markets. It was a new system, but it still had the paternal roots of the old feudal system of Europe. Critics would argue it still was a type of economic dependency of the lower class on the wealthy; and like any concentration of wealth, it could lead to abuse. Still, unlike Europe, the wealthy class was not a permanent aristocracy. Workers could rise up the class ladder, and the wealthy would also occasionally fail in their investments. Many of O'Hara's workers would become the great area capitalists of the nineteenth century. O'Hara would, however, become part of a wealthy family with branches even today.

Regardless of O'Hara's motivation for philanthropy, he advanced civilization on the frontier, building churches, poorhouses, and schools. The old family wealth never caused the social unrest of Europe because the American worker had the opportunity to follow in O'Hara's footsteps. O'Hara's fortune is remembered today for Schenley Park in Pittsburgh. Mary Cogan was the granddaughter of General O'Hara. She married a

Captain Schenley and left Pittsburgh for England, but her real estate holdings remained. On her death in 1903, these real estate holdings were estimated at $50 million. It took years to sell so as not to depress the market. In the end, the family gave massive donations of land and money. Land donations include today's Schenley Park, the land where the Carnegie Library stands, and the Fort Pitt blockhouse at the Point.

The Scotch-Irish view of capitalism was uniquely American and nationalistic. It was based on hardworking, self-reliant, and independent members, who supplied the infrastructure for the whole community. Realizing the importance of community to the individual and the whole without the feudal or patriarchal dependence of Europeans, community, like government, was for and by the people. It was the duty of the wealthy individual to spread the wealth, not that of government. While the Scotch-Irish proved highly competitive capitalists, they had a passion for helping the less fortunate. This was rooted in their hatred of the British aristocratic system where the poor were doomed to a life of illiteracy and inability to move up in class. The Scotch-Irish wealthy would initially build the community's hospitals, schools, libraries, churches, soup kitchens, and civic centers when no such government programs existed. Such a system depended on the religious values and morals of its citizens. It is why Alexis de Tocqueville saw religion as the glue of early America and its capitalistic system and education as its foundation.

The Scotch-Irish brought a love of freedom, capitalism, and the idea of free education for youth. As the Scotch-Irish fled British oppression to America in the 1700s, they brought a love and culture of elementary and high-level education. They saw free education as insurance against oppression. For the middle class, the Scotch-Irish started library associations, which, for a fee, lent books. In Europe, scientific and philosophical societies were for the aristocrats and wealthy, but the Scotch-Irish organized them for the middle class.

It was a tradition that went back to the Scottish Enlightenment. In Scotland, the literacy rate was an amazing 80 to 85 percent. Most Scottish towns in 1750 had their own lending libraries. Successful Scotch-Irish felt it a duty to give to community education. The Scotch-Irish Presbyterian school system came with them to the American colony. By the time of the American Revolution, America's literacy rate was almost the highest in the world (second only to Scotland) at 70 percent to 75 percent, while England's rate was only 50 to 60 percent. France and Italy were under 40 percent.[9] York County's Presbyterian schools were popular with the Germans as well as the Scotch because of their high standards. Presbyterians made up the majority of roving "subscription" teachers. The Western frontier had an impressive literacy rate of 65 percent in the early 1800s. This literacy rate, coupled with the high average wealth, allowed Americans to read and buy books in large numbers. This literacy rate turned the Western frontier of Pennsylvania and Ohio into the seed of the American empire.

The Scotch-Irish in the 1700s created frontier log cabin universities. Many of America's colleges such as Princeton, University of Pennsylvania, University of Pittsburgh, Washington and Jefferson, University of Cincinnati, Miami University, Ohio University, Transylvania University, Allegheny College, Geneva College, Grove City College, and Westminster College, owe their creation to Scotch-Irish log cabins. The mixed and pragmatic college curriculum was a result of the Scottish educational system. Transylvania University in Kentucky in the early 1800s was the "Harvard of the West."

Lexington's Transylvania College had built a national reputation. At the time Transylvania was making a name as the West's best college, and was the first college west of the Alleghenies to have a medical college in 1810. Transylvania University had been started from the Presbyterian Church by a group of local Scotch-Irish activists. By 1823, Transylvania was one of the best in the nation with 400 students and a 6,000-volume library. In the 1820s, it graduated an average of 500 students a year. Educators at Transylvania even sent an agent to Europe with $17,000 to purchase more books, which had been granted for that purpose by the state legislature. These frontier colleges taught business accounting and applied science for the first time.

Cincinnati followed Pittsburgh in 1800 as a Scotch-Irish center of capitalism. Cincinnati showed how education would lead to innovation and economic growth. Capitalists came to realize that investing in education meant more profits in the long run. It was a linkage that had never been understood in Europe, where education was limited to the aristocratic class. Cincinnati was also blessed with heavy industry in the 1820s, having five steam engine manufacturers, three steamboat manufacturers, several iron foundries, and cotton-gin makers. It was also the literary and publishing center of the West. In 1826, Cincinnati publishers had turned out 61,000 almanacs, 55,000 spelling books, and 30,000 primers. Cincinnati had one of the nation's best public school systems, with about fifty schools operating in 1836, and one of the nation's first high schools. Cincinnati was the center of the political movement for tax-supported public schools. A tax of two mills was levied in Cincinnati. The city had tax-supported school districts, and its teachers averaged $300 a year salary with a range from $200 to $500 a year. Many of the Cincinnati schools were solid two-story brick buildings, allowing for graded classes.

Educational philanthropy would be the mark of Scotch-Irish industrialists such as James O'Hara, Isaac Craig, Andrew Carnegie, Edgar Thomson, and Thomas Mellon. Furthermore, equal opportunity through education became a cornerstone of the American system. Philanthropy would be the link between the workplace and the community, offering an American alternative to an aristocratic feudal system at one extreme, and European socialism at the other. Europe's struggle with industrialization and labor would change the world, including America.

Three

European Industrialization, Master Entrepreneurs, and Worker Utopias

---

The American Industrial Revolution was decades behind that of Europe; however, changes in Europe would influence the evolution of industry in America. The Industrial Revolution would break down the crafts and guild system of Europe as well as the feudal system of unskilled labor. The feudal system, regardless of its reinforced class structure, was paternal. While the guild system was paternal, it was much more fraternal, with guild shops averaging about four to six workers. Apprentices did the menial labor as they learned their craft. Journeymen were the main producers, while the master managed the shop. The shop also functioned as a living unit, offering room and board. The guild of a given craft established standards of work including wage scales. Guild membership was restricted but had the political support of the government and the church. Production was slow, steady, and high quality. The crafts shop was ill suited to meet the quantity and complexity of machine production, but America would offer opportunities for these displaced craftsmen of Europe.

America's plantation factories and frontier industries were far behind the sweeping Industrial Revolution of Europe. Interestingly, it was the advance of Dutch technology in textiles in the 1600s that was a harbinger of the Industrial Revolution. The Dutch harnessed wind power and automation to reduce the cost of textile manufacture. In Holland, thousands of laborers lost work to these technological advances, which would be part of the Pilgrims' motivation to sail for America. The Dutch advance hit the British textile industry hard by the 1620s, particularly in the Puritan districts of England.[1] The falling textile prices resulted in British layoffs and labor riots in the 1600s, creating a new wave of Puritan immigrants to America in the 1630s and 1640s.

Europe was in a state of flux, tearing down social norms to meet the demand of the Industrial Revolution by the 1700s. Machines were replacing the guilds in the cotton and textile markets. The wealthy aristocratic class was given special permits from the king to open factories without guilds. The rationale was that cheaply produced clothes could be shipped economically to suppress American industry. The national British strategy was successful but at the expense of the guilds. Wages were rapidly falling. Skilled labor was drastically replaced, while the need for unskilled labor exceeded supply. Part of the supply shortage resulted from the resistance of skilled workers to work for low wages. The demise of the skilled craftsman family head created the supply of women and children to feed the family and pay bills. Unemployed skilled workers joined the working poor of women and child laborers. The distribution of wealth deepened as Europe's middle class of skilled workers was eliminated. By the early 1800s, 70 to 80 percent of the European population was estimated to be the working poor. The industrial urban environments saw the rise of poorhouses and debtor prisons as both the guild system and the feudal system passed into history. City slums replaced the feudal village as the home of unskilled labor. By the 1810s, the Industrial Revolution had brought social unrest to the streets. Guild members formed groups of revolutionaries to burn emerging automated factories in the dead of night.

Amazingly, it was government that proved the most flexible in changing to the new environment. The old aristocracy set up monopolies in industries in cotton by royal charters. The new wealthy landlord class controlled the evolving factories and Parliament. Parliament proved supportive of long hours and low wages for the newly emerging class of free laborers. The working poor remained unrepresented in the European political system.

Some European nations such as Germany tried to support the skilled laborers, but cheaper goods from automated British factories crushed that effort over time. By 1800, England owned the world cotton market, and its huge influx of money had replaced the financial losses associated with the American colonies. England invented machines and manned them with cheap labor, eliminating any possible world competition. The combination of the factory system and automation created a surplus of free laborers, driving wages down.

The British Industrial Revolution created a type of dark, hellish world for the laborers. The cotton weaving factories were dangerous and required 10- to 12-hour days. Child laborers were required to keep the machines manned. High-paid middle-class skilled workers became a new class of unemployed workers. The number of handloom weavers had dropped from a peak of 100,000 in Scotland in 1800 to 84,560 in 1840, and 25,000 by 1850.[2] In Britain by 1815, it was estimated that over 50,000 weavers alone were unemployed. The new factory used women and children to reduce the cost of unskilled labor. Furthermore, the displaced skilled weavers started a type of guerrilla warfare. This movement, known as the "Luddite" movement, was named after a fictional leader, "Ned Ludd." Around 1810, the Luddites started to raid factories in the night, smashing and burning machines. The movement lasted only a few years, with many of its leaders being publicly hanged. In labor-short America, machines tended to create jobs versus destroying them.

The deskilling of Europe continued to accelerate into the 1840s. Less radical unemployed skilled workers tried to address the problems of unemployment. The Rochdale Society of Equitable Pioneers, founded in 1844, was an early consumer cooperative of unemployed workers. The original store was in Lancashire, England. It was one of the first to pay a patronage dividend. The Rochdale Pioneers' cooperative became the prototype for societies in Great Britain and formed a basis for modern cooperatives. The Rochdale Pioneers are most famous for designing the Rochdale Principles, a set of principles of cooperation that provide the foundation for the principles on which co-ops operate. The movement spread to over 1,000 cooperatives in England. They expanded into selling their own wares as well. The cooperative store model would be tried by later capitalists such as Milton Hershey and Andrew Carnegie to help workers. The cooperatives of the 1800s did little to address the real issue of unemployment and factory work.

The home life of these industrial laborers was even worse than the factory environment. The industrial slums were covered most of the time by dark sulfurous smog. Families were packed into apartments with limited heat. Sewage was dumped in the streets, mixing with horse manure. Disease was everywhere. The hardest thing was the realization that there was no upward movement. Children, if they survived, could expect no better for their families. The working poor, like earlier serfs, were a permanent under-class. However, unlike the feudal serfs, they lacked social safety nets and paternal help. For many, the poorhouse offered a better alternative.

Poorhouses (also called almshouses or workhouses) were tax-supported institutions to which people were required to go if they could not support themselves. The Act for the Relief of the Poor of 1601 made parishes and local communities legally responsible for the care of those within their boundaries who, through age or infirmity, were unable to work. They were started as a method of providing a less expensive (to the taxpayers) alternative to what we would today call "welfare." Industrial growth increased the number of workhouses. This growth was created by the Workhouse Test Act of 1723 by obliging anyone seeking poor relief to enter a workhouse and undertake a set amount of work, usually for no pay. People requested help from the community Overseer of the Poor (sometimes also called a Poor Master), an elected town official. If the need was likely to be long-term, they were sent to the poorhouse instead of being given relief. Sometimes they were sent there even if they had not requested help from the Overseer of the Poor. That was usually done when they were found guilty of begging in public. By 1840, a number of laws were enacted to pay for a system that was overburdened.

The abuses of the European Industrial Revolution towards unskilled workers and the displacement of skilled workers would lay the groundwork for social revolutions across Europe in the next few decades. The need for women to work would break down the social structure. More so in Europe, women went to work to maintain the family income, much like what was seen in America of the 1970s. The darker side of cheap labor was the use and abuse of children. Dickens's novels shocked the world with their stories of child labor. Furthermore, unskilled laborers in Europe had little hope of ever owning land or property. These laborers were merely subsistence laborers. The great machines of the Industrial Revolution had clogged the streets of Europe with unemployed workers and the working poor. A whole generation of skilled workers felt betrayed by their governments. Debtor jails became the breeding ground for social unrest. The 1840s saw the rise of socialists and anarchists rioting in the streets. In general, America needed labor more and offered more opportunity for the poor, which led to significantly higher wages. It would also spark massive immigration to labor-short America. Abuses occurred in America, but the extreme labor shortages in many areas favored a more humane approach.

The decline of the craftsmen in America was just as dramatic as in Europe, but took a different path. First was the impact of the American Revolution, which weakened the guild system of the European governments. Freedom meant minimum outside influence on the crafts. Freedom and equality translated to the crafts shop. This transformation has often been described as "Artisan Republicanism." Labor historian Sean Wilentz summarized observations of America at the time by Alexis de Tocqueville and James Boardman: "Both men, in their search for America, stumbled on what remained of a distinctive system of meanings, one that associated the emblems, language, and politics of the Republic with the labor system, social traditions, and the very products of the crafts."[3] While republican principles had changed the guild crafts system, the bigger impact would be economic.

American master craftsmen and their crafts were being challenged by semi-manufactured, cheap goods from Europe. The crafts guilds lacked the centuries of traditions found in Europe. To stay competitive, master craftsmen started to bastardize the crafts system, breaking the years-long training procedure from apprentice to journeyman to master. American masters created "half apprentices" or skilled laborers to reduce the wage and cost structure.[4] Young American workers were happy to "learn a trade." The use of cheap labor allowed for more rapid and less painful conversion to the factory system of production. Lacking the tradition of guilds and experiencing a labor shortage, America flowed more smoothly into the factory system; but as in Europe, a new social structure of skilled and unskilled was evolving in the workplace.

In America, the crafts economy would develop into a crafts production economy. Wages for skilled and unskilled labor were often ten times that of Europe. Ultimately, the situation would lead to the skilled crafts unions of the United States. With no overriding guild rules and restrictions, an American craftsman rose quickly to master as demand for goods, not guilds, created the shop-owning master. Often unskilled laborers would rise through the ranks to master. These capitalist masters often invested in multiple shops. They became entrepreneurs creating multiple workshops, warehouses, showrooms, and exporting companies. The earliest and most famous of this class of manufacturing capitalist was New York's Duncan Phyfe, a cabinetmaker. By 1815, Phyfe employed over 100 journeymen in three shops and numerous warehouses.[5] His Regency-style furniture was shipped all over America via a distribution system similar to the one made possible by the earlier cooperation between trades seen in the manufacturing town of Lancaster in the 1700s. Phyfe and similar master entrepreneurs formed the General Society of Mechanics and Tradesmen to foster bonds between trades. Thus, cabinetmakers were able to hire or employ metalworkers to build their furniture. The society even formed banks to help finance projects. The master still maintained a benevolent and family approach to his journeymen. The system, however, was too big; and by 1820, workers started to band together for wage demands.

Actually, the movement toward journeymen associations in the United States had started in the 1790s, but it was restricted to the artisan republic. Journeymen formed these early organizations to counter the entrepreneur associations, which were changing the craft shop system to corporate shops. From 1800 to 1820, these journeymen organizations were resisted by the master entrepreneurs. When larger trades such as shoe-making formed journeymen associations, they were opposed in court. In general, the courts saw them as a conspiracy and ruled them illegal based on English law.[6] Still, in America there were no uprisings as seen in Europe, as workers also believed that the republican principles of the revolution would take hold in the workshop. As these corporate shops grew to 300 or more employees, this view would change. The workshop, as a true family, was lost as the owners could no longer know the individual names of their workers. Strong religious values still maintained the earlier paternalism, to a large degree.

The problems of the Industrial Revolution for the worker were noted almost from the very beginning. The abuses of the British factories were well known throughout the world. In particular, Britain had come to dominate the world's cotton manufacture with its highly automated factories. The factory system not only threatened the crafts guilds but the social fabric of the nation. The use of young children working 12 hour days for 6 days a week was part of the problem, even in America. Britain needed to keep its low-cost labor and machinery advantage to stay ahead of the Americans, who were the source of the raw cotton. England had built its first automated cotton mills in the 1770s. Initially, these mills were powered by water; but within a few years, the steam engine would further automate and speed production. Smoke filled skies, child labor, and overworked, poorly paid women became the face of Britain's Industrial Revolution. There were reformers and visionaries in Europe who proposed a type of paternalism to replace the loss of the guilds and the feudal systems. Government regulation was slow in coming, and reformers arose from the private sector.

One of the most enlightened of these reformers was Robert Owen (1771–1858). Owen was part reformer, socialist, prophet, utopian, manager, and capitalist. Often called a communist or a socialist, Owen was really a different kind of capitalist. Still, today he is hailed by communists as an example of working socialism. Amazingly, he is also hailed by capitalists today, such as the American Management Society, as a classic manager and father of personnel management. It is rare (there may be no other example) that a pragmatic system is praised by capitalists, communists, and socialists. It appears that Owen had found a type of Holy Grail in the management and treatment of workers. He certainly defined an approach to allow socialism to work within a capitalistic environment. Owen's approach did have some major drawbacks when extended beyond a small community.

As a young salaried mill manager, Owen became convinced that highly motivated workers contributed more to efficiency and productivity than the machines. Still, Victorian logic was to invest in new machinery rather than improving the working environment by spending on the workers. Unlike the social reformers, church leaders, and utopians of the time, Owen argued the case for improved working conditions for return on capital. He maintained that slave-like, struggling workers were highly inefficient. He argued that money spent on the worker would return, "not five, ten, or fifteen percent for your capital so expended, but often fifty, and in many cases a hundred percent."[7] The American Management Association today considers Owen's 1813 address to manufacturers a classic in management. The famous quote from that address reads: "Your living machines may be easily trained and directed to procure a large increase of pecuniary gain. Money spent on employees might give 50 to 100 per cent return as opposed to a 15 per cent return on machinery. The economy of living machinery is to keep it neat and clean, treat it with kindness that its mental movements might not experience too much irritating friction."[8]

Robert Owen would be referred to by many paternal capitalists such as Andrew Carnegie, George Westinghouse, and H.J. Heinz, as their inspiration. Owen would become the father of paternalism in manufacturing as well as in communal manufacture. He would argue that the paternal treatment of workers was in the interest of the manufacturer, always seeing the matter from an economic view versus any religious or social activist view. Unlike many paternal capitalists, Owen saw worker happiness, not community philanthropy, as the best form of capitalism. Owen himself preferred the term "paternal."[9] This approach was far different from that of Andrew Carnegie or John Rockefeller, who gave much to the general communities, such as libraries, while their workers struggled in a hell on earth.

Robert Owen would test his beliefs in the manufacturing village of New Lanark, Scotland. The village was initially a product of the Industrial Revolution founded by David Dale and cotton machinery inventor, Richard Arkwright, on the River Clyde in 1786. Robert Owen originally came to manage these extensive cotton mills in 1799. Cotton mills of the Victorian period were notorious for child labor, injuries, and low pay. Victorian mills tended to be located in poor industrial urban districts. The workers with their low pay were left to their own wits to live in these ghettoes. Workers and children were packed into apartments lacking heat and running water.

Owen had been critical of the government and the state church in allowing abuses such as child labor. He soon looked to develop an experimental manufacturing complex, becoming a managing partner in 1800. Unlike other reformers, Owen hoped to show the profitability of happy and well-treated workers. Owen's ideas of an integrated working community have earned him the label of socialist, but Owen was actually motivated by profits. Still, Owens saw community and working factories as integrated. He believed success in the factory required healthy and educated communities. In an 1813 address to fellow manufacturers, he espoused a capitalistic view of communal manufacturing: "A well-directed attention to form the character and increase the comforts of those who are so entirely at your mercy will essentially add to gains, prosperity, and happiness; no reasons except those founded on ignorance of your self-interest, can in the future prevent you from bestowing your chief care on the living machines which you employ; and by doing so you will prevent the accumulation of human misery."[10]

New Lanark became an alternative successful model for the industrial world from 1800 to 1825 under Owen's leadership. Today New Lanark is noted as a UNESCO World Heritage Site. Some of Owen's radical ideas show just how bad the abuses of the time were. Owens established at his mills in New Lanark that children could not work more than ten hours, could do no night work, and had to be ten years old to work. These rules were proposed to Parliament in 1813 as well but found no political support. Owen built nurseries for the children of working mothers to assure a head start in education. New Lanark also had free schools for older children. He also set up schools for further adult education of his workers. For younger mill workers, manual arts training in wood and iron was available and formed the source of needed crafts workers in the village. To pay for employee free education, Owen used the profits from his company stores. Many of the child workers were urban homeless and poor and were commonly exploited in the early industrialization of Britain. In 1817, Owen employed about 500 poor children from the cities.[11] These poor children were provided excellent rooms in a well maintained boarding house. They were provided free education and training.

Education was based on a nondenominational approach. All religions were accepted, but the moral guides tended to be based on Judeo-Christian principles. Owen accepted the state churches of Britain but often criticized them for not addressing such moral issues as child labor. Direct religious training was considered the responsibility of the parents. Moral living was stressed, however, in New Lanark schools. Taverns and drinking were purposefully restricted to eliminate drunkenness. For the orphan children, Owen established an Institute of Character Foundation. The books used in New Lanark schools were similar to the moral, nondenominational *McGuffey Readers* of nineteenth-century America. Unfortunately, Owen carried his moral requirements for workers too far, as would Henry Ford with his sociological department a hundred years later. Both Owen and Ford monitored the lifestyles of their workers. Indirect punishments, such as public scrutiny, were used to maintain a code of conduct. This idea of imposing a code of moral conduct was often a result of the paternal approach and would prove a major weakness. The approach's strength was it was firmly rooted in capitalism, not religion.

New Lanark was owned by a group of capitalist partners who received a return on investment probably averaging 20 percent. The village had around 2,000 residents in the 1810s. Wages were much higher than in England. Owen firmly believed that high wages led to more productivity.[12] Later in life, he would experiment with many forms of wage systems, but at New Lanark, there was no direct employee profit sharing. Owen also avoided layoffs in bad times by using the workers for village improvement or using the time to train, realizing that loss of a paying job was one of the workers' greatest fears. It was a concept used successfully in the 1980s in Japan. During the American cotton embargo of 1806, New Lanark workers received full wages for the year. The benefits given to the employees were extensive. Workers received low-cost housing, reduced prices for necessities through a company store, and free education and health care. Street and house maintenance were supplied by the village. There was a system of health care, disability insurance, and retirement, into which the workers put one-sixtieth of their wages. Owen maintained a system of higher wages at New Lanark but would later experiment with hours of labor as the standard for community currency.

Owen also pushed and experimented with reduced factory hours and increased breaks. He viewed the waste of time and materials as a result of overworked employees. Owen developed many of the same employee principles that would lead the Japanese revolution of lean manufacture. Reminiscent of Toyota's lean manufacturing approach today, Owen argued that "greater attention by workpeople in avoiding breakage or waste of time might increase output, and that in his experience, shorter hours work did result in closer attention."[13]

Robert Owen was not alone in his early paternal approach in Britain.

The manufacture of the very icon of the Industrial Revolution, the steam engine, was based on a paternal approach to the workers. The approach could be found in the company of James Watt and Mathew Boulton at the Soho Engineering Foundry in 1800. The foundry had started making steam engines in the late 1700s, but it was the sons of the founders who in 1800 shifted to a paternal approach. Albeit less extensively, they applied many of the ideas of Owen. The foundry walls were routinely whitewashed to improve the lighting. Houses were rented to workers as part of their pay. The owners implemented a welfare system to help the unemployed and injured workers. The company instituted the Mutual Assurance Society to supply these benefits. The owners rationalized their implementation of benefits as a necessity, as noted by biographers: "Still further to increase the attachment of workmen to Soho and keep his school of skilled industry."[14] Soho employed skilled workers as the company had invested much in the development of these skills. This paternal approach allowed Soho to break with guild traditions by placing a foreman in charge versus a master craftsman. The use of a foreman was something new at the time. In general, skilled workers found this paternal approach a major improvement over guilds. The paternal capitalism was self-serving, but consistent with Adam Smith's core principles. The Soho approach would become popular in the early coal and steel industries of America.

In 1825, Owen brought his ideas of utopian manufacturing villages to the United States. Communal manufacturing villages were not new to America. Radical religious groups had founded highly successful communities throughout America. The Shakers, a radical Quaker group, had successful villages in New England and Kentucky. The Harmonists had villages in Pennsylvania and Indiana. The Zoarites had a successful manufacturing community in Ohio. These were tight-knit religious communities, many of whom believed a millennial prophecy that the world would end in 1900 and practiced celibacy. These self-contained villages often generated much income from selling their quality products to the outside world. Shakers were known for their wood products, Zoarites for high-quality cast iron products, and Harmonists for wine and an array of consumer goods. Both the Harmonists and Zoarites also invested their profits in outside stock. The Harmonists became a major investor in the Pennsylvania Railroad. These communities were far more socialistic than New Lanark, with labor sharing versus pay. They were true collective communities, similar to the *kibbutz* of modern-day Israel. Owen established his new radical communist manufacturing town in Indiana by purchasing a previously established religious commune of the Harmonists.

New Harmony, Indiana, was established by the Harmony Society in 1814 under the leadership of German immigrant George Rapp. The town was originally known as Harmony. The Harmonists built a new town in the wilderness about 25 miles from the Ohio River mouth of the Wabash, and 12 miles from where the Ohio makes its curve first before the mouth. In 1819, the town had a steam-operated wool carding plant, a cotton mill and spinning factory, a horse-drawn and human-powered threshing machine, a brewery, a distillery, vineyards, and a winery. Manufactured goods included cotton apparel, flannel, and wool cloth, yarn, knit goods, tinware, rope, beer, peach brandy, whiskey, wine, wagons, carts, plows, flour, beef, pork, butter, and leather goods. The 1820 manufacturers' census reported that 75 men, 12 women, and 30 children lived in Harmony. The town functioned as a religious commune sharing everything.

The problem started as New Harmony rapidly grew to over 800 people. Many of these were freeloaders. In 1824, the inhabitants decided to sell their property and return to Pennsylvania. These Harmonites became known as Rappites and built a new communal town in Economy, Pennsylvania, outside of Pittsburgh.

When Owen came to America in 1825, he, too, moved more to socialism and a collective community (the root of communism). With the intention of creating a new utopian community, Owen purchased the 30,000-acre Harmonist village of Harmony, Indiana, and renamed it New Harmony. Owen would apply his own views on this new project. On February 5, 1826, the town adopted a new constitution, the New Harmony Community of Equality, whose objective was to achieve worker happiness based on principles of equal rights, equality of duties, and equality of pay. Cooperation, common property, economic benefit, freedom of speech, kindness and courtesy, preservation of worker health, acquisition of knowledge, and obedience to the country's laws were included as part of the constitution. The original Harmonists returned from Pennsylvania as Owen recruited artists and craftsmen. He believed he could establish a social utopia and moved away from any capitalistic principles. While eliminating all remnants of religion, Owen imposed his own beliefs of free love, elimination of marriage, temperance, and equality of pay in what became known as a "Declaration of Mental Independence."[15] The elimination of private property and equality of pay were far different from the principles of New Lanark. New Lanark had been Owen's economic vision while New Harmony was his moral vision. Still, Owen hoped to produce goods for commercial profit as well as a return on investment to wealthy supporters. New Harmony lacked the glue of a strong shared religious vision to function as a collective society. Owen had taken his vision too far. New Harmony became a financial failure but became a popular community of freethinkers and artists. While Owen would continue to be a popular writer, New Harmony never approached the successful economic model of New Lanark. Owen's legacy principle was that capitalism has the propensity towards greed and corruption that requires boundaries set by moral values, religious guides, and/or government regulation. But socialism was not a pragmatic solution.

Recently and retrospectively, Owen has become a favorite in segments of the socialist movement, His only success, New Lanark, was rooted in capitalism. In fact, his socialism experiment with manufacturing proved an abject failure. There were a number of smaller, less successful socialist communities in the United States in the 1830s and 1840s. Charles Fourier (1772–1837) was a French social theorist who elaborated on a vision for a utopian society organized along socialist principles of martial liberation, cooperative organization, women's liberation, and human interaction. Fourier's principles were clearly radical in Puritan America. Many of these utopias were founded by the transcendentalist movement of New England. Transcendentalists of the 1840s believed in the perfection of the individual instead of reform of the larger society. The individualistic nature of transcendentalism gave it more of a spiritual direction than a social quality, one that also influenced later utopian movements. The most

Old Economy Village in 1904 (courtesy Carnegie Library of Pittsburgh).

important of these communities was Brook Farm, established in West Roxbury, Massachusetts, in 1841. Residents hoped to free themselves from the capitalist world so as to work as little as possible, all the while enjoying the fruits of a libertarian culture. Unlike their European counterparts, American transcendentalists such as Ralph Waldo Emerson embraced the quest for a higher moral law. Fourier based communities were very similar to the hippie communities of the 1970s versus an experiment in worker satisfaction. These experiments, like the old plantation system, could not maintain the growth and industrialization of America. Still, America would experiment with hybrids of utopian communities and the factory system needed for industrialization. Many future paternal capitalists such as George Westinghouse, Andrew Carnegie, and H.J. Heinz would study these early communal systems and apply some of their useful approaches to workers.

Another successful model for American work communes was a mix of capitalism, socialism, and religion in the 1800s. This was often called Christian communism. Equality of pay and wealth had always been the root of problems for these manufacturing communities. Success seemed to be in members working for the greater glory. In effect, Christian communism was a variation on the monastic Benedictine model of prayer and work. The American version of economic monasticism was seen in many of the Shaker communities in New England and Kentucky. The Shaker model was very close to the Puritan experiment. Families owned their own farms, but all excess production became communal. The community took care of the disabled and young but did not tolerate any form of freeloading. Like the golden days of European monasticism, the Shakers did hire outside workers for general labor jobs. Full admission to the society required review by the Trustees.

The Shakers focused on developing skills in woodworking. Their products were used in the community, and all excess was sold to outside buyers to generate capital. An elected group of Trustees marketed outside sales and used the funds for communal purchases. The development of skills was a very satisfying career for most Shakers. Their woodworking skills and wood products are still admired to this day. They vertically integrated their woodworking operations, becoming manufacturers of equipment and supplies such as nails. They proved highly creative and inventive with the development of tools such as the circular saw. While religious unity was their strength, it also became a weakness in their expansion. While never mainstream, these communes did make contributions to manufacturing paternalism and worker productivity.

Another group of religious separatists came from Germany in the 1800s, many of whom were unemployed skilled workers. The Zoarites settled in 1817 in Zoar, Ohio. More religious than economic by nature, they formed a communistic society as a means to remain together. Food was scarce the first winter. Because some families had not yet cleared their land or bought tools, they had to work on neighboring farms. The next season, each Zoar family cultivated its own acreage, but yields were insufficient to feed themselves and pay the land debt.[16] Thus, in 1819, the original plan of private land ownership and cultivation was scrapped and the commune was born.

These German craftsmen proved to be highly adaptable and creative. The small community contracted in 1825 to extend the Ohio Canal through their village. The canal connection opened their farm and manufactured products to Cleveland, Pittsburgh, and Cincinnati. Zoar produced a wide range of wood, iron, tin, and clay products. They also built a large brewery. Highly skilled as iron workers, they built two iron blast furnaces that rivaled the quality of iron made in Pittsburgh and Cleveland. Their pig iron was sold at a premium in American industrial markets. While selling raw pig iron, they also built iron foundries at Zoar to produce stoves which became popular throughout Ohio.

Like other American manufacturing communities, Zoar experimented with and pioneered personnel management. Workers were allowed to change careers every five years. This was necessary to reduce personnel problems caused by equal pay. This type of career rotation proved highly effective at improving the morale with the more skilled workers. Unskilled workers often rotated jobs daily. One weakness was communal education; children remained in a general nursery until they were fourteen. Families did live extremely well as Zoar was a huge economic success. Like those of other religious separatists, the community died out in 50 years, leaving millions of dollars to be distributed to the few remaining members.

The economic success of these communal manufacturing towns was clearly due to the high morale and productivity of their workers. The challenge for industry was to somehow bring these paternal practices to city factories and urban environments. Many nineteenth-century industrialists studied the amazing productivity advances of communal manufacturing. Industrialists such as Henry Ford tried to emulate some of these communal practices with his workers by distributing seeds to employees for their gardens and producing fresh bread daily for employees.

Four

Lowell and Rockdale

Communal manufacturing was never a pragmatic answer to the problems created by the Industrial Revolution, which pitted the unskilled labor against skilled labor and the advance of automation. At the heart of this struggle was the morale of both the skilled and the unskilled worker. The European craftsmen or skilled workers faced the rapid industrialization of the late 1700s. For centuries, the guilds and government had maintained high wages for craftsmen. The guild system also controlled supply and demand. Skilled crafts by the 1700s were highly regulated. The Industrial Revolution would change the face of manufacture and labor in Europe by destroying the guild system and introducing the factory system. In America, the old guild structure would prove more open to industrialization and automation. American guilds would transform into crafts unions.

In America, the delineation of competing visions of agriculture and industry would evolve as the nation evolved. By the dawn of the 1800s, the nation had a developing textile manufacturing sector in New England. America was learning to produce glass bottles, guns, gunpowder, stoves, farming implements, and pig iron. Even Thomas Jefferson marveled at the industrial growth of a young America. Yankee industrialists had smuggled in new automated looms from England, enabling American textile manufacture to move to high productivity levels. The acceptance of automation had given American textile manufacturers an advantage over the labor-intensive British industry. British anti-automation proponents known as Luddites had held England back. Americans, with their inherent labor shortage, looked to automation, which became an American success story. As Europeans resisted automation out of job loss fears, Americans, partially out of necessity, embraced automation. Automation resulted in price reduction, and price reductions opened up more markets. Cheaper products such as glass, iron, cotton, and wool were produced by automation as well. The result was industrial growth and more job demand. It was labor shortages that would restrict the industrial growth in America. Immigration became a necessity to keep the American economic engine running.

Many see the invention of the steam engine or the rise of the iron industry as the catalyst for the change, but it was cotton that changed the world. Cotton would break the guild structure of Europe and usher in the factory system on both continents. Cotton created the necessary demand for rapid automation. It was cotton that bought the factory system to America. Of course, it was the automated cotton textile industry that gave rise to reformers such as Robert Owen. It was even cotton that brought Andrew Carnegie and the steel industry to America. Even Pittsburgh was the "cotton city" prior to steel. While cotton inspired the greatest surge in invention and automation, it would simultaneously entrench slavery in America.

Cotton, however, was totally controlled by England's highly industrialized mills. England's automated production had destroyed the early American hand-driven industry. The country controlled the cotton market by forbidding the sale of their specialized machinery in America. Parliament also used dumping of product to destroy any newly rising American mills. For the seeds of the cotton industry to sprout, it would take special protection from the American government. Henry Clay, congressman of Kentucky and Speaker of the House, would initiate a reindustrialization plan for America. Clay had taken particular note of the industrial boom before and after the War of 1812. Clay's spies recorded the following from a speech by Henry Brougham in Parliament in which he declared, "It was well worthwhile to incur a loss upon the first exportation, in order, by the glut, to stifle in the cradle, those rising manufactures in the United States."[1] Henry Clay and his emerging Whig Party were ready to protect America from such international monopolies through trade tariffs.

Economic embargos of the war and high prices had resulted, not in a collapse of American production, but in a surge. Eli Whitney's cotton gin had encouraged a booming Southern plantation system to grow cotton, most of which was shipped to England for processing. In the 1790s, a Quaker merchant, Moses Brown (Brown University is named after him), teamed up with Samuel Slater to build a cotton textile mill in Rhode Island; but the industry took advantage of the shipping problems and embargo leading up to the War of 1812 to bring money and innovation into cotton textile manufacture. A Boston merchant, Francis Cabot Lowell, visited the automated cotton textile mills of England. England earlier had banned the foreign sale of power looms to prevent American competition. Lowell studied and memorized machine designs, and returned to America to "reinvent" power looms, using what today we call "reverse engineering." For capital, Lowell brought in a number of merchant families to form Boston Manufacturing Company. The opportunity provided by the war attracted the shipping fortunes of New England. What was really unique was Lowell's financing plan, using a joint-stock arrangement versus a partnership. Partnerships often ended with the death of a partner, but Lowell's stock arrangement would allow the firm to move on after the death of any partner. His system is the basis of today's corporation.

The War of 1812 created a major boom in textile production. In addition, demand for cotton clothes soared as these new mechanical looms could create complex patterns. In 1800, America had 2,000 spindles; by 1810 there were 80,000, and by 1812 there were 500,000 spindles! As Lowell built a number of mills, massive amounts of labor were needed. He also needed to keep overhead low, since England was dumping cheap product into the American market. Henry Clay would develop a scientific system of tariffs to allow America to compete. England, of course, was using cheap child labor in industrial sweatshops. The embargo created a boom for American textile manufacturers with 105 new textile mills in 1814 alone. In 1831, forty million dollars were invested in textile mills that produced 230 million yards of cloth. The problem was the labor shortage, which created a rise in child labor at the cotton mills. In 1820 in Massachusetts, 45 percent of the cotton mill workers were children; it was 55 percent in Rhode Island. By 1831, America had 800 textile mills employing 38,000 women, 18,000 men, and 4,000 children. Cotton mills were emerging in places like Pittsburgh, Lexington, and Cincinnati. Central Ohio had a growing wool industry as well. Henry Clay's American system of protection appealed to these new industrialists and their cities.

Unlike the case in Europe, the Industrial Revolution created a labor shortage in America. Industrialization and automation created a need for laborers who had never been needed before. As an agrarian nation, America had been content to import manufactured goods. Farmers had also been trained to make needed products at home. Companies needed to attract labor from farms as well as from children and women.

The town of Lowell, Massachusetts, became the center of American manufacturing. Lowell recruited some Irish immigrants, but a larger, cheaper labor force was needed, so manufacturers turned to Yankee farm girls in Massachusetts, New Hampshire, Vermont, and Maine. Lowell manufacturing did offer a better environment than that of British mills, but not for purely paternal reasons. The mills needed to attract American workers in New England. About 17 percent of the workforce would be young single women. The pay was $1.85 to $3.00 a week, including discounted room and board. The pay was less than that of men but three times that of a head maid. The workday was 12 hours (with breaks), and the week was 6 days long. The ages of the workers varied from 15 to 25. A woman was required to sign on for a year, and the average length of stay was three years. The work week seems long, but it was equivalent to that of farm work. The factories had an infirmary, but employees were charged to use it. Lowell also hired seasonal workers such as schoolteachers. But money alone could not win out against the beliefs of the New England Puritans, who believed women should be in the home. They also viewed women who worked as having destroyed their reputations.

To win over the Puritan stock of New England, Lowell created a revolutionary work environment. Boardinghouses were managed by a strict "house mother," who assured strict social norms. The wholesome environment included schooling and free lectures. The mills were clean and safe. Responding to the criticism of Puritans, mill owners applied a strict moral code to the working village. House mothers maintained strict rules including curfews, dress codes, and restricted interactions with men. Courses were given in housekeeping and cooking.

The girls were "encouraged" to build saving accounts with part of their pay. The nearby town, designed to be a "commercial utopia,"[2] was built and controlled by the company. Cleanliness and a crime-free environment were paramount in its operation. Women were expected to attend church services routinely; not attending was cause for dismissal. The girls were encouraged to become active in church including becoming Sunday school teachers. The boardinghouses promoted biblical studies as well. The young girls were taught sewing and cooking. They only averaged about three years of employment, so the Lowell boardinghouses were a type of prep school, aided by the town's circulating library. This type of industrial prep school approach would be adopted by later paternal capitalists such as H.J. Heinz. The boardinghouses had well-stocked libraries, and reading clubs were mandated. Girls published a famous literary magazine known as the *Lowell Offering*.

Another reason for the paternalism of the Lowell mills was political.[3] The great debate of the 1820s was over the protection and growth of American industry by protective tariffs. The cheap prices of cotton fabric produced in England had prevented the development of American mills. The

British attempted to destroy the American textile industry by dumping huge quantities of British textiles on American docks. The British similarly dumped cheap pig iron to suppress the American pig iron industry. The Democrats and President Andrew Jackson argued the promotion of American manufacturing would only bring the social abuses of Europe to America. The Federalist-Whigs of New England argued American manufacturing would be different. Industrialists studied and made the necessary changes to eliminate the abuses of the British factory system.

The mills won the praise of British muckraking novelist Charles Dickens. Dickens only visited Lowell for a day, but as he was the great critic of British industrialization, his positive review carried much weight. While the working hours were actually longer than in Britain, Dickens was impressed that the boardinghouses had pianos and libraries.[4] Certainly the literary endeavors of the Lowell girls would have impressed him. The prep school approach using young girls was much different from the life-long sentence of women to factory work in Britain. Critics argue that the company put its best foot forward, but that it was no different from companies today. Still, even President Andrew Jackson was impressed by his visit. These American mills and related communities were a successful option to the extremes of communal manufacturing and British industrialization.

It certainly was arguable whether the Lowell area was "Camelot on the Merrimack." Clearly, it was dramatically different from Manchester, England, the iconic city of the Industrial Age. Manchester's skies were thick with smoke from the coal-fired steam engines. In Manchester, orphans manned the cotton mills. Children roamed the streets and often lived in alleys. Housing consisted of rooms holding six to eight. Streets and gutters filled with sewage. Life expectancy among Manchester's poor was 17 years.[5] Lowell was a dramatic improvement over Manchester, but work was still hard and dangerous. The breathing in of cotton fibers caused brown lung or byssinosis. It is estimated that 70 percent of early New England cotton workers died from respiratory illnesses.[6]

Henry Clay, presidential candidate and Speaker of the House, often toured these mills and became their popular defender; thus, one of the mills was named after him. Clay argued the "American system" was proactive and a positive experience for workers. Women were given new opportunities via their work in the mills. The corporation started savings banks and encouraged savings. The system became popular with poor New England farmers whose daughters averaged about four years working at the mills. These mills employed 6,000 women and 1,600 men by 1820.

The major shareholder families—the Lowells, Appletons, Cabots, Lawrences, and Jacksons—would dominate New England economics and politics and helped form Clay's Whig party. The Whigs, and later the Republican Party, became great defenders of protection of American industry to maintain wages and income. Lowell capitalists became known as the "cotton Whigs" because of their ties to the South.

The Lowell mill girls became famous, as did the approach of the mill owners towards them. Much like Walmart today, both the praises and denouncements were passionate of the working conditions at the Lowell mills. In the 1840s, the mills became the focus of a state investigation.[7] This investigation was completed in 1845 and was very favorable. The Lowell capitalists also proved to be philanthropists, building hospitals, parks, churches, and museums throughout the area. Still, the Lowell experiment as a paternal economic model has to be considered a mixed bag. The model of a preparatory experience to attract young girls to the workforce prior to marriage would be emulated successfully, decades later, by industrialists such as George Westinghouse and H.J. Heinz.

The impact of the benevolent approach of the Lowell mills on American industry is unclear. The Lowell model, unlike that of Owen, was not philosophically based, but centered solely on profitability. It was popular with many Whig politicians and capitalists. Many of the benevolent adaptations at Lowell were to address the overall labor shortages and overcome Puritan objections to using women in the workplace. The cotton industry was expanding throughout the Northeast and Middle Atlantic states. In general, the industry faced a labor shortage and a productivity challenge from better-equipped British mills. The success of various religious communes and the Lowell experience did suggest that worker satisfaction and improved workplace environment could address both issues. Unfortunately, the second generations of the Lords of Lowell were less benevolent and paternal, and the system eroded to one of employee abuses in the 1850s. Some of this was the result of nineteenth-century globalization, which put the American mills under large cost pressures, competing with cheap foreign labor and raw materials. Many Whigs argued that lack of protectionism had forced the American cotton mills into this unfair competition.

Others argue that Lowell capitalists, at least in the late 1840s, used paternalism to prevent the kind of labor unrest commonly seen in Europe. Labor unrest was considered a result of the boring work environment of automated factories.[8] Unrest in Europe had created a wave of immigration to America, and more and more of these immigrants were replacing women in the mills. As profits decreased during and after the Civil War, much of the paternal environment disappeared. It became more profitable to use European immigrants with less paternal benefits.

The Lowell experiment, for all practical purposes, ended with the Civil War. During the war, and despite the Union attempts to blockade, Southern cotton was shipped to England, strengthening their industry, until the South embargoed Britain for its refusal to recognize the Confederate states' independence. The Lowell mills struggled as the Union Army opened up captured plantations, but profit losses destroyed the business. The New England mills that survived the war were far different operations. After the Civil War, the industry was under attack for working conditions and health and safety hazards by the press and government. Government and unions made inroads into the industry. The workers' pay and conditions improved, but at a cost to the manufacturers. Local and state government added more regulation and taxes. By the late 1890s, many of the mills were in need of major renovation. Still, the attitude remained that the textile industry was here to stay. The workers were now low-paid immigrants, and profits were razor slim. Lowell would be remembered for its paternalism, but as profits shrank, many paternal practices were eliminated. The final blow was the full elimination of protective tariffs. The work went overseas under the banner of free trade, but it really pushed child labor to poor unregulated countries or industrial sweatshops.

Some historians have suggested a broader movement of the early 1800s was seen in what might be called "Christian industrialism," tying it to the spiritual awakenings of the eighteenth century.[9] Christian industrialism would appear to be less of a movement than the confluence of industry and the Great Awakening in early America. The Rockdale district of Delaware Valley was another early cotton manufacturing area that tried to bring community and factory into a mutual arrangement. The Rockdale manufacturers looked to build a Christian community and use it to foster a productive workforce. They focused on giving money to community churches and schools versus attempting corporate ownership of the community. This was the more common approach of the early capitalists, similar to the Scotch-Irish capitalists of Western Pennsylvania and the early Pennsylvania iron plantations. Rockdale, however, was more a mix of the paternalism of Lowell and the old Pennsylvania manufacturing plantations. The Rockdale workers were male immigrants lacking the family bonding that was found in Lowell. These shifting immigrants required more of a patriarchal approach. A number of Christian capitalists arose to face this new challenge.

Probably the greatest of these evangelical capitalists was John Crozer (1793–1866). Crozer came from Puritan stock and became a strong Baptist. He had built his cotton mills near Chester, Pennsylvania, in the area known as Rockdale, with much struggle. Biographers have called him part manufacturer, part lay evangelist. He rebuilt the town's houses, schools, and churches. He ruled his employees, demanding they attend church and be of moral character. While better than most, he still required his workers to labor ten hours in a poor working environment.

Crozer is often pointed out in the debate on these pre–Civil War capitalists. He represented a type of ambivalence as to the nature of their philanthropy. Skeptics see at least some of the giving as self-serving. Crozer and the other cotton lords benefited from a more skilled and motivated workforce. Even Crozer noted that his charity assured workers would stay in the community during times of unemployment and underemployment.[10] The mix of capitalism and philanthropy is as complex as the individuals involved. At best, one should realize that capitalism with philanthropy is better than capitalism without. Clearly, in America there was an implied obligation of those blessed with wealth to give back.

The Rockdale mills were located along the banks of Chester Creek in Delaware County, in southeastern Pennsylvania, between Philadelphia and Wilmington. The Rockdale model was more patriarchal than paternal. The Rockdale mills and communities were overlooked by the owner or his manufacturer's mansion. These mansions were up the hill from the creek or river bottom factories and mill worker tenements. The workers' houses were rented to them. The community churches and other social institutions were the gifts of the patriarchal owners. Some mills also had a mill superintendent who lived closer to the workers. As the owners gained wealth, they often moved away to fashionable districts, leaving the mill superintendent to tend to the operation of the mill. The mill manager became a new class of manager. In addition, the foreman level evolved into a managerial class as the wealthy owners moved to cities. The focus of the owners was more on building the community than on the workers themselves.

The working conditions at the Rockdale mills were fair to poor by low British standards. However, the Rockdale mills offered opportunity. A worker who was a natural leader or processed leadership skills could advance to the managerial class. By 1850, a Rockdale mill worker made about $28 a month while a supervisor could expect $65 a month.[11] This opportunity to advance in pay and class offered a magnet to the mill for ambitious youth. The influx of immigrants in the 1840s led to abuses and the breakdown of paternalism. Cheap immigrant labor spread to cotton mills to industrial cities such as Pittsburgh.

Lowell's cotton girls had put up with long hours, in part, because of the benefits and the short commitment to the work. Immigrant workers saw the job as a lifelong commitment. The immigrant workers were not supplied housing, and they were forced to live in low-cost slums. Long hours were not tolerated well by the immigrants. Mill owners switched to children. The 1840s and 1850s saw a number of strikes as a response to these abuses. Major strikes by women cotton factory workers protesting 12-hour workdays occurred in Pittsburgh in 1845 and 1848. The strikes led to an 1848 state law limiting workdays to ten hours and prohibiting children less than twelve years of age from working in cotton and textile mills. Higher costs would lead to the loss of the cotton mills in pro-union cities such as Pittsburgh. Because of the importance of the cotton mills in New England, the elimination of the 12-hour workday was slow to be enacted.

Five

Crisis in American Labor: Class, Skilled, and Unskilled Laborers

American labor was a far different mix from that of Europe. America had a strong middle class of craftsmen—also known as artisans and mechanics—which had been key to the American Revolution. They faced the same threat of industrialization as did those of Europe; but as they formed the political core of America, their fate would be much different. America had also become the refuge of many European craftsmen. In addition, America was short of the unskilled laborers needed for industrialization. It also lacked the ready sources of women, children, and displaced craftsmen to fill factory jobs. This would require new ideas like those imposed at Lowell for the expansion of industry. Paternal practices were a necessity to operate the factories. Like Europe, America would struggle with labor and industrialization, but its path would be far different from that of Europe.

Besides the labor market itself, America was far different publicly and socially. Europe had a serf-aristocrat mentality, while America had a middle class, property opportunity, a desire for educational opportunity, a belief in Creator-given rights, and a love of freedom. These differences would make the struggle with industrialization more difficult on a personal level. America would have its abuses, but the solutions would be more consistent with American principles. Of course, in fairness, the slaves are often forgotten in our labor history. Slavery, however, left its mark on

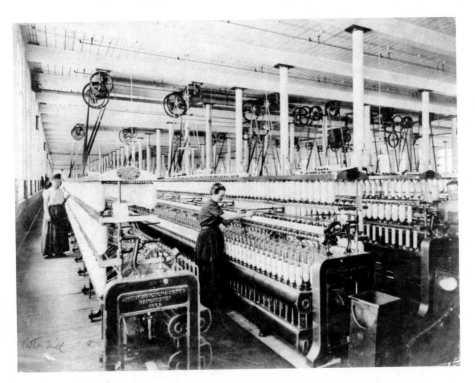

Women workers at Lowell ca. 1900 (Library of Congress).

labor even in the North. The Democratic Party was a national party with deep Southern roots. The Democrats supported slavery while opposing the capitalists of the North. They saw America as an agrarian society supplying raw materials to Europe, which had been its colonial heritage. Cotton was the country's main export to Europe, whose factories, in turn, produced cloth to be imported into the United States. Democrats opposed the tariffs of Federalists and Whigs to promote industry because they feared retaliation tariffs on raw cotton by Europe.

The politics of protectionists and slavery would align with the North-South divide. The North had never fully considered the use of slaves in their growing factories because of their early resistance by the middle class and the craftsman class. Border states also approached slavery differently. The Jamestown colony model would eventually lead to slavery and an aristocratic society in the South. The views on work and the individual varied greatly between Jamestown (Virginia) and the Plymouth model (New England). Both were royal colonies with governors reporting to the king. Land distribution became the key to many differences between the two colonies. The tobacco industry of Virginia did require capital and manpower beyond that of the small crafts-oriented industries of New England. Small tobacco farmers did try to succeed without slavery, but were opposed by the government. The granting of land in Virginia opposed the small farmer and favored wealthy investors. Successful large planters were favored to obtain new land, thus slavery spread.

Unfortunately, America was slow to learn the economic inefficiencies of slavery. Men held by physical, economic, or mental chains are never very productive. But even in America's dark history of slavery, some enlightened plantation owners realized economic freedom was key to productivity. Northern and Upper Southern tobacco planters moved from the daily over-seeing and feeding of captive workers to a task system. Slaves, once they completed tasks of the plantation owner, were free to plant gardens, build homes, and care for families. They were allowed to have rifles to hunt food and had property rights. The productivity and profitability of these Upper Southern tobacco plantations was far superior to the fully imprisoned slaves of the Deep South.

Northern capitalists feared the Southern aristocrats using slavery might move into manufacturing of iron in the 1840s. The emerging indus-trialization of iron making in the North was manned by Irish immigrants and native labor. The South, however, was building an iron industry in the border states through the use of slaves. Virginia and Tennessee had devel-oped very competitive iron factories using slaves. A Northern economist in 1847 argued the dangers to Northern workers, stating, "The slave labor in Virginia at the cost of $120 a year would soon destroy the Pennsylvania iron industry, which paid $300 a year for labor."[1] Northern capitalists often used such fears to force lower wages and subdue strikes. The result was a strong alliance of the workers with the antislavery movement.[2] This alliance of Northern labor and the antislavery movement would result in the for-mation of the Republican Party from the Whig Party. It would be the root of a Republican protectionist platform from Abraham Lincoln (a former Whig) to Herbert Hoover. It would push capitalists to treat their workers better.

The real change in the labor market in the first half of the nineteenth century came from Irish and German immigration and urban industrial-ization. The building of the Erie Canal opened the floodgates of Irish immigration in the 1820s. The Erie Canal would connect the western mar-kets to New York City and the world through the port of New York. The canal dropped freight transport costs between Buffalo and New York from an average of $90 a ton to $4 a ton. A person traveled the canal at five cents a mile. Work for the canal began on July 4, 1817. The states were short on native-born laborers to meet the needed thousands and advertised in Europe for laborers. In general, wages were at least three times higher than those of Europe. The work was extremely hard, requiring hand digging, hauling dirt, tree stump removal, and tree cutting. Much of the path was marshy, and workers faced the threat of contracting malaria. Hundreds of skilled masons from Germany came to help line the canal with stone and clay. The canal, by the time it was completed in 1825, had brought tens of thousands of Irish to America.

Initially, English, Welsh, and Irish were recruited from the poor of New York City. The pay was $12 a month plus food and board. By 1820, labor was becoming short and wages rose to fifty cents a day. Agents were sent to Ireland to recruit laborers as the canal building slowed for lack of labor. Irish immigrants came by the thousands to work at eighty cents a day including room, board, and a ration of whiskey. Some of America's first incentive pay systems were developed on the Erie Canal, offering the Irish extra whiskey for achieving goals. Labor shortages forced wages up to one dollar a day by 1825. The recruitment and paternalism of the canal managers would be a model for future labor-short industries such as steel and rubber.

The men worked ten to fourteen hours, but the food and wages exceeded anything known in Ireland. Breakfasts of eggs, mush, ham, potatoes, pancakes, and cornbread were common for canal workers. Lunches were packed for them to eat during a half-hour break. Dinner was loaded with a variety of meats. The Irish tended to settle along the path of the canal, finding work operating the finished waterway. The canal was an Irish network for future Irish immigration. The Irish in New York started to face discrimination by groups such as Tammany Hall and upstate Federalists. By 1819, Irish immigration was about 6,000 a year (about 3,000 for the canal); while in 1827, it was over 20,000 a year. In 1832, Irish immigration reached 60,000 a year as other states begin massive canal building, and crops started to fail in Ireland. The number of worker deaths on the canal was extremely high, with as many as 1,000 workers a year lost to malaria, and maybe another fifty to rattlesnakes. Even after the Erie Canal was completed, it employed 8,000.[3]

When the canal building slowed in the 1830s, it created a new source of cheap labor needing work. Some of the Irish moved to the cotton mills, and others moved to the booming urban industries such as furniture, shoes, and clothing. The canals created demand and volume that led to the American "factory system." The canals would change American labor and capitalism forever. The tariffs, extended canal trade, and government contracts produced volume levels for consumer products and food never previously encountered, allowing a shift in many industries from a crafts system to the factory system in the Northeast.

New York City became the key seaport on the east coast as grain from the Midwest moved to New York on the Erie Canal. The impact of the canal on New York can be seen in the fact that in 1800, the port of New York accounted for 9 percent of America's exports; and by 1860, it was 62 percent. The population of New York in 1820 was only 123,700, but rose to 814,000 in 1860. In 1825, the year of its completion, the canal carried 212,000 barrels of flour, 562,000 bushels of wheat, and 435,000 gallons of whiskey, most of which was for export.[4] The success of the Erie Canal inspired canal building in Pennsylvania, Ohio, and Indiana. By 1830, New York City was the center of American manufacturing. Demand for these consumer goods forced the conversion of crafts shop into factories. The centralized craft manufacturing shop would be the missing link in this transition, similar to that seen in Lancaster wagon making during the 1700s. The demand for low-cost ready-made clothing caused a rapid industrialization of the clothing trades. Demand for clothing and the stream of famine-driven immigrants of the 1840s caused rapid specialization of work in the clothing industry. Unskilled cutters became the labor core of the old tailor craft while a small group of skilled workers maintained a crafts posture. There was a pride and status attributed to skilled workers. Mobility, the key to attracting both skilled and unskilled workers in America, was different from the class rigidity of Europe. The same happened in ready-made shoes, furniture, and construction. American urban industrialization took a similar path to that in Europe. The difference was segmentation in these trades to three classes: unskilled, skilled, and the managerial class. The skilled and manager classes would evolve into a strong middle class. In many industries, skilled laborers made more than the supervisors. Yet, there was a strong pull of opportunity for laborers to rise to the managerial class. Many would start to call this part of the "American dream." It was this mobility and hope in the future that drew many to America.

While America was developing into a new crafts model, Europe was either resisting automation or fully embracing it. The revolutionary 1840s in Europe had caused the crafts guilds to be banned and be replaced with a type of trade union. In addition, socialism was evolving in Germany as an alternative to capitalism. German crafts guilds formed a policy that banned automatic looms in order to protect crafts jobs. In 1847, there were 2,262 automated looms versus 116,832 handlooms. The crafts system, to a large degree, was institutionalized. The problem was that cheaper machine-made cloth from England flooded Germany, crushing the overall industry. Like the Luddites of England, Germany learned globalization and automation could not be resisted. In the 1840s, many German craftsmen had gone to France to learn their trades; but France followed the German approach to free trade in the late 1840s, and German manufacturing and crafts all but disappeared. German craftsmen looked next to the United States to establish their old trades. German locksmiths, tailors, shoemakers, cigar makers, brewers, bakers, brick makers, and others headed for America. In America, these craftsmen tried to merge crafts with union protection again.

The crafts also caused a division in the labor movement of the last half of the nineteenth century. The union movement was confronted with the opposing needs of skilled and unskilled laborers. The Knights of Labor and the amalgamated (crafts) unions were in competition for the same workers. The main difference between the Knights and these amalgamated unions was that the Knights were organized by industry and the amalgamated by trades. The Knights favored representing both skilled and unskilled workers within an industry and were more likely to accept unskilled immigrants. The amalgamated favored representation of skilled workers, opposing the membership of unskilled. Amalgamated represented the "tonnage" workers paid by the tons produced. The amalgamated called their basic unit a lodge while the Knights called theirs a "forge." The amalgamated unions were in America's main industries such as steel, iron, and glass. The Knights were concerned with broad labor issues such as the eight-hour day and working conditions. The amalgamated was focused on wages, crafts control, and pay scales. In 1882, the amalgamated unions were in most of the steel mills and mines with some competition from the Knights. Generally the amalgamated unions would fail because they represented a declining group of workers as automation took place. In steel in the late 1800s, about 70 percent of the workers were unskilled. When the amalgamated union called a strike for higher wages, the majority of workers were left out. They would learn the hard way without solidarity, a strike would fail. The root of the problem remained the advance of automation, which eliminated the crafts. Some crafts formed trade associations to control the workplace.

The American labor market took on a unique bastardization of the old crafts in heavy industry such as iron, glass, and coal mining in 1850s. This semi-crafts model would last until complete automation took place in the 1880s. The skilled iron makers known as puddlers would use the master craftsman as the head of a working crew of skilled and unskilled laborers. The skilled iron workers formed one of the first ironworker trade associations, which were called the "Sons of Vulcan." They restricted entry into the craft and kept methods secret. Welsh and English puddlers controlled these "forges" or shop unions in Pennsylvania. These trade unions did not protect the lowest and most mistreated unskilled laborers. These iron puddlers were paid by the amount of steel produced. The iron company subcontracted, paying the master puddler for the iron made. The master then paid the skilled workers and unskilled laborers. The wage was around $9 a ton, which for 10 hours of work per day might translate to $15 to $20 a week. Actually, the puddler was the master craftsman and received the $9 per ton; he, in turn, paid a handful of men on his crew. A crew worked five "heats" of about a half-ton each per ten-hour day. The lowest-skilled man on the puddler's crew made around $4 for the week. This was better pay than most front-line managers and foremen. Puddlers and iron rollers were considered the "worker aristocracy" of Pittsburgh. Even the puddlers broke with the crafts model by using unskilled workers in work once done by apprentices. Most of the unskilled laborers not in the Sons of Vulcan were paid around 70 cents a day. These unskilled mill laborers did not belong to tonnage production crews and made up the majority of the mill workers. The ten-hour day became the standard of the puddling crews.

The invention of the Bessemer process in the late 1860s would challenge the need for the master puddler and his crew. By the 1880s, Bessemer steel was quickly replacing wrought iron in tonnage usages such as railroad and bridge building. A single Bessemer converter could produce as much as twenty times the output of a full day's work of the puddler in 40 minutes. Furthermore, the Bessemer steel operating crew required much less skill than the puddler and his crew. New capitalists such as Andrew Carnegie and Benjamin Jones would apply the new technology without the use of puddling crews, hiring unskilled cheap immigrant labor instead. Ironically, Carnegie embraced the advance of technology and the elimination of the crafts system that had broken his father and made it necessary for the Carnegie family to come to America.

Coal mining used a similar semi-crafts model and had the skilled workers represented by an amalgamated union. The American mines attracted Welsh, Cornish, and Scottish master coal miners who could earn three cents a bushel, which was far better than Europe was paying. This translated into six to eight dollars a day, which was above the two dollars a day earned in Europe. These miners were considered craftsmen and specialists, having served long and arduous apprenticeships in Europe. They were also independent operators being paid for their level of production, and hiring their own unskilled laborers to load coal. The coal company paid the master miner-operator directly, who, in turn, paid his workers. These early miners were piece-rate and were free to determine their own working hours. They were responsible for their own equipment such as candles, shovels, picks, and "lard" lamps. By the late 1880s, the company took over worker control, paying each worker based on skill levels or a single unskilled rate. The miners would form an amalgamated union before full transition to a trade union. The initial unions in America would only represent the skilled workers. Unskilled labor depended on the benevolence of the owners. The eventual unionization of both skilled and unskilled into unions by the end of the 1930s would be the first step in the end of paternal capitalism.

From 1882 to 1900, capitalists such as Andrew Carnegie finished off the remains of the large crafts unions. The year of 1882 was one of strikes in the steel and iron industry. These were centered on the problems that had started at Pittsburgh Bessemer Steel at Homestead. The problem was much more complex than a struggle pitting the rich capitalists against the poor laborers. First, as we have seen, the poor immigrant laborer was excluded from union membership. These crafts unions were for skilled workers only. Second, the pressure to confront the union didn't come only from the boardroom or the owners, but from the evolving managerial class. Lower and middle management was frustrated by the pay scales of the union skilled workers. The steel foreman, for example, worked the same twelve-hour day as the steel puddler or blast furnace man but was paid considerably less. Usually, the foreman made half the wages of the highest-paid union worker. In the 1880s, a blooming mill roller made about $6.00 a day, a blooming mill foreman about $2.50 a day, and an unskilled laborer about $1.00 a day. The blooming mill superintendent made about $6 a day. The average worker of the period made about $1.65 a day, so there was little public support at times for these crafts unions. The internal control of the union by various nationalities, along with crafts rivalry, created internal opposition. Still, companies often lost public support because of their unilateral lockouts in recessions. The other part of the problem was a fear of the unions by the owners. Part of it was a control issue, but another part was European unionism, which was socialistic, political, and often violent. The newspapers were full of stories of the violence and socialism in Europe, and the American Railroad Strike of 1877 had put fear into the general population.

Burning of Union Station, Pittsburgh, during the 1877 Railroad Strike, first published in *Harper's Weekly 1877* (Library of Congress).

The glass industry was one of the last to switch over to automation and unskilled labor. The skilled glassworkers were the aristocrats of America's skilled workers. In the early 1890s, the glassblower made the equivalent of $28 an hour today. The glass workers had a structured system which consisted of a "gang" headed up by the blower or master craftsman, followed by the assistant blower, gatherer, assistant gatherer, and servitor. The industry used child labor for unskilled work. A glasshouse might have 8 to 14 gangs working on various shifts and furnaces. In addition, the gang was supported by a group of usually 4 to 8 who handled the glass in various stages of production. The first effort to unionize the flint glass workers was in Pittsburgh in 1858. The organization was known as the Glass Blowers Benevolent Society and again focused on the blowers; it most resembled a European guild. The Benevolent Society continued as a secret organization without much success. It wasn't until 1878 that the Knights of Labor brought a number of eastern unions together in the United Flint Glass Workers. This union represented at least the whole gang except the unskilled boys (the handling boys, making up the biggest fraction of employees, were left out).

The struggle of the crafts and skilled trades in the mid–1800s became the struggle of the unskilled immigrant by the late 1800s. Unions, which

**Looting during the Railroad Strike in 1877, first published in *Harper's Weekly*
(Library of Congress).**

had favored the skilled laborers, had to adapt for the unskilled immigrant
worker. Capitalism, in its quest for efficiency and low cost, could be cold
and uncaring. Some capitalists, however, found productivity gains in the
fair treatment of workers. The immigrant laborer had become necessary
in most industries by the 1890s, and Ireland was no longer big enough to
supply the demand. The Slavs and Hungarians of Eastern Europe became
the new source of American labor.

The invention of the glass-blowing machine by Michael Owens in 1905
changed the labor balance as had the Bessemer process in steel. The commercial version in 1908 known as machine A could produce twelve beer
bottles per minute or 17,280 in a 24-hour period. This compared to hand
production of 2,880 per day using a crew of six men and boys.[5] The skilled
glassblower was essentially eliminated, and unskilled labor became the
standard. As had been the case with steel and mining, immigrants flooded
into the workforce. They lacked the basic needs, however, and the city
governments were unable to finance the needed housing, hospitals, and
social needs. In an age without taxes, the immigrants needed to look to
the company and capitalists for their most basic needs. To a degree, paternal capitalism became a necessity and an integral part of doing business.

Six

Early Paternal and Employee-Driven Capitalists

The Puritans, the Lowell cotton mills, and Owenite cooperatives were, to some degree, special communal cases of industry. Men like James O'Hara had pioneered the importance of developing community to attract labor to an urban center. The first industrialist to take the concern of laborers and apply Christian principles and develop community using profits made from industry was Peter Cooper. Cooper (1791–1883) was an American industrialist, inventor, philanthropist, trade protectionist, and candidate for president of the United States. He rose from a pre–Civil War class of craftsmen and mechanics that developed the industrial foundation of America. He designed and built the first steam locomotive in the U.S. and founded the Cooper Union for the Advancement of Science and Art in Manhattan. Cooper would be one of America's wealthiest by the mid–1800s. His roots went back to colonial New York in the 1600s. The Cooper family had come from England searching for economic opportunities, had fought passionately for America's freedom. Having suffered for lack of education, Cooper believed that equality of education and opportunity to obtain it was the key to industrial democracy. He linked the success of American industry to its educational system. In particular, Cooper hoped to open opportunities for young apprentices to become factory owners and inventors. Cooper's blend of capitalism and philanthropy was known as "Scientific Humanism."[1] Others called it paternalism or paternal capitalism.

In 1808 at the age of seventeen, Peter apprenticed to a coach maker on New York's Broadway and Chambers Street. His salary was $25 a year plus room and board. While treated fairly, he looked at apprenticeship as a type of economic slavery. At the end of his apprenticeship, Cooper was employed at a factory for $1.25 a day making machinery to shear cloth. Cooper proved a successful businessman, buying the patents for new machines. Saving and investing, he opened and sold a number of manufacturing businesses. Still, coming from a lower-class family, Cooper was frustrated with the apprentice system and limited opportunities for youths. A young Cooper would find himself in the middle of the struggle between the transition of the apprentice system and the more generalized skilled labor in America.

A biographer described his early experience: "At every stage, however, he found himself hindered by lack of thorough knowledge. Moreover, he found that his lack of education crippled him in an attempt to make other men understand and appreciate his fruitful ideas. As an apprentice, he resolved to do something for apprentices."[2] For Cooper, a more important matter than attracting labor was offering American youth an opportunity and realizing the nation needed well-trained youth. He wanted youth to have the success and opportunity he had enjoyed. By the late 1840s, Cooper was a very wealthy businessman.

Years later, Cooper and his son-in-law, Abram Hewitt, purchased land around Baltimore and started an iron-making business to support the building of the Baltimore & Ohio Railroad. In 1828, Cooper developed a new version of the steam engine locomotive known as the "Tom Thumb." To improve his iron parts, Cooper began developing new methods in the puddling of iron. He would go on to build wire mills, supplying wire for the first transatlantic cable and many Roebling bridges, which he also financed. In the 1850s, Peter Cooper expanded his manufacture of steel rails, wire, and beams at his Trenton Iron Works. He would become the first to apply the Bessemer process and open-hearth process in the steel business. In 1854, Cooper's fame rose as he teamed up with Cyrus Field to build the transatlantic cable.

Now Peter Cooper would be on the forefront of a second wave in American immigrant labor and the rise of unskilled labor using technology. Cooper tried to soften that transition of labor. Trenton Iron was a good place for workers in both skilled and unskilled labor. Workers were provided with houses and the company store offered supplies at cost. While Cooper was known for his fairness, he didn't build a reputation for his employee relations. He would become more involved in worker education and training on a broader scale. Cooper had lived through the deskilling of workers and believed education was the best insurance for the American worker. Learning a single skill was no guarantee of a productive career. For the unskilled worker, the future was even bleaker. Cooper saw the problem as bigger than any one company or industry. In this respect, Cooper was more of a philanthropist than a paternalist.

Cooper's fortune grew, and as a prominent New Yorker, he was asked to serve on the city's education committee. Cooper would fight hard for free public education. During this period, he formulated the idea of an educational institution with the purpose of "to be ever devoted to the Union of Science and Art in its application to the useful purposes of life."[3] This unique free educational institute was called the Cooper Union for the Advancement of Science and Art, which became known as the Cooper Union. There was nothing else like Cooper Union in the 1850s. The Union offered education on all levels from self study to college. Cooper Union was the first private college to admit Jews, blacks, and women. The Cooper Institute would offer night classes for adult students in science and business. It was also open to women and supplied free lectures and training for all. Its library was the only one open to the poor in New York, and was open at night for the working class. The library, in its first year, had over

Peter Cooper cartoon from *Puck Magazine* in 1902 (Library of Congress).

3,000 patrons a week.[4] Not surprisingly, the Cooper Union building was the first four-story fireproof structure built with wrought iron beams from his mills. This New York building would cost $600,000 alone.

The United States Commission on Education reported the following on the facilities of Cooper Union: "These afford a remarkable example of the intelligent application of a great charity. Their purpose is the technical instruction of the laboring classes, which is accomplished through the agency of a free library and reading room, free lectures and two classes of schools, viz., the Evening School of Science and Art and the Art School for Women."[5] Cooper would have the help of his son-in-law, Abram Hewitt, in the building of Cooper Union. Hewitt would run the many business ventures as Cooper turned to philanthropic and social endeavors as the years passed.

In the 1860s, the Union offered a three-year course in science and engineering. Cooper brought in guest speakers from all walks of life. Abraham Lincoln in 1860 gave a speech at Cooper Union that many believe won him the presidency. Lincoln heralded his protection of American industry that would become the cornerstone of the Republican Party platform until 1930. The Cooper Union became a center to free educational lectures. Other early speakers included Mark Twain and Susan B. Anthony. In addition to Lincoln, the Great Hall would be a speaker platform for seven presidents, also including U.S. Grant, William Taft, Teddy Roosevelt, Woodrow Wilson, Bill Clinton, and Barack Obama.

In the 1870s, these lectures ranged from exploration to scientific invention. His School of Design became popular with women, offering certificates in art and photography. Cooper Union was the first major institution to embrace the training of women in typewriting (as typing was known at the time). In the 1880s, Cooper established an Inventors' Institute, which had a museum of inventions and new devices. It also functioned as an incubator for new inventions. The institute also had working mechanical models for the education of young boys. Cooper had been a prolific inventor, with inventions varying from steelmaking to Jell-O. Peter Cooper believed the encouragement of invention was key to the nation as a whole. Peter had been encouraged as an apprentice to invent, and one of his early friends had formed a group of apprentices to encourage invention. Part-time alumni of the Inventors' Institute would include Thomas Edison and August Saint Gaudens. Thomas Edison developed the iron-sulphate chemistry responsible for his stock ticker in the Cooper Union laboratories.

Cooper was greatly influenced by his religious beliefs. "The production of wealth is not the work of any one man, and the acquisition of great

Peter Cooper statue ca. 1901 (Library of Congress).

fortunes is not possible without the co-operation of multitudes of men."
He believed it to be the responsibility of the wealthy to exercise Christian
charity because "a good human intelligence," he explained, "feels bound
to use all its powers to accomplish the greatest good [for] the greatest
number."[6] Cooper was a Unitarian, but the Union was open to all. He had

many Quaker friends who had also influenced him. Cooper did feel, as did the founders of the country, that God should be part of education. Not only did Cooper see this institution as God's work, but as an ethical force in the world of business. Cooper saw a strong connection between community and business.

Cooper was also known for his generosity and charity to the poor. One donation included $10,000 to supply shoes for poor children. Peter Cooper also proposed social programs to help the unemployed. Cooper, like many industrialists, realized the biggest worry of workers was the loss of a steady income. During the 1873 Panic, Cooper proposed an extensive public works system for the unemployed. Cooper opened his library to the poor in the Panic of 1873, giving away half-dollars and dollars for a total of as much as $1,500 a week at times.[7] He offered free education to needy workers.

Cooper saw capitalism as national in scope. He argued domestic capitalism and free trade with other countries could not be equivalent. He wrote books and pamphlets on the necessity for a high protective tariff to keep American workers employed. He became an important voice before Congress on labor and manufacturing. In 1877, Cooper ran for president as a candidate of the Greenback Labor Party. The party's name referred to the non-gold backed paper money, commonly known as "greenbacks," issued by the North during the American Civil War and shortly afterward. The party opposed the deflationary lowering of prices paid to producers entailed by a return to a gold- or silver-based monetary system, which was the policy favored by the dominant Republican Party.

He broke with the Republicans over the need to pay off the national debt and reduce taxes. Cooper ran in support of the unemployed, ending free prison labor, shorter working hours, ending the rising government debt, and ending the massive inflow of imports into the country. While defeated, Cooper would politically support the protection of American industry through tariffs his whole life. Cooper was always concerned that his efforts to educate and train workers would be lost to foreign imports. On a local level, Peter Cooper fought hard against the corruption in New York of Boss Tweed and Tammany Hall. The Greenback Party would merge with and form a segment of the Republican Party.

Cooper stood out in an age of political and business corruption. He was the antithesis of the robber barons. A journal report of Cooper's funeral best distinguished him from the robber barons of the time, noting "that the only people not attending the funeral were those 'who attended Vanderbilt's ball the previous night and were probably not over their spree,' and the crowd who went to Philadelphia to witness the launching of Jay

Gould's pleasure yacht, *Atlanta*, whose absence would purify the moral atmosphere at the Cooper funeral."[8] While many great capitalists such as Andrew Carnegie claimed Cooper as their guide, few could stand up to his ethics, charity, and honesty. Cooper was truly a once in a hundred years birth. Certainly, Cooper has no equal today.

For the last twenty years of his life, Peter Cooper's energies were focused on the Union as his industrial empire maintained his fortune. During his life, he gave over a million dollars to the Union; and on his death, he left another $200,000. The year of his death, the Union required another $300,000 to repair the building, which the Cooper children supplied. By the beginning of the twentieth century, the Union was struggling to meet its broad mission of education for the public. In 1902, another group of capitalists came to its aid. The list included Andrew Carnegie with a donation of $600,000, H.H. Rogers of United States Steel with a donation of $250,000, and Peter Cooper's brother, William, with $340,000.[9] Cooper had few critics, but he did have his share of political enemies. In time those enemies disappeared, and Cooper's legacy grew with the Cooper Union.

Another great paternal industrialist and early philanthropist, Joseph Banigan, would come into the scene in the 1860s. Joseph Banigan came to America around 1848 as part of a great wave of European immigrants. A lot of these immigrants were called "forty-eighters" for the peak year of 1848. The Irish came with the failures of the potato crops. The Banigan family found help to get to America from the charity of Irish workers in the state of Rhode Island. Joseph's father remained a poor laborer struggling to feed his family. Rhode Island had been founded by Roger Williams, who had fled Puritan Massachusetts, and was a colony with no official religion. As such, Rhode Island had always welcomed Catholics, and was open to Irish immigrants, who found opposition in most other states. Still, in Providence, Rhode Island, the Know-Nothing Party, a secretive anti-immigrant political faction, was active. Banigan would see the hatred of bigotry early on in Providence. The young Banigan, at nine years old, started with the New England Screw Company that employed mainly women and children. Banigan went on to become a jeweler's apprentice for a few years.

In 1860, Banigan married Margaret Holt and went to work for his father-in-law in the new rubber industry. At the Providence Rubber Company, Banigan entered the booming rubberized shoe market. Eventually, he would partner with John Haskins and others in the Roxbury India Rubber Company, the first licensee of Charles Goodyear. Banigan and Haskins would form a new company, Goodyear India Rubber Stopper Bottle Company, in Roxbury, Massachusetts. Banigan proved an ambitious and quick learner. He became the plant's operating manager and expert in rubber production. After the Civil War, Banigan moved to Woonsocket, Rhode Island, and started the Woonsocket Rubber Company. He became known for his hiring of struggling Irish immigrants.

Woonsocket Rubber manufactured rubberized shoes and later boots for miners. While the rubber industry was located in New England, booming business made skilled workers in short supply. Woonsocket Rubber would invest in turning unskilled Irish laborers into skilled workers. Banigan became known for paying premium wages and donated much to the community of Woonsocket to make it attractive. Banigan, however, demanded much from his Irish workers, tolerating little of the drinking holidays so popular with them. Banigan also improved factory safety procedures, including firefighting, since fire was the commonest cause of major damage. Working hours and conditions were improved over those of the overall rubber industry. The paternal approach gave Woonsocket productivity and cost advantage over his competitors. Banigan proved a brilliant businessman, vertically integrating his operations into raw rubber and cotton production. By 1878, Banigan had over 800 employees and had eliminated the use of children.

Banigan proved very progressive in his approach to the workers. He and his workers were Irish Catholic and knew well oppression, famine, poverty, and lack of income. The 1870s and 1880s were a time when fatalities and injuries were common in American industry. Worker injuries often left the families without incomes. The Irish fraternal organizations, such as the Knights of Columbus, offered death and disability, paying about $300, a year's wages. Banigan became an active supporter of the Knights of Columbus. At Banigan factories, a $1,000 check and paid funeral expenses were given to the family. Injured workers received full wages while recovering, as well as paid physician fees.[10] Disabled workers were given light labor jobs for life. Most of Banigan's private charity will never be known. It was typical of the Irish to keep their charity private or it wouldn't count fully in the eyes of God.[11]

Banigan would become the first Catholic millionaire, but he never forgot his roots nor his faith and ex-countrymen. During recessions, Banigan often gave unemployment checks to help his workers. He gave freely to the community and church charities. Banigan would be inducted into Pope Leo XIII's Knights of St. Gregory for his philanthropy. Leo XIII was known as the labor pope because of his concern for abuses throughout the Industrial Revolution.

While most of Banigan's giving was private, he did have some major public projects. In 1882, Banigan purchased land and built a brick facility for the Little Sisters of the Poor to house 350 homeless. Banigan gave extensively to orphanages, mostly Catholic, but he required an open-door policy to any child in need. In 1895, Banigan built a special orphanage for toddlers less than four years of age, who had become wards of the state. He gave tens of thousands to St. Vincent dePaul and the Sisters of Mercy to help the poor. Similarly, Banigan built homes for the disabled. He donated much to the building and maintaining of hospitals. A special project was the building of the St. Maria's Home for Working Women. This home helped disabled, sick, and unemployed women. Banigan would build a Catholic university in Providence. Also, Banigan became the main donor for the establishment of Brown University, a Baptist school. Banigan established scholarships for poor Irish students. Similarly, he gave money to Mormon educational institutions. Banigan served personally on the boards of these organizations. He even had a full time manager at his rubber company to help with philanthropy.

Paternalism did not spare Banigan's rubber factories from labor problems. In the 1880s, Banigan and the labor movement itself were in disagreement about the role of unions. The rubber industry, like most of America, had highly paid skilled crafts workers and unskilled laborers. In rubber, the most elite of the skilled workers were the bookmakers and rubber cutters. These elites made as much as $3 an hour based on piecework. Unskilled laborers made between 50 cents to 75 cents an hour. Two unions were fighting over the workers. The crafts union modeled after the national American Federation of Labor was mainly interested in only the skilled workers, while the Knights of Labor wanted to represent both skilled and unskilled. The problem with the Knights is they had no interest in paying by skills. The Knights in Banigan's factories broke with the national leadership by forming local assemblies of skilled workers only. The Knights did suggest that the unskilled workers form their own assemblies, but they would have to negotiate separately with the company.

Banigan, like most industrialists of the time, had little liking for the union. Like most of the nineteenth-century industrialists, he had gone from rags to riches. Even the paternalists had little support for unions. For Banigan, it was a matter of control; he had little tolerance for a third party in the business. Banigan was always more of a benevolent autocrat, and this was his company. The union was after more than wage improvement; it wanted to reduce to an eight hour day, to protect against arbitrary firings, and to eliminate poor treatment. Even a morally good man like Banigan could, at times, have abusive approaches. Banigan had demanded that his employees attend church services, something the union totally opposed. He also would not guarantee uniformity of his supervisors' behavior. Banigan would also see his workers as ungrateful if they joined a union. His Irish workers had tempers, too. It was not that they didn't trust Banigan or weren't grateful, but the fear of unemployment or the inability to feed their families dominated their working lives. Banigan's factories were won over by the secrecy of the Knights of Labor.

Banigan was a capitalist first. He was in an industry which was facing rapid automation and invention. Labor was costly but the labor pool was shrinking. The Knights of Labor in 1880s had a strong hold in the industries of the East. The situation was a lot like globalization today. The unionization of the glass industry had forced companies to move from New England to the West in search of cheap labor. British control of the raw rubber market also put East Coast rubber at a disadvantage with imports. Fear reigned on both sides in labor disputes, and there were few winners. Banigan, the autocrat, had little time for the union at his rubber plants. In 1885, facing competition from more automated competition, he reduced the wages of his skilled workers, though leaving them still above the industry average. Banigan fired a union leader as well, bringing on strikes at his various plants. The strikes drew national publicity, and even the Vatican put pressure on Banigan, a Knight of St. Gregory, to compromise. With the help of a local priest, the disputes were settled.

Within a few years, the Knights of Labor would pass away and give rise to the American Federation of Labor, but it would take until the 1930s to fully unionize the rubber industry. Joe Banigan would fight for the American rubber industry through automation, protective tariffs, vertical integration, and building trusts. He grew his company and merged with others to form the United States Rubber Company in 1892. United States Rubber would become the largest rubber company and later became Uniroyal. The company would be one of the first twelve stocks to make up the Dow Jones Industrial Average.

Joe Banigan became a model for giving back to the workers by building community. Banigan's death in 1898 brought a huge gathering of Catholic bishops to mourn a man who had done so much for the poor. It was said that thousands of nuns prayed for him in his final illness after he had given so much to the church. Still, Banigan had his detractors, such as the unions. Banigan, however, would be the model for the industrialization and immigrant workers. Capitalists would have to integrate immigrants into nativist communities. Many would fail to meet this challenge; others would rise to it.

Seven

Robber Barons and the Questioning of Capitalism

The unequal distribution of wealth, stock scandals, opulent living, and the greed of Wall Street have been decried as the down side of capitalism. Most of these highly publicized issues became problematic in the Railroad Age of the 1850s, 1860s, and 1870s. Worse yet, corrupt capitalists would align with corrupt politicians in Tammany Hall and the Tweed Ring. The corruption would lead to America's first great depression in 1873. These excesses and abuses put a negative face on capitalism. With capitalists like William Vanderbilt, Jay Gould, Jim Fisk, and James Hill, paternalism became an exercise in public relations with little concern for the working man.

The 1860s would see the first major American business scandal. It would tie corrupt politicians and financiers into a national crisis. The scandal would be the legacy of the administration of Ulysses Grant. At its root was a natural contraction in the economy after the Civil War, but it is best remembered for the first "Black Friday," when the gold market in New York crashed on September 24, 1869. The crash was the result of a political scam and scandal. The stock market plummeted 20 percent and agricultural products plummeted 50 percent. The result was a short but severe disruption in the economy, making headlines across the nation. The railroad industry crashed also, due to overexpansion and its role in the gold market. The crash would eventually lay the groundwork for the Panic of 1873.

The Crisis of 1869 was started in the expansion of credit to finance the Civil War. The North had large gold reserves, but these were quickly used up in the first two years of the war. In 1862, the Legal Tender Act permitted the use of paper money and took the government off the gold standard. The Act authorized over $150 million in paper money. Paper money was issued with little backing, in the form of notes known as "greenbacks." Such a rapid expansion of credit created massive inflation as the war ended. Greenback dollars dropped to 35 cents in equivalent gold. The low gold value gave the government an opportunity to use gold to pay off the war debt.

The Grant administration decided to start using gold for a payback plan. Since the government controlled most of the market, it, in turn, controlled the price. However, speculators could make money if they could discover the timing of the government gold sales through leaks in the Grant administration. The general plan was far from secret, but certain speculators had an insider in the administration. Financier Abel Corbin was the president's brother-in-law and was close to Grant. Corbin would, in Grant's presence, argue against the government selling gold, but got President Grant to appoint his friend Daniel Butterfield as assistant treasurer of the United States. Butterfield planned with Wall Street financiers and railroad barons Jim Fisk (1835–1872) and Jay Gould (1836–1892) to corner the gold market. Butterfield tipped them off to when the government was to sell gold. Quietly, Fisk and Gould proceeded to corner the gold market by buying massive amounts.

By the end of August 1869, the government payback plan had been very successful in bringing down the debt. The money supply and the price of gold remained steady as $50 million of the national debt was reduced. The government varied the moves in the market, believing that based on the market indicators, they had held off speculation. However, Fisk and Gould, with the help of insider information, were sitting on a mountain of low-priced gold. It was only with the rapid rise in gold price in late September that the government realized the scam. One problem was the brazen attempt to include more government officials in the scam.

As Grant implemented his payback plan, gold started to drop in value. Fisk and Gould would move in and buy at these low prices. Gold hit a pre-low of $130 an ounce. Gold prices started to rise as Fisk and Gould hoarded gold. The government was moving about $4 million of gold in the plan. The total gold market was small, being estimated around $15 million, so Fisk and Gould had gained control of the market. They could now drive the price of gold up, making a huge profit. Slowly the price of gold started to rise with the hoarding of speculators. By late in the year, a $20 gold piece was worth $26 in gold. In September, gold hit a high of $162 an ounce (a high that would take a hundred years to hit again). Once the public fully realized what was happening, Grant ordered $4 million in gold to be sold on the market. As the gold hit the market, a selling panic set in; the price plummeted in a few minutes, destroying many unknowing speculators and small investors. Grant's brother-in-law was bankrupt, but Fisk and Gould were able to escape with little harm. The stock market followed with its own crash, spreading the harm to more innocent investors. A large number of brokerage houses were pulled into bankruptcy.

The crash of the gold market caused a major decline in wheat prices, hurting American farmers. In 1869, the American harvest had been bountiful, and farmers had hoped to sell wheat in Europe at high prices. Instead, farmers suffered major financial losses that led to bankruptcies throughout the Midwest. Now American farmers saw the corruption of Wall Street financiers as never before. It was during the same period that Gould and Fisk became involved with Tammany Hall, the New York City political ring. They made Boss Tweed a director of the Erie Railroad, and Tweed, in return, arranged favorable legislation for them. Tweed and Gould became the subjects of political cartoons by Thomas Nast in 1869.

In 1869, the full impact of an earlier scam of Fisk and Gould surfaced. The Railroad Act of 1864 had created an economic boom, but with it came the seeds of destruction. The Railroad Act created a system of corruption that made many Wall Street insiders rich, crushing farmers and small investors. This Act showed the worst of government involvement in such projects. It created a new stock company called Crédit Mobilier to aid the government. Crédit Mobilier set the supplier contracts. If a hammer cost a dollar for Crédit Mobilier, they might charge three dollars to the Union Pacific. The company could also overcharge for the actual cost of iron track laid. Crédit Mobilier generated a dividend for the stockholders (most of whom were Wall Street insiders) at the expense of the government. The Union Pacific Railroad was a network of corruption, where for every $3 spent by the government, less than $1 went to actual construction. In the early 1870s, there was a true bubble in railroad stocks.

The scandal spread to Congress. Congressmen and others purchased shares at a discount and could reap enormous capital gains simply by offering their discounted shares to a grossly undersubscribed market, where demand was high for shares of such a "profitable" company. These same members of Congress voted to apportion government funds to cover the inflated charges of Crédit Mobilier. Americans were shocked as never before at the sheer magnitude of the financial corruption. The great mansions of these financiers were no longer admired, but seen as ill-gotten.

Jim Fisk's social scandals were also constantly making headlines. As part of a scandal with a New York prostitute, Fisk was murdered in 1872, before his corrupt business scandals were fully known. Jay Gould lived until 1892 and continued to build a railroad empire. The public had learned to resent these financiers. Ultimately, Congress investigated 13 of its members in a probe that led to the censure of Oakes Ames, a New York Republican, and James Brooks, a Democrat from New York. A Department of Justice investigation was also made, with Aaron F. Perry serving as chief counsel. During the investigation, the government found that the company had given shares to more than thirty representatives of both parties.

These scandals would weaken the stock market and expose the building bubble in railroad stocks. The railroads were undercapitalized and not producing profits. Grain prices had continued to fall, further increasing railroad losses. New York banker Jay Cooke was behind the railroad stock bubble with the overselling of Northern Pacific stock and bonds. Cooke had been heavily involved in financial scandals with the Canadian government and caused Prime Minister Sir John A. Macdonald to lose his office. To the public, Cooke's shady financial dealings were covered by his philanthropy.

The Northern Pacific was in dire need of capital, and Cooke couldn't sell bonds because of the current atmosphere of unsavory rumors. In early September of 1873, some small railroads went under and a stock panic started to build. On September 18, 1873, known as Black Thursday, the large investment house of Jay Cooke failed. Black Friday, September 19, brought the failure of others, and a full-blown panic was initiated. The market crashed. The Panic of 1873 hit the nation hard. The panic lasted five years with 30 percent unemployed and another 40 percent working for less than seven months a year. Nationally, a quarter of the nation's 360 railroads failed, as well as twenty thousand other businesses. Nationwide, three million would lose their jobs, while daily wages fell 25 percent. Unemployment nationally was running over 25 percent for years. Business activity dropped by 33 percent; and for the first time, beggars were numerous on American streets. It would become the nation's second greatest depression, and the average American blamed Wall Street.

No amount of philanthropy would change that tarnished image of capitalists. While the 1860s and 1870s hurt the image of most capitalists, operating capitalists (versus Wall Street and bankers) such as Andrew Carnegie were still admired. There was even a split internally between the bankers and financiers versus the industry builders. The bankers wanted free trade and no protectionism, since they made their money on the volume of imports and exports, not on American industry. Still

Protectionism cartoon of Andrew Carnegie in 1893, first published in *Harper's Weekly* (Library of Congress).

another image problem for American capitalists overall was the development of wealthy American aristocratic families. The Astors and Vanderbilts would represent this new phenomenon in the 1870s. These aristocrats were removed from the workers they controlled through their banks and stocks. Furthermore, much of their philanthropy went to the places where they lived, such as New York, or to their causes, not the workers.

Cornelius Vanderbilt (1794–1877) and his son William and 12 other children became the face of America's wealth. When Cornelius died in 1877, he had amassed the largest fortune accumulated in the U.S. at that time, totaling $100 million (about $2.6 billion in today's dollars). In the early 1850s during the Gold Rush, a time before transcontinental railroads, Vanderbilt launched a steamship service that transported prospectors from New York to San Francisco via a land route across Nicaragua. His route was faster than an established route across Panama and much speedier than the other alternative, around Cape Horn at the southern tip of South America, which could take months. Vanderbilt's new line was an instant success, earning more than $1 million (about $26 million in today's money) a year. He used these profits to invest in railroads in the 1860s.

Cornelius Vanderbilt teamed up with James Fisk and Jay Gould in a number of railroad deals. He gained control of the New York Central in 1869. By 1873, he successfully linked New York to Chicago by rail. During the Panic of 1873 and the resulting depression, Vanderbilt began construction of Grand Central Terminal in New York City. The name Vanderbilt became synonymous with high living. Cornelius Vanderbilt's descendants went on to build grand mansions on Fifth Avenue in New York and many luxurious "summer cottages" in Newport, Rhode Island, along with the palatial Biltmore Mansion in North Carolina.

Vanderbilt was an active but reserved philanthropist, giving to a limited number of philanthropic causes including the YMCA, funding to help establish the Metropolitan Opera, and creating an endowment for the College of Physicians and Surgeons at Columbia University. In 1880, he provided about $1 million for Vanderbilt University in Nashville; but even here, it was an endowment fund that required the money be invested in Vanderbilt's railroads. He left most of his fortune to his son, William.

New York bluebloods such as the Astors, Vanderbilts, Roosevelts, Hydes, and Goulds made up the top of the list of the "400" wealthiest. Their inherited wealth dominated New York's Fifth Avenue. The parties and balls exceeded those of Louis XIV, whom they openly tried to emulate. The New York press showcased the aristocracy with wide coverage of the elites' parties and affairs. The public followed it as they would a soap opera today. New York's wealthy were of English ancestry. The important religion was Anglican and Episcopalian. Their universities were Harvard and Yale. The source of their wealth tended to be banking and financial investment versus making, building, or inventing things. Their "factories" were the banks of New York. They were elitist and saw class distinction as important. They even established a line of royalty. They hated the "nouveau riche." They were truly the leisure class and found work vulgar. Philanthropy was looked at as a necessity and was limited to the arts and higher education for the most part.

After the passing of the Panic and Depression of 1873, in the 1880s, the wealthy class became even more opulent. The public and politicians came angered at these public displays. The new emerging industrialists such as Carnegie, Westinghouse, and others were embarrassed by the mansions and parties of the "400." Furthermore, these older millionaires often looked down on the more recently successful as the working rich. The press started to look at the philanthropy of the rich in a Marxist framework; that is, it covered their guilt (robber baron theory) or was used to keep the poor happy and in their place (welfare capitalism). After the Panic of 1873, there would be decades of questioning capitalism. Many Americans would turn to socialism and Marxism as a solution to uneven wealth distribution. Marx simply framed the argument around greed and a conspiracy to oppress the lower classes. The behavior of the wealthy class in this period of 1880 to 1900, called the Gilded Age by Mark Twain, would inspire an economic theory to explain it.

The Theory of the Leisure Class: An Economic Study of Institutions (1899), by Thorstein Veblen, is an economic treatise and detailed social critique of conspicuous consumption as a function of social-class consumerism. Vablen proposes that the social strata and classes and the division of labor of the feudal period continued into the modern era.[1] The lords of the manor employed themselves in the economically useless practices of conspicuous consumption and conspicuous leisure as did this new class of American wealth. The middle and lower classes were employed in the industrial occupations that support the whole of society. Veblen saw philanthropy as a class responsibility as well as a means to maintain the class system. In this respect, Veblen's view was similar to the negativity of Karl Marx. Marxism held private charity in contempt. Philanthropy, according to Marx, represented a bourgeois solution to the proletarian problem. It was considered, like religion, an instrument of capitalist manipulation, an opiate of the masses intended to numb and ultimately incapacitate the working class.

Veblen also suggested that many great industrial philanthropists did it for vanity. This certainly cannot be fully refuted, yet there are examples that find some limitations in Veblen's theory. Many of the American capitalists were anonymous donors, such as George Eastman. Eastman was the founder of Eastman Kodak, the entrepreneur who turned photography from a profession with prohibitively high startup costs into an affordable hobby for the middle class. America's best-known bad boy of capitalism, Henry Clay Frick, gave over $200 million away, mostly anonymously. Even Rockefeller provided some $70 million to the University of Chicago, while insisting that not a single building bear his name—even rejecting an image of an oil lamp on the university seal, worried that it would be seen as a nod to Standard Oil.

In retrospect, Rockefeller took on the face of robber baron in the last quarter of the nineteenth century. Rockefeller's methods were highly competitive and cutthroat, but the 50 percent drop in the price of kerosene was a favorable result for consumers. Rockefeller's philanthropy did little to mute the criticism of the huge profits of his Standard Oil Company. He absorbed and destroyed his competition over the years. Rockefeller had taken 80 percent of the oil market by the 1874. By 1890, Standard Oil had over 90 percent of the oil refining capacity in the United States. Its size and power allowed it to continuously cut costs and prices, crushing the competition. The United States government sued, using the Sherman Anti-Trust Act of 1890. In 1892, the Supreme Court ruled Standard Oil an illegal monopoly. Standard Oil superficially complied, but retained control of the boards of the individual companies into which it had been subdivided. In 1899, the company reorganized in New Jersey, where state law allowed a parent company to own stock of other companies.

In 1902, journalist Ira Tarbell (sister of an executive of a competitor) wrote a series of magazine articles on the abuses of Standard Oil. Her book, *The History of Standard Oil*, became a classic in capitalist literature. Tarbell's father had been bankrupted by Standard Oil and the fight became personal. Her book was a story of greed that turned the public against all trusts. The trust-busting administration of Teddy Roosevelt took on New Jersey Standard Oil in 1904. After years in court, the ruling found that Standard Oil violated the Sherman Anti-Trust Act, stating that Standard's dominant position in the industry was due "to unfair practices, to abuse of the control of pipelines, to railroad discriminations, and to unfair methods of competition."

Rockefeller was a cold individual, yet he was a generous philanthropist and applied paternal employee practices. One historian noted: "Rockefeller was extremely generous with his employees, usually paying them significantly more than the competition did. Consequently, he was rarely slowed down by strikes or labor disputes. He also believed in rewarding his most innovate managers with bonuses and paid time off if they came up with good ideas for productivity improvements."[2]

Other historians argue philanthropy by men such as Rockefeller was guilt-driven.[3] Most overlook that philanthropy for many was imbedded in capitalism. It improved morale and productivity. The truly paternal capitalist was far less interested in philanthropy than in creating a highly motivated and loyal employee. This breed of capitalist was more consistent with Robert Owen, but employee relations and even philanthropy cannot be reduced to generalized philosophies. Philanthropy was and is very individualistic, promoted by moral and cultural training and background, rather than by vanity or guilt. For many capitalists, philanthropy was part of the profit motive.

The excesses of the Gilded Age had soured the public on capitalists, industrialists, bankers, and financiers. Still, there was a growing group of capitalists who saw paternal treatment and philanthropy to worker communities as a profitable endeavor. During the Gilded Age, a quiet revolution was taking place in the workplace and worker communities. The ideas of Robert Owen and Peter Cooper would be favored again. Capitalists such as H.J. Heinz, John Wanamaker, and George Westinghouse would update paternalism for the twentieth century. There would be, however, another group that would use paternalism as cover.

Eight

New Breed of Paternal Capitalists

The rise of American industry in the 1850s would change the face of capitalism, philanthropy, and employee relations. Industry would create a demand for unskilled immigrant labor. The Puritan village had given way to the industrial city, which started to look more like England's Manchester than Plymouth, Massachusetts. While the immigrants fueled the Industrial Revolution, they also created a new problem for the community. The immigrant worker was feared and created a social challenge to the American city. The immigrant worker needed to be integrated into the community and workforce. Capitalism changed for both the worse and better, as did the nation. The Irish invasion of workers had only been a prelude. Education was still the most important feature in the development of the nation, but the new immigrants had to feed their families. Industrial philanthropists would be needed to feed the poor and build hospitals and schools.

Peter Cooper would have many followers in educational philanthropy, but the new immigrant workers would offer new educational challenges. Joe Banigan had conquered bigotry against the Irish in Rhode Island, but a new wave of Eastern European immigrants stirred new hatreds. Immigrant workers faced racism and lacked the most basic of needs. Industrial philanthropists needed to realize that charity had to begin at home. In addition, the true paternal capitalist is not primarily a philanthropist, but a capitalist interested in worker productivity.

John Wanamaker (1838–1922), the Philadelphia department store magnate, would assure an advanced education for his employees. Wanamaker would focus on educational benefits for his employees as well as the community and the nation. This was much different from the community scope of Peter Cooper or even Joseph Banigan. Wanamaker was one of a new breed with men like H.J. Heinz, George Westinghouse, and J.C. Penney who that believed charity began at home with their employees. Wanamaker was certainly aware of the criticism of many philanthropists who gave much to the community while their workers slaved for little. Wanamaker would pioneer employee education, benefits, and fair treatment.

One of Philadelphia's great philanthropists and civic leaders, John Wanamaker, grew up in the German section near Philadelphia in a strong Methodist tradition. The family would later switch to the Presbyterian Church, and Wanamaker became active in prayer and Bible groups. In 1850 at age 12, he became an errand boy for a publishing company at a wage of $1.25 a week. He soon found a higher paying position ($2.50 a week) at a clothing store. Health problems, however, forced the young Wanamaker to move west. After several years, Wanamaker returned to Philadelphia to become the secretary of the newly formed Young Men's Christian Association (YMCA). At an exceptional salary of $1,000 a year, Wanamaker had found his passion.

In 1861, Wanamaker made a major career change and opened a small clothing store. He based his business on customer satisfaction with a money-back guarantee. He also guaranteed the lowest price or a refund. Using newspaper advertising, Wanamaker pioneered new marketing and sales methods. By 1871, Wanamaker built a new store in Philadelphia, employing 43 salesmen, 70 cutters, and 20 clerks. Sales had gone from $24,000 in the first year to over $2 million in 1871.[1] From the beginning, Wanamaker applied Christian principles in his business and employees. He refused to have any work done on Sunday and required absolute honesty from his employees. In a few years, Wanamaker had branch stores in Pittsburgh, Baltimore, Richmond, Louisville, and St. Louis.

Wanamaker's real revolution came in 1875 when he purchased the old Grand Depot of the Pennsylvania Railroad for a new kind of department store. This new type of store would handle a massive variety of goods. It would have a restaurant on the first floor. It would be one of the biggest stores to use electricity to light it. Employees were offered extensive training and managers were sent to Europe to study retailing.

Wanamaker was one of the nation's most progressive employers. In the 1870s, employees with over six months of service were given a week of paid vacation. Wanamaker offered death and disability insurance for his workers as well as health benefits. He was one of the earliest to offer pensions for his employees. For his older employees, Wanamaker established health and athletic clubs. As the company grew, Wanamaker added doctors and dentists for his employees based on the model of his friend, H.J. Heinz. Wanamaker demanded, in return, a high level of personal hygiene and moral conduct.

Wanamaker developed a school for his employees' advancement known as the "store school," or more formally, the John Wanamaker Commercial Institute. In 1878, Wanamaker established a school of instruction for his employees. Wanamaker's stated goal: "to enable those who are doing the day's work and earning a living to get a better education to earn a better application."[2] For the older employees, attendance was voluntary and consisted of night classes. For those under 16, Wanamaker made it obligatory. These younger students attended classes in the morning before going to their work stations. Each student attended two sessions a week, learning a full college curriculum as well as business methods. Some students were given night classes after receiving a hot meal in the store dining room. Wanamaker employed over 20 teachers from the daily schools of Philadelphia. For more advanced students, foreign languages were offered. Older employees, who were required to go abroad for business, were also given language courses. These store schools included extensive military training for the young students. The young cadets were used during the Spanish-American War and later during a call up by President Wilson for duty on the Mexican border.[3] Wanamaker included a store school with each of his new stores.

Wanamaker's success with employee education drew him into community education. Wanamaker, like Peter Cooper, developed a passion early for the improvement of public education. In the 1880s while growing his business, Wanamaker worked with local churches to expand Sunday schools for bible education of the young. Wanamaker's experience with the YMCA had convinced him that youth needed more than Sunday school to develop moral character. He selected a small church (Bethany Church) to try a neighborhood experiment. Wanamaker supplied the buildings for a neighborhood industrial school to train youth in practical trades. The church managed the program. The school was open to all at a nominal fee. Wanamaker believed the school should be self-sustaining. The school, by 1889, had over 500 boys and girls taking a variety of courses such as bookkeeping, drafting, cooking, telegraphy, printing, engraving, and sewing.

The Bethany School experiment would become the model for the community colleges of today. In 1890, Wanamaker expanded his ideas in the building of the Williamson Free School of Trades, for which he was a trustee. Wanamaker used the funds left by his friend, Isaiah Williamson. Over forty buildings were built by students taking carpentry and bricklaying. Wanamaker managed over two million dollars left by Williamson and actually increased the trust. Over the years, Wanamaker expanded this school project into the Wanamaker Institute of Industries, which still operates today. When Wanamaker found there was no college preparatory school for girls, he founded one in 1882. It became known as the Wellesley School, since the teachers were supplied by Wellesley College.

Wanamaker would serve on the Philadelphia school board and as a trustee on the Pennsylvania State Military School. During his decades of service on the school board, he fought for improved ventilation and sanitary conditions in city schools. Wanamaker was also known for his vigorous support of higher salaries for teachers.

A neighborhood development project, one of Wanamaker's greatest achievements personally, was known as the Bethany Brotherhood. It was a men's organization founded in 1890, and it provided religious instruction and fellowship to area worshipers of the Presbyterian faith. It was a social club for young men. Wanamaker built a three-story building on Philadelphia's South Street. The building included game rooms, a swimming pool, library, museum, dining hall and lounge. It was to be a social Christian club. To encourage thrift, Wanamaker founded the First Penny Savings Bank to be part of the club and neighborhood.

Throughout his life, Wanamaker was a devout Presbyterian. He worked with the Bethany Sunday School for many years. Even during his busiest moments as a department store entrepreneur, he actively worked on the national Sunday school movement. Pennsylvania State Sunday School Association was the founding work of Wanamaker. He served for twelve years from 1895 as its president until the election of his close friend, Pittsburgh capitalist H.J. Heinz. Wanamaker also served as vice president of the World Sunday School Association. He would travel the world often with H.J. Heinz in an effort to establish Sunday schools and Christian men's clubs. Wanamaker founded several Presbyterian churches as well, including the Bethany Memorial (today called Bethany Collegiate) Church in 1865, the John Chambers Memorial Presbyterian Church in 1897, and the Bethany Temple Presbyterian Church in 1906. He also maintained ties with the YMCA during his business career and contributed to the development of YMCA buildings all over the world.

Wanamaker's success in the community brought him into politics.

He became Postmaster General under President Benjamin Harrison. While Wanamaker proved creative as Postmaster, he was dragged into a number of controversies and scandals. Wanamaker also had his critics in business as he took a hard stand against unionization. Wanamaker never had the slightest labor problem at his stores, but as a prominent Republican, he was often characterized as an anti-union extremist. Wanamaker, like so many other capitalists of the period, feared the socialist element in the union movement. He argued that, with good management, a union was not needed. The problem, of course, was that most capitalists were far from Wanamaker's Christian ideal.

Still, even Wanamaker had his critics (or in Wanamaker's case, skeptics), who referred to him as "Holy John" and "Saint John," as he often was depicted in cartoons.[4] These skeptics criticized the purity of his motives: "For Wanamaker, economic and symbolic capital blended with one another in his relationships with his employees and public, the latter being patrons of his store. He changed his economic capital into symbolic capital. These activities created misrecognition of his benevolences which were turned into economic capital through greater employee loyalty, long-term consumerism resulting from savings, and a demand for more expensive, quality merchandise as a result of education. Wanamaker reduced prices in times of crisis and reduced profits, hence misdirecting public thinking that he cared more about personal relations and community than business. This action, in turn, brought more patrons into his stores and increased his economic capital."[5] While this type of criticism questioned his motives, Wanamaker's approach still represents the highest ideal of practical capitalism. Paternal capitalism is always capitalism first. Wanamaker represented the group of capitalists who gave back some of those profits.

In the end, Wanamaker's public bronze statue would merely say "citizen." He raised money for many causes such as the relief of famine in Ireland, the treatment of yellow fever in the American South, and victims of the 1913 Ohio River flood. On the day of his funeral, the city closed all public schools and flags were lowered to half-mast. His pallbearers included the governor of Pennsylvania, the mayors of Philadelphia and New York, the chief justice of the Supreme Court of the United States, and Thomas A. Edison. Wanamaker's type of capitalism would put pressure on others such as Marshall Field in Chicago, who became a reluctant philanthropist, feeling it was expected of him. This is not to cast a moral judgment on Marshall Field, which must be left to a higher court. Capitalists have the right to do what they please with their money in our democratic society, but men like Wanamaker set a new standard.

Men like John Wanamaker, H.J. Heinz, and others in the last part of the nineteenth century were part of a debate on the accumulation of wealth. America was itself in the middle of the great debate of capitalism and socialism. In Europe the abuses of workers had led to socialism and an unholy alliance of unions with political parties. The followers of Karl Marx had come to America to take over the union movement. Socialism would not find deep roots in America, but it did change capitalism to a more paternal system.

Marshall Field (1834–1906) was born in Massachusetts to Puritan stock going back to 1650. Field worked his way up from the farm. He made his mark in retailing by his honest and fair treatment of the customer. Field eliminated unethical merchandising practices. He was known for refunds and consistent pricing that became standards in quality retailing. Field's employees were also instructed not to push products on uninterested customers, as was common practice in stores of the period. Field employees received job-related training, as opposed to a full educational curriculum. While not a high-wage employer, Field offered many benefits. The ninth floor of the department store had an employee cafeteria, music room, and gymnasium. Employees were offered paid vacations and half time for sick days. Marshall Field had the Puritan belief of giving to community, but he lacked the passion of a Wanamaker or a Cooper.

Marshall Field was often found lacking in his comparison to John Wanamaker. However, Field fostered a strong legacy with his bequeathal of eight million dollars to the Natural History Museum of Chicago. Wanamaker's vision of a better world for workers was lacking in capitalists such as Marshall Field. Although Field was also a cofounder of the University of Chicago with John D. Rockefeller, his employee relations were often considered poor. John Wanamaker's moral code and Christian view made him a superior employer to Marshall Field in Chicago. Field's store came under state investigation for his low pay of women. Although Field's wages for women were not much less than those of Wanamaker, Field offered them few benefits. Like Wanamaker, Field opposed unions; but Field was more aggressive in the radical and tough Chicago labor market. He fired employees with union contacts and employed spies to monitor employee activity.

Philip Armour (1832–1901) was another Chicago capitalist and philanthropist who lacked the truly paternal approach of Wanamaker. Like Field, Philip Armour was a reluctant philanthropist. Armour and Company owned fourteen acres in the stockyards in Chicago. Philip Armour's packing house employed an efficient new killing and cutting line. Rather than have one man butcher one hog, each worker stood in one spot and completed one task. The animals, hanging from a line by their legs, would proceed from one workstation to the next until every saleable piece was separated for the market. Armour's famous disassembly lines have been the Zeus of industrial mythology, having been called the inspiration of Henry Ford, Michael Owens, and many others. And every part of the animal was sold. Along with meat, Armour sold glue, oil, fertilizer, hairbrushes, buttons, oleomargarine, and drugs, all made from animal byproducts. Low-grade meats were canned in products like pork and beans. This efficiency reduced the pollution that the factories created. Yet, operating without strong federal inspection standards, the meatpackers sometimes allowed contaminants to adulterate the meat, such as rat droppings, dead rodents, or sawdust. Spoiled meat or meat mixed with waste materials was packed and sold.

Armour, who built low-cost houses for his workers, was often cited for low pay. At a time when the living wage for a five-member family was $15.40 a week, the workers at Armour and Company only earned about $9.50 a week. Armour fired and blacklisted union leaders and employee activists who demanded higher wages. Yet Armour was known for his generosity to the poor. This type of paradox was common with many capitalists of the time. Armour's anti-union view was consistent with that of Wanamaker and almost all capitalists of the time, but Armour lacked the true compassion for the workers, or at least was blinded by his union hatred. Workers often labored for 12 hours a day, seven days a week. Safety measures and benefits were nonexistent. While pay was much higher than in Europe, it had the perception of being too low. In reality, American laborers were making five to ten times that of equivalent industries in Europe. The length of the working day was considered particularly oppressive, but it was standard for the period. A national labor organization, the Knights of Labor, was gaining popularity with its campaign for an eight-hour day in Chicago. Armour opposed the labor movement and was drawn into the Haymarket Riot in Chicago in 1886.

Even Amour's business practices came under criticism and scrutiny. The publication of Upton Sinclair's *The Jungle* in 1905 exposed decades of unsanitary practices, but its main focus was the poor treatment of the workers at the Armour plant. At the time, Sinclair was a Chicago socialist active in the movement. His earlier works had been failures, but *The Jungle* would make him an overnight sensation. For months in 1904, Upton Sinclair worked a 12-hour shift in the Chicago stockyards while living in a hut. Sinclair's novel was meant to send a socialist message of the oppression of immigrant workers. He ends the novel with a socialist orator shouting: "Organize! Organize! Organize! Chicago will be ours!" Sinclair would be disappointed despite his success, as his anti-capitalist message was lost amid the furor over the exposure of unsanitary practices. Sinclair noted: "I aimed at their hearts and by accident I hit their stomach."[6] In fact, most Americans had no stomach for socialism. His socialist message had held up the publication of *The Jungle* with big publishers. It was first published in 1904 in a socialist paper but then picked up by Doubleday in 1906. While Armour's legacy was hurt, he shook it off, stating, "I have no social ambition but to run Armour Company."[7]

Chicago in the 1880s was on the front line of the clash between European style socialists and unions with American capitalism. The practices of Field and Armour made Chicago ripe for a clash of systems. Poor treatment of workers strengthened the socialist and union movements. In Chicago, the socialists had hi-jacked the union movement. The poor working environments and community ghettoes often allowed the socialists to make a strong case for European-style unions. Public support went back and forth. The violence of the Haymarket Riot turned the public against the socialists temporarily. The bigger problem of the socialist movement was the church, which was just as problematic as the capitalists. Anti-religious socialist views engendered opposition to these more radical movements in the churches of America. Socialists saw the church as an institution of the rich to pacify poor workers. In particular, the Catholic Church, which represented a majority of immigrant workers, stood firmly against the socialist movement. This did not take away the church's opposition to the poor treatment of workers by some capitalists. Certainly, many capitalists had gone too far in their poor treatment of workers. Capitalists like Armour saw the need to do something for the workers to pacify them.

To characterize Armour as heartless or even uncaring would be going too far, but Amour's inflexibility, poor labor relations, and unsanitary meatpacking methods hurt his legacy. Still, for many he is known as a philanthropist. He gave away over $50 million in philanthropic endeavors. The American culture seemed to demand that its capitalists give to community. Many capitalists like Armour and Field would become reluctant philanthropists. Armour donated over one million dollars to establish the Armour Institute (Illinois Institute of Technology), a coeducational training school. He also created the Armour Mission, an educational and health care center. Armour was typical of many Gilded Age capitalists, who gave much to the community while neglecting some of the very workers who built his fortune. These capitalists stand in stark contrast to men like Peter Cooper, John Wanamaker, and many later paternal capitalists. Unfortunately, capitalists like Armour dominated the headlines, but there were true paternalists as well. Capitalism had to change in its approach towards workers.

One of Wanamaker's protégés was the Pittsburgh pickle and ketchup king, H.J. Heinz (1844–1919). Heinz had worked for years with Wanamaker on the Sunday School Association. They often exchanged ideas on employee relations. Heinz, like Wanamaker, would give to both his employees and the community, but there was an emphasis on his employees. While Heinz's employee benefits were the best of the period, he was not a high payer or a union supporter. His outstanding application of the Golden Rule in his company's vision was a powerful motivator; and Heinz Company never experienced a strike during the 70-year period.

Heinz, a German, had studied the chocolate companies of Germany and their paternal approach. Heinz would travel often to Germany to study

John Wanamaker ca. 1902 (Library of Congress).

factories. The German paternal capitalist movement that Heinz observed in 1886 was a reaction to the trade unions and socialists of Germany. Employee health was one of the fundamental concerns of German factory paternalism, and common to Heinz's approach. Heinz had personally observed a socialist riot in Holland that killed 24 workers. He realized that in Europe and America, the problems faced by workers had to be addressed for the good of all.[8] Heinz would become one of the great paternal capitalists of the time. He also built employee-oriented factories.

There was a doctor and a dentist assigned to his factories. Heinz was one of the earliest to relate dental health to overall health. Health care was extended to all in the employee's family. Heinz's workforce was a bit unique in its majority of younger women. These women workers were often daughters supplying additional family income, and young married immigrant wives working to buy a house or start a family. For immigrant families, Heinz offered English classes and citizenship classes. Home skill classes, such as sewing and cooking classes, were also offered to these young woman employees to prepare them for marriage. A job at Heinz was the ideal employment for a young girl prior to marriage.

There was, of course, a sound business reason for these benefits as well. Pittsburgh was labor short, with most men being employed in the steel mills; Heinz had to attract young women to work for him. Furthermore, the 1880s was a heyday of the socialist movement in America, which threatened capitalism. Like German capitalists, many American industrialists saw paternalism as a means to combat socialism and the rise of unions.

On a personal level, Heinz would help single mothers and career working women with college classes at the local Duff's Business College. He also offered upward mobility for such women into the management ranks. Heinz would be one of the first employers to offer pensions and disability insurance. He offered lunches to his employees at cost. Lunchtime concerts were commonly given. The women were given uniforms, and the company paid for laundering. Heinz maintained summer camps for vacations of employees and their children.

Heinz's giving was often overlooked by the press in favor of the big-dollar gifts of local steel magnate Andrew Carnegie to libraries and museums. Even more forgotten are the instances of out-of-pocket help given to an employee in need. Heinz also included many charitable expenses in the company's operating expenses. Employees who could not afford good working clothes were often given them by the company. One year, Heinz approved a corporate fund to feed street beggars, one of the little-known legacies of this unusual capitalist. Heinz was always there to help the poor and unemployed. He went further to address the needs of immigrant workers than his neighbors, Andrew Carnegie and Henry Frick.

Unlike the other great capitalists of Pittsburgh, Heinz did not move to New York or Florida but stayed in the community. Heinz got personally involved in community projects, serving on city commissions for pure water, sewage control, and air pollution from 1900 to 1911. Pittsburgh had led the nation in the number of typhoid fever cases due to lack of a sewage system and water pollution from the steel mills. Heinz chaired the water commission that eliminated typhoid fever, which killed his wife. He also led the effort to reduce air pollution from coal burning. He converted his own factories to clean-burning natural gas.

Heinz's philanthropy was more personal and less public than his fellow capitalists. His donations focused on religion, social services, hospitals, schools, churches, and individuals. He rarely made press headlines like Carnegie. Heinz's giving was more likely found in church newsletters. His biggest philanthropic effort was the Sunday School Association, working with Wanamaker. Heinz had spent years personally teaching Sunday school. Even in his darkest business days, a young H.J. Heinz would show up to teach on Sundays; and when traveling, he always found a Sunday school to drop in on. Heinz gave of his time, talent, and treasure to the Sunday school effort. He belonged and was an executive director of the Allegheny County Sabbath School Association, the Pennsylvania State Sabbath School Association, the International Sunday School Association, and the World Sunday School Association. He always combined Sunday school visits with his world travel; and in later years, he traveled the world to spread the application of Sunday school.

Heinz was particularly sensitive to the local community's inability to deal with the flood of immigrants. A Heinz philanthropic effort in this area was the Sarah Heinz House. The Sarah Heinz House at the time was considered a "settlement" house. Settlement houses had become an extension of paternal capitalism in Pittsburgh and Chicago. They were outreaches to the children and the immigrant tenant-house families. The Kingsley House of 1895 in Pittsburgh was one of the first. Settlement houses functioned as well-financed YMCAs. Many, like the Kingsley House, focused on the learning of life skills, citizenship skills, and work skills. The settlement houses also offered adult courses in language and citizenship for immigrant families. These settlement houses, while often formed by churches and financed by industrialists, were ecumenical, although Christian-based. The YMCA had been limited in its approach until it developed the ability to integrate its membership with Catholics, who made up the majority of immigrant workers.

Heinz built a Christian-based settlement home but steered clear of any direct religious tie. The house motto was: "Youth, Recreation, Character, and Service." He did require a temperance oath, but this was acceptable with all faiths for youths. Sarah Heinz House was to be a Christian house that showed Christian principles by action, not preaching. The founding principles were based on the Golden Rule. This was a front-line operation open to any child of need. Heinz wanted to get poor city kids off the streets and give them an option other than gangs. Most of the kids in the Pittsburgh streets were Catholic immigrants, and Heinz realized that they needed help, too. As always, Heinz was ecumenical in his approach. He noted at the June 6, 1915, dedication of the Sarah Heinz House: "I do not know what percentage of the young people connected with this work is Protestant or what percentage is Catholic. Furthermore, I do not want to know. No sectarian bias will influence the work of this institution.... It is our desire to surround the boys and girls of the neighborhood with such good influences that they will never want to depart from the right paths."[9]

Nine

American Patriarchal or Philanthropic Capitalism

When most Americans hear the term paternal or welfare capitalism, they think of industrial philanthropist Andrew Carnegie (1835–1911). Carnegie, however, was not paternal in the style of Owen. His capitalism was best described as patriarchal or philanthropic. Carnegie saw himself as destined to help mankind while ignoring the needs of the very workers who supplied his fortune. His approach to his workers would give paternalism a bad name. Carnegie was, however, the leader in community philanthropy. Carnegie believed he was destined to educate the world. He believed this was the role of the capitalistic class. His philosophy was a strange mix of Puritanism, deism, and classism. He had even broken off from the traditional Calvinist faiths of Scotland, with Carnegie's father joining the radical Swedenborgian Church. The union of faith and charity is a central tenet of the Swedenborgian Church, yet Carnegie saw charity as philanthropy, not better treatment for workers.

As an employer, Carnegie had many shortcomings. His workers lived in industrial slums. What Carnegie offered to his employees was an opportunity to rise through the ranks by hard work. His managers, known as the "Carnegie Boys," were true rags-to-riches stories. His employees rose based on merits in an application of survival of the fittest in the workplace. A young Catholic, Charles Schwab, rose to president of the company, when Catholics in most companies could never become managers. Carnegie offered opportunity, which became an organizational strength. Still, for the average worker, Carnegie Steel offered only a daily 12-hour routine, and employees struggled to feed their families. Carnegie's years of philanthropy did change him, and he would at least try to make restitution to his former workers.

Carnegie's philosophy of giving focused on creating avenues of opportunity. Carnegie truly believed in the idea of social Darwinism and survival of the fittest. He maintained a close relationship with Herbert Spencer, the great British philosopher of social Darwinism. Carnegie would even have Spencer's bust carved on his great architectural frieze of the world's great philosophers in his Pittsburgh library. Yet when Carnegie brought Spencer to tour his Pittsburgh mills, Spencer noted that a "six months stay here would justify suicide."[1] Also, Carnegie's giving methodology was clearly on the Spencerian approach: "In bestowing charity, the main consideration should be to help those who help themselves."[2] This methodology fits well with the strict Puritan view versus a broader Christian view of charity.

One of Carnegie's early and few ventures into paternal capitalism, focusing on his workers, was a cooperative store for the workers. Carnegie was a student of the Rochdale Society of Equitable Pioneers and the British cooperative movement. The cooperative would require worker investment, which attracted Carnegie to the approach. The workers were not interested in such an investment, however, and the cooperative effort of Carnegie failed.

The many great libraries and community centers that Carnegie gave back to his steel communities were of little value to his overworked steelworkers of the time. These steelworkers lived in industrial slums. Carnegie gifts would, however, benefit greatly the descendants of these workers. The very nature of giving did transform Carnegie in his later life. Years after his retirement and his prodigious library giving, Carnegie would finally give a package of retirement, insurance, and health care to the former laborers who had made his fortunes.

Carnegie himself felt he was applying Puritan principles of money and business.[3] He offers proof that one cannot make generalizations about individual capitalists; each one's behavior is a function of personal beliefs and experience. Amazingly, Carnegie would break ranks with other philanthropic industrialists, such as John Rockefeller, over an important tenet of capitalism. Carnegie maintained that he would not create an aristocratic family line but would give all his money to charity. He left only enough money for his wife and daughter to live out their lives in comfort. He believed money would destroy the motivation of any descendants. Few capitalists would follow his lead. So after having saved six years to make the trip from Scotland, Carnegie's great-grandson would visit Carnegie's first mill in Braddock, Pennsylvania.

Andrew Carnegie had been born in 1835 in Dunfernline, Scotland, the son of a hand weaver. Ironically, the Carnegie family and his father were true victims of the Industrial Revolution in Europe, which destroyed the craft of weaving. Power looms drove John Carnegie out of business, finally forcing the family to migrate to the United States in 1847. They came by boat and canal to Pittsburgh, which at the time had booming cotton mills. The family settled in Allegheny City (today Pittsburgh's north side), where many Scotch immigrants worked in the cotton mills. John Carnegie, a master weaver, refused to work in the automated mills, so Andrew needed to help the family. His father died a broken man, unable to adjust to the changes in skilled labor. Young Carnegie found a job as a bobbin boy in a local cotton mill at $1.20 a week. He worked 12-hour days, six days a week. Sundays were strictly reserved for worship and rest in this Scotch-Irish Presbyterian area. Interestingly, it would be Carnegie who would later force Sunday work in his steel mills. He also attended night school at Pittsburgh's Duff's College, which had been built decades earlier by early capitalist James O'Hara. Carnegie would take accounting courses at Duff's College.

Andrew Carnegie's real break came at age fourteen when he landed a job as a telegraph boy delivering messages to Pittsburgh businesses. The telegraph was a new technology, the line arriving in Pittsburgh a few months before Carnegie had arrived. He took to the work and expanded on it by learning Morse code and telegraph operation. Carnegie took messages throughout the city to the area's wealthiest capitalists and became friends with many of them, including the "King of the Pig Iron Aristocrats," B.F. Jones. Jones offered an example of a true paternalist. He was known for his fair treatment of workers and was also a leading political link in the alliance of protectionism and paternalism.

The story of Carnegie's oil investment started with an 1862 visit to Pennsylvania oil country with his brother's friend, William Coleman, who was in the iron and coal business. Prior to the trip, Carnegie had made some small investments in oil based on advice by his East End friends. He then purchased a $40,000 share in an oil venture known as Columbia Oil. Carnegie and Coleman even dug a "lake" (known today as "Carnegie's Pond") to hold oil in hopes of a future shortage. In the end, oil seemed in endless supply, and the stock returned over 400 percent! Not surprisingly, the president of Columbia Oil was Charles Lockhart, who would be a future founder of Standard Oil, and who would be a future model for

Carnegie. It is also suggested that Carnegie's experience with Columbia Oil was his first taste of philanthropy. Columbia Oil provided housing and had built a library for the town of Columbia Farm.

Carnegie started in the iron industry in 1867, buying Union Mills in Pittsburgh. Even though his own father had been broken by the crushing of the crafts system, Carnegie would make his fortune on transitioning to automation. Even before automation, Carnegie worked to break the crafts union of skilled iron puddlers. The puddlers were actually a true guild with secret meetings and practices. In 1867, Carnegie locked out the puddlers' union (Sons of Vulcan) at the mills in hopes of breaking the union and its strike. The strike spread to other Pittsburgh iron and steel mills. In late 1867, the producers raised a fund to recruit poor Germans in Europe. The next two years would bring a wave of cheap German laborers who would train to be puddlers. At the same time, they were used to lower wages and replace the bottom of the labor force. The combination of cheap labor, the breaking of trade and crafts unions, and a booming iron market made Carnegie a millionaire by 1869. Although the replacement of the highly skilled puddlers was the least successful strategy employed by Carnegie and the other manufacturers, the replacement of the day laborer with a cheaply paid immigrant laborer proved extremely profitable. Actually, the wages of the puddlers increased, too, as they hired some of this cheaper labor for their crew to compete with Carnegie!

Carnegie turned to the new product of steel. Iron was needed as the raw material for steel, and it was here that Carnegie used the new Bessemer process to end skilled crafts in the industry. The Bessemer process, like the automatic loom, would eliminate millions of skilled jobs. On a European trip in 1872, Carnegie stopped in Sheffield to see the inventor, Henry Bessemer, and his steelworks. Carnegie returned to Pittsburgh determined to build a steel mill. That mill was his Edgar Thomson Works at Braddock, Pennsylvania. Named after Edgar Thomson of the Pennsylvania Railroad, the mill was to make steel rails, replacing wrought iron. Carnegie and his partners endured the Panic of 1873 to see the mill roll its first rail on September 1, 1875. Carnegie would convince his old friends at the Pennsylvania Railroad to use steel rails instead of puddled iron ones produced by skilled workers. This move would be the beginning of one of the world's greatest industrial empires. In 1901, Carnegie became the world's richest man when he sold his massive steel empire to J.P. Morgan for $480 million. Carnegie would retire full time to philanthropy. Carnegie's rags-to-riches story made him an extremely popular figure with the public.

Carnegie Steel in Homestead, Pennsylvania, 1899 (Library of Congress).

Carnegie and his partners would give much to the mill communities, but many argued it would have been far better to give back to the workers in wages and benefits. Even Carnegie would agree with that argument near the end of his life. Carnegie was far from a true paternal owner of his steel mills. In 1889, Carnegie donated his first library and community center to the mill town of Braddock. Still, the majority (about 70 percent of the workforce) of his unskilled laborers didn't have the time to use it. The poor immigrant workers worked 12 hours a day for long stretches of days. The unskilled majority of steelworkers made less than the average American worker ($340 versus $450 a year), but wages were only slightly above the poverty level. Landlords often abused the industrial slum worker. There were overcharges for rent in many cases. A two-room apartment might run $7–$11 per month without toilets, baths, and heat. Fuel costs were about $30 a year (coal heating). The two rooms would house a family of six with a possible sub-renter or two.

Nearly half of the wages were used to feed their average family of five.[4] Some typical food prices were: corned beef at six cents a pound, coffee at fourteen cents a pound, flour at two cents a pound, and butter at twenty-two cents a pound. Bread was around five cents a loaf, and potatoes were thirty-nine cents a bushel. A pound of ham was about eleven cents, and a pound of crackers was four cents. Ketchup in prepackaged bottles ranged from fifty cents to a dollar a bottle. Ketchup from the grocer's barrel was around thirty cents a gallon or forty cents for a pint bottle, which was a considerable amount based on wages of one dollar to a dollar and a half a day. Ketchup, however, was popular because it added spice to an extremely bland diet. Other costs were a dollar for a man's shirt, a linen handkerchief was five cents, a wool blanket was $2.50, and a gallon of whiskey sold for $3. A starter house would cost around $2,000 to $3,000.

The conditions in the mill slums of Braddock and Homestead were horrific. The slums were at river level and flooded constantly. Streets were mud. Pigs and chickens roamed the streets. Sewage went directly to the streets as in Europe's industrial cities. Alcoholism was a way of life. The Catholic Church did offer education and disability insurance for the children. The churches also offered language and citizenship courses for adults. The workers still poured in, finding long-term opportunity missing from the industrial slums of Europe. The system's saving grace was the mobility of the immigrant workforce that averaged less than a generation in the slums. The mill slums in many ways offered a gateway to America for poor immigrants; and eventually Carnegie's museums, libraries, and community centers would be used and appreciated by later generations.

Carnegie looked at himself as a developer of American society. He was patriarchal in his approach. He would give 1,679 libraries worldwide, including the mill towns. Even his libraries, built by the nation's best architects, came with a catch. The community was expected to supply the books. The donation of books, at least in the mill towns, often came from local Carnegie managers. Of course, patriarchal is far better than the pure greed of many capitalists such as Vanderbilt, who lived as the world's greatest kings, wanting to establish aristocratic families for America. Carnegie truly believed that the rich should give all back to society and personally did so. He believed in giving to those who could help themselves.

The problem was Carnegie believed many like him were destined to distribute the wealth on their terms. Carnegie stated, "'Superior wisdom, experience, and ability to administer' made the man of wealth the ideal 'agent for his poorer brethren ... doing for them better than they would or could do for themselves.'"5 Carnegie's view was very aristocratic and more feudal than paternal. Unfortunately, many capitalists believed in this destiny-driven view that even had precedence in the Calvinistic beliefs of the Puritans. By contrast, paternal capitalists, such as Westinghouse and Heinz, saw a high-paying job and benefits as the best philanthropy. Even Carnegie's rich partners, Henry Clay Frick and Charles Schwab, gave more directly to the workers. Frick would give over $300 million, in mostly anonymous donations, to hospitals, poor children, education, and local charities. Charles Schwab built hospitals and schools to train skilled workers. He also maintained thousands of jobs during the depression to keep workers employed.

The public fascination with the mythical Carnegie would come to an end in the 1890s as labor problems and bloodshed made the headlines. The press would never again print the favorable articles about Carnegie that had dominated in prior years. Articles would decry the hypocrisy of Carnegie's giving and worker benefits.

Carnegie's flagship steel plant of Homestead Works was the site of bloodshed that changed public option. The gathering of forces at Homestead led to the downfall of many industrial icons in America. It was here that America's strongest union faced America's largest company of Carnegie Steel, leading to industrialist Andrew Carnegie's Waterloo. It was the beginning of the end of the Amalgamated Association of the Iron and Steel Workers; but like the Alamo, it would be the rallying cry of American unionization for decades. The Homestead Strike changed management, the union, and the public's view of concepts like property rights and European-style union socialism. It also challenged the idea of paternalism in the workplace.

Both the Carnegie empire and the Amalgamated Association of Iron and Steel Workers approached July 1892 at the peak of their power. Carnegie was the richest man in the world, and his company was the biggest and most profitable. Homestead was one of America's great melting pots as Slavs and Hungarians poured in to fill the thousands of unskilled jobs created in America's largest factory. Many ambitious immigrants saw the slums of Homestead as paved with the gold of opportunity. The local native population of skilled laborers were angered by this new influx of unskilled workers. The Amalgamated union was a skilled crafts union that excluded the unskilled labors in the workforce. The ethnic mix would become a major complication in the struggle. This strike was far from America's bloodiest or biggest, but it is one of the most remembered. It also changed the perception of philanthropy and paternalism as offsetting virtues.

The buildup to the 1892 Homestead Strike started at the 1891 convention of the Amalgamated Association of Iron and Steel Workers, a few miles downriver at Pittsburgh. The convention had 261 delegates representing 24,068 members. It was America's largest crafts union representing the skilled crafts workers of the iron and steel industry. The union, however, was fighting the inherent changes of industrialization and technological automation. Like the earlier fight for survival by the weavers of Europe, it was a struggle for the skilled crafts model versus unskilled technology. The Amalgamated was opposing disturbing trends that eroded the skilled crafts system infrastructure. The union was holding to its skilled apprenticeship system of seniority, controlling the amount of production that could be scheduled, and banning overtime until all crafts workers were employed. The union remained opposed to the entry of any Eastern Europeans such as Slovaks and Hungarians, who were the unskilled fraction of the workforce. As the possible strike approached in July of 1892, hundreds from the national press filled Pittsburgh hotels as both sides fought for public support. National politicians came also, as they framed the conflict as part of the tariff-free trade debate of the time. The Democrats cited Carnegie's profits and poor wages as a failure of the years of protective steel tariffs to help the workers. Homestead had been recognized by both Andrew Carnegie and the union as the location of Armageddon for the showdown of labor and steel management.

The real battle was, for the most part, against the advance of technology and automation which was reducing the skill level needed. Homestead represented a stand for management as well as reinforcement of property rights and control of the means of production. Carnegie had purchased the failed Homestead Bessemer steel mill and gutted it, putting in the latest technology. Carnegie and his general manager, Henry Clay Frick, had eliminated hundreds of skilled workers. Carnegie had brought in thousands of Eastern European unskilled workers and was expanding their role in the operations with technology. Furthermore, the economy of 1892 was now in a downturn, which gave Carnegie the upper hand that he had played so well in the past. This time, both Frick and Carnegie overplayed their hands.

The union skilled workers at Homestead numbered 800 out of about 3,800 total employees. The Amalgamated Association of Iron and Steel Workers represented an even smaller group of 325 highly paid and skilled workers. The wage argument was initially concerned with those 325 workers, leaving the lower skilled and poorly paid unskilled workers unrepresented. Even more surprising might be that the average American worker at the time made $8.50 a week, while a union skilled steelworker at Homestead averaged $35 a week.

Seeing the downturn in the economy, Carnegie designed a new type of wage package. The proposal would tie skilled steel rollers' wages to the price of steel. His argument was that the worker should be invested in the risk of the marketplace. In terms of a percentage cut, the new proposal from Carnegie meant a cut from 40 percent to 20 percent. The 3,000-plus unskilled laborers joined the strike, having no place to go and nothing to gain.

In early June, Andrew Carnegie wisely left Pittsburgh for a vacation in Scotland. On June 25, 1892, Frick closed off negotiations and started plans for a lockout. Meantime, reporters worldwide were flooding into Pittsburgh. One paper estimated there were at least 135 journalists from all over the globe. Homestead was international news.

Frick set up an 18-foot wooden fence topped with barbed wire and allegedly fitted with rifle slots. Sewers from the mill were provided with gratings to prevent an underground attack. Arc light searchlights were also installed on twelve-foot towers. It was rumored (falsely) the barbed wire was electrified, using Westinghouse's new alternating current. Pinkerton had been advertising in Western cities for armed guards at five dollars a day plus food and lodging. They mustered these raw recruits in Chicago, a mix of college students, drifters, and laid-off workers. The union similarly prepared their forces, which included the unskilled workers. They patrolled the river, railroad tracks, and bridges. Assuming scabs would be sent in, scouts on horses were sent down and up the river to warn the town of any approaching company men.

Things had reached the breaking point in Homestead as the saloons filled up and effigies of Carnegie, Frick, and others were hung on telegraph poles. Frick laid out his plan to have the Pinkerton guards enter the works, turning it into a fort. They would enter via the Ohio and Monongahela Rivers. The union had managed to gain the support of the unskilled workers, which surprised Frick and Carnegie; but it was a weak alliance. The unskilled workers were caught in the middle and could only hope for a quick settlement.

The Pinkertons moved by two river barges on the Ohio River to the Homestead plant. The barges had been purchased and converted to covered troop carriers. These were floating forts described as "Noah's Ark." They were equipped with dining halls and kitchens, complete with a hired steward and twenty waiters. The barges landed at the mill and the Pinkertons disembarked, armed with Winchester rifles. There was some pushing at the mill, and then shots rang out. Three steelworkers were killed on the spot and dozens wounded. The rioters fired an old twenty-pounder Revolutionary War cannon, missing the barges and hitting and killing a steelworker. A small number of the Pinkertons were wounded as well and retreated to their floating forts. Inaccurate cannon fire and shots continued as the Pinkertons huddled in their floating forts. The huddled Pinkertons had some protection but lacked air conditioning, and the barges were becoming sweaty iron furnaces. Homesteaders added to the barrage by tossing dynamite. Telegraph wire reports to Washington and Congress brought calls to repeal the tariffs that had helped Carnegie Steel. Meanwhile, the Homesteaders poured oil on the Monongahela River and started a few surface fires. The Pinkertons were overwhelmed and raised a white flag. The count was 13 dead and 36 wounded. Captured Pinkertons were forced through a crowd of angry workers who freely beat them with clubs.

The sheriff struggled to find deputies, and the union leadership in Homestead struggled to regain control of the town. Union men in Chicago talked about sending men and guns. The United States Congress debated daily. The governor finally sent troops after Pittsburgh political bosses pulled every string possible; still, the troops were not greeted in Homestead. Rails were torn up to slow the trains, but the troops were in place by July 12. With the town under military control, Congress sent a special committee to hold hearings. Union President Hugh O'Donnell called unsuccessfully for a national boycott of Carnegie steel products, and Samuel Gompers came to help support the unsuccessful boycott. Homestead did become a magnet to socialists in the United States.

Things changed again as the socialists entered the crisis from places like New York and Chicago. The socialist and anarchist movements in the United States had been following the action at Homestead and hoped to use it to their political gain. The most radical left fringe was the anarchists, who even rejected the minor organizational bent of Karl Marx. The anarchists had always looked for opportunities to get involved in labor strife. They were best known for the Haymarket Riots in Chicago. For them, the capitalists were the chief evil of the world. On July 23, a clean-cut socialist and activist in a suit, Alexander Berkman, entered Frick's office at the Chronicle-Telegraph Building on Pittsburgh's Fifth Avenue. Berkman had arrived alone in Pittsburgh around July 16 with a little money and a gun, and wearing the suit his girlfriend, Emma Goldman, had purchased for him. Berkman rushed in and fired, hitting Frick in the shoulder. Frick fell, and Berkman fired again, hitting Frick in the neck. Berkman's entrance into the crisis changed things. The union wanted no part of Berkman's act. While the press continued to villainize Frick, they also hailed his courage and nerve. Frick survived and remained in control from his bedroom. His bravery and resolve were amazing.

The religion of the mill workers was Catholicism, and the local priests and press saw more evil in anarchists and socialists than capitalists. An editorial in the *Catholic World* in 1893 noted: "The distribution of wealth is frightful in its very inequalities. Still I do believe that the socialist system is radically and hopelessly wrong. I do believe that the American workmen can right their wrongs by the machinery at their disposal and without violating of votes any law human or divine."[6] The public across the nation was concerned about the existence of anarchist cells in major cities and the rising tide of socialism, which forced unions to expel known socialists. The public, having little stomach for the use of Pinkertons and troops in labor disputes, turned against the union and Carnegie's style of capitalism. For the next few years, Homestead would be debated in major newspapers across the nation.

Democrats felt they could carry Western Pennsylvania for the first time since the formation of the Republican Party in the 1850s. This would challenge the alliance of protectionism and paternalism. The American union movement pulled away from the socialism, violence, and political role of unionization seen in Europe. Unions also realized the importance of full representation and solidarity. Torchlight parades in Homestead had floats portraying "protectionism" as black sheep, as politicians injected their own brand of racism into the crisis. Senate Democrats came to Homestead to hold hearings. Homestead cost President Harrison and the Republicans the election, and the Democrats would effectively repeal the great protective Tariff of 1890. Carnegie's name would forever be tarnished. However, the union was crushed, and it would not be until the 1930s that Pittsburgh mills would again be unionized.

Carnegie would donate one of his greatest libraries to the city of Homestead. The Carnegie Homestead Library was opened in 1898 and was a massive community center. It was an imposing Renaissance brick fortress, considered at the time to be the largest free library in the world. The main floor had a 20,000-volume library, a 1,000-seat auditorium, a 36-foot by 68-foot swimming pool, a billiards room, clubrooms, and bowling alleys. The second floor had a basketball court, running track, and exercise room. The library offered a wide variety of lectures and classes for the improvement of the worker. Henry Clay Frick donated a Steinway

Homestead Strike from *Harper's Weekly* in 1893 (Library of Congress).

piano to the Homestead Library at a possible cost of $80,000. To a large degree, Homestead was propped up by the capitalists to show that workers could pull themselves up. Many American cities, such as Detroit, looked at Carnegie's money as tainted after the Homestead Strike and refused his libraries.[7] Carnegie would never again find the favor of the press, and philanthropy became more suspect. Press cartoons often showed libraries being built on the backs of poor laborers.

In his 1920 *Autobiography*, Carnegie defends his philanthropy, an altruistic mission. In his book, he hopes to publicize the "Carnegie Myth," but it is based on facts. This Carnegie image appears much closer to that of Peter Cooper. Carnegie, like Cooper, remembers his struggle as a young unskilled worker, lacking access to education. Carnegie remembers how a wealthy industrialist, James Anderson, opened his personal library to help young boys. Carnegie was an American patriot interested in advancing American culture and exceptionalism. His lack of concern for his unskilled workers is still a paradox, given his own rise as an unskilled worker. It is, however, true that Carnegie often justified the means based on the end improvement to society. It was an argument not accepted in Homestead.

Carnegie argued that philanthropists had to focus their giving on projects to improve society in general (each in his view of what was needed). Carnegie libraries were given more and more to towns that had no relationship to his old factories. Carnegie would use the famous Pullman Strike of 1894 as a rationale for rejecting the idea of giving back directly to his workers. He argued against this type of "paternalism" as "pauperizing."[8] Carnegie ran his philanthropic operations as his business. He would start to question his old views as he grew older. His remorse led him to address his workers of decades earlier who had made him wealthy.

In 1900, Carnegie sold his steel company to J.P. Morgan. He then spent the last 18 years of his life giving away all his money. Giving seemed to change Carnegie; he began to regret the treatment of his mill workers in amassing his fortune. Andrew Carnegie established a pension and insurance program for the old workers of the Carnegie Company, which was now a division of United States Steel (USS). This applied to just under a third of the total 200,000 employees of United States Steel. In addition, Carnegie set up the Carnegie Relief Fund for his old workers. The Carnegie Relief Fund offered a pension and disability insurance. The Carnegie Relief also offered a $500 death benefit with $100 additions for surviving children (in addition to any other insurance held by the worker). Disability payments were based on the nature of injury but went as high as $5,000. Pension benefits were based on wages at retirement and years of service. A laborer making $37 a month would receive an average of about $5.60 a month, and a blacksmith making $80 a month would retire at $17.50 a month. At the time it was one of the best in the company. Still, many saw Carnegie's change as too little too late.

Similarly, Carnegie's managers, who became millionaires with the sale of Carnegie, would give another estimated $600 million back to society in the form of hospitals, churches, community centers, poor homes, relief funds, schools, and parks. Carnegie's partners proved more altruistic in their approach to giving. Henry Clay Frick, for example, gave away over $250 million anonymously to hospitals and community services. Most of the old Carnegie managers and partners publicly regretted the poor treatment of their workers. Still, their end of life generosity was unequaled in other countries. And for the better part of two centuries, American hospitals, libraries, and colleges were dependent on industrial philanthropy. Colleges included some of the nation's best, such as Princeton, Stanford, Rutgers, Brown, University of Chicago, Dartmouth, Carnegie-Mellon, and hundreds of smaller ones. Even state colleges depended on these donations; for example, the electrical engineering department at Ohio State (George Westinghouse), chemical and metallurgical engineering at the University of Pittsburgh (Charles Schwab), and metallurgical engineering at the University of Michigan (Carnegie partners).

Ten

The Failure of Pullman City

George Pullman (1831–1897) would represent paternal capitalism at its worst, but it didn't start out that way. Pullman would show that, like capitalism itself, paternalism could fall prey to abuses and greed. Pullman's worker city started out as an altruistic project, which soon became a source of profits. Profits, of course, had been the basis of such noble worker cities as New Lanark. While his profits were reasonable, in light of an economic recession and strike, they seemed out of line. Pullman was labor friendly, but he was hardheaded and a poor communicator. He was no George Westinghouse. Pullman's abuses would lead for an opening for the socialist movement of the period to show the weakness in the sincerity of paternal capitalism.

George Pullman was born in 1831 in Brocton, New York, near Buffalo. His family were Universalists but had Puritan roots. A young Pullman worked as a clerk in several businesses before going into the railroad service business at 27 years of age. Pullman didn't invent the overnight sleeping coach; it had been around for two decades. He would improve and customize it to make his fortune. In 1858, Pullman remodeled the sleeping cars for the Chicago & Alton Railroad with much success. The remodeled and ornate coaches were revolutionary. Saving his capital, Pullman opened a workshop in Chicago (today it is the site of Chicago Union Station), forming the Pullman Palace Car Company. Pullman spent over $20,000 to produce a coach car known as the Pioneer at a time when a normal sleeping coach cost $2,000. The Pioneer would become famous in housing the funeral party of Abe Lincoln, which rode from Washington, D.C., to Springfield, Illinois, for the president's burial.

With the popularity of the Pioneer, Pullman continued to build sleeping coaches for various railroads; and by 1867, he had 48 cars in operation. One of the early purchasers of the Pullman cars was the then superintendent of the Pennsylvania Railroad, Andrew Carnegie, who would become a significant stockholder in the company. Actually, Carnegie had formed a company to compete with Pullman but saw the successful possibilities of a merger. Carnegie's ties with railroad executives assured success. In the Panic of 1873, Carnegie sold his share in the Pullman Company to maintain the building of his steel empire. Pullman would expand into "hotel" cars, which would offer first-class cruise. By the end of the 1870s, Pullman and his company ranked as the most successful in America. Pullman built his mansion on Chicago's Prairie Avenue, where his neighbors were Philip Armour and Marshall Fields. This trinity of Chicago capitalism would reflect some of the worst of Gilded Age paternal capitalism.

Pullman's Chicago plant had built a reputation as a well paying company. The Chicago labor market would prove to be the most difficult.

Pullman City, 1892 (Library of Congress).

Chicago was the front line for the socialist movement in the United States, but the Chicago labor market lacked supply. Often benefits were given to attract workers. The Pullman Company offered free transportation to and from work, and the cost to the company was estimated at $8,000 per month or about 20 cents a day per employee.[1] In 1880, when Pullman asked workers to pay for half the cost, it resulted in a bitter strike. The experience led Pullman to envision the development of a manufacturing community built around a new manufacturing facility. The actual idea had long been in the making as Chicago unionists and socialists had become more violent, and moving out of the poor immigrant neighborhoods seemed to make for a more stable workforce.

During one of his European trips in 1873, Pullman visited the Owenian factory town of Saltaire, England. The factory town was built by Sir Titus Salt (1803–1877) in 1853, and historians believe Pullman was inspired by Saltaire.[2] Titus Salt operated a woolen factory in Bradford, England, which produced a very special woolen fabric from Russian sources. Bradford was a booming industrial city with all the pollution of industrial England. Cholera epidemics were common and often crippled wool production. Salt faced many of the same problems of the Chicago industrialists. Bradford had seen violent struggles in the 1840s and 1850s as a center for the working-class Chartist movement. Social reformers decried the slums of Bradford and the living conditions. Socialists had entered the union movement, and there had been violence. The great novels of Charles Dickens had addressed the social slums of earlier nineteenth century England. In the 1870s, British author Charles Reade's novel, *Put Yourself in His Place*, addressed the rising violence between unions and factory owners. It is known that George Pullman had read and been impressed by this novel.[3] Titus Salt had studied the earlier manufacturing village of New Lanark and hoped for a similar solution. Salt built his new factory in the clean and beautiful Aire Valley. When Pullman visited Saltaire, many were hailing the village as appeasing labor without the formation of a union.

Titus Salt had built a manufacturing village with a population of 6,000. The village was comprised of workers' homes, which rented at competitive rates. The homes did return a profit to Salt of 4 percent.[4] Interestingly, the higher the position at the factory, the bigger the house. The factory was located in this beautiful, well-kept city. Saltaire had a hospital, library, community center, church, schools, and parks, all built by Salt. Salt, like Robert Owen, became interested in creating a social utopia. Salt banned the use of alcohol in his community. Overall, like New Lanark, Saltaire proved a successful model for paternalism. Pullman would borrow many concepts from Salt. The popularity of Salt's approach to workers saw the formation of the Society for Promoting Industrial Villages.

Titus Salt would be remembered as a kind employer in a time of slave-like laborers. Titus Salt became England's most popular industrialist, with over 100,000 lining the streets for his funeral in 1877. Unfortunately, the free-trade policies of the British government would make the woolen industry unsustainable, and Saltaire would fade into history. Today, like New Lanark, Saltaire has been designated a UNESCO World Heritage Site for its pioneering of humanitarian ideas. Pullman also saw it as a successful alternative to socialism.

In 1880, George Pullman started to build a worker utopia based on Saltaire around his Chicago factory. Pullman built a city for his workers of the time. It would be a true industrial city, similar to that of Krupp Steel in Germany and the old industrial towns of Robert Owen. The idea was utopian in scope but would be profitable for the company. Like most utopian plans, Pullman planned to impose a set of moral rules on the workers as well. One historian comparing Pullman City to Saltaire noted: "The principle was the same: openly avowed paternalism as an alternative to fist-in-the-face corporate militancy."[5] Pullman City was also compared to Fourier-type utopias as well: "Like Brook Farm and even earlier New Harmony communities, it was idealistic; but unlike them, it was the result of hard-headed business decisions and thus more likely to succeed."[6] However, the labor problems in Chicago at the time even rivaled the socialist unrest in Europe.

Pullman ran Pullman City as a profit center in the vein of Robert Owen. It would be the nineteenth-century version of New Lanark. Pullman publicly stated that philanthropy was not his goal because he wanted to attract a better class of workers willing to help themselves.[7] It was to be an inspirational and motivational city for workers away from the problems of Chicago. Pullman began construction of his city in 1880 on five thousand acres of land, fourteen miles south of Chicago near Lake Calumet. By 1885, the population reached 9,000, including 3,000 children. The city housed 4,000 employees and their families. Single laborers were housed in block row houses; and as in Saltaire, skilled and managerial employees merited detached homes. Managers and skilled workers also merited more features in their houses. Executive and skilled laborers were located nearer to the parks and lake. Pullman would bear the cost of construction and upkeep with a 6 percent return on capital.[8] Workers were required to live in Pullman City, where Pullman ran all utilities, services, and rent for a profit. He charged rents 25 percent higher than surrounding neighborhoods, but the amenities were considerably more. In addition, Pullman purchased water from Chicago at four cents per thousand gallons and sold it to his town at ten cents. Houses included front porches and backyards, something missing in the industrial slums.

Clergy were charged rent on churches, and the library charged a fee, too. Still, consider worker slums in Chicago, which lacked clean water, sewage systems, and paved streets. Pullman foresaw a safe and crime-free environment. The houses were of sturdy brick versus the wooden firetraps of Chicago's industrial slums. In fact, Pullman City became known as America's first all-brick city. Saloons were on every block in Chicago, adding to the high crime rate. The overcrowding and poor sanitation of the Chicago industrial slums were described as "prime breeding ground for dreaded pestilences such as cholera and tuberculosis."[9] Crime and prostitution were out of control in these industrial slums. Youth in the slums could expect little in their future. Even the hardcore socialists were impressed with the cleanliness and safety of Pullman City.

Pullman City, like earlier industrial utopias, was a dictatorship with all governance being from Pullman himself. He tried to control good upkeep through company inspectors. He would allow only one bar in the whole city, while Chicago averaged two per block. Inspectors were used to maintain clean water and a functioning sewage system. The better homes had indoor plumbing and bathtubs. Residents were expected to be properly attired at all times. Offenders would be evicted after failing to heed frequent warnings. Pullman, however, can be faulted for overreach in his attempts to control the town's social norms. A recent study noted: "Choices of activities were also planned, and George Pullman selected all the types of books available in the library and the performances at the theater."[10] Socialists saw Pullman City as a "gilded cage." Other industrialists, such as Andrew Carnegie and J. P. Morgan, saw it as socialism.

Pullman wasn't the first to try to profit internally from "paternal" capitalism in America. The great coal and steel capitalist, Henry Clay Frick, had also set up grocery stores and houses for his workers in the coal fields. A mining industry study in 1884 showed how much the company stores were really a company abuse.[11] The state survey of coal companies showed that around twenty percent of a coal company's profits were attributed to the company store, while Pullman's stores were designed to make a more reasonable six percent. Some might argue that even Robert Owen made a profit from his company stores, but his margin was much smaller than the mining company's profits. Pullman City profits were returned directly to the workers, as occurred in Owen's case. Pullman did avoid the negative image of the company store by bringing in independent merchants. In Pullman's case, he rented space to merchants who built beautiful arcades that rivaled our malls of today. Pullman City had its own bank. By the late 1880s, people were coming from the world over to see this worker utopia. When the 1893 World's Fair came to Chicago, Pullman proudly arranged tours for fairgoers. Pullman also had a scale model built so that all of the 35 million fairgoers might see his utopia. The Pullman utopia would not, however, survive the oncoming financial crisis in the economy.

Like so many paternal capitalists, Pullman didn't know how to handle economic downturns effectively. Carnegie had tried unsuccessfully to tie wages to product prices in the marketplace, with little success. Pullman tried to save jobs through pay cuts with even less success. Pullman, like Henry Clay Frick in the coal mining industry, did not reduce rents in turn. Workers no longer saw the company town as a true benefit. It was a major mistake that brought violent strikes to both industries. Interestingly, a century earlier, Robert Owen had dealt with the problem: he kept people working and reduced rents in bad times.

The once hailed utopian Pullman Company and town would be the

Worker housing for workers at Pullman City, 1893 (Library of Congress).

location of a major labor strike in the economic downturn of 1894 that would spread like the Great Railroad Strike of 1877. At its peak, the Pullman railroad strike would involve over 250,000 people in 27 states and last three weeks. The violence resulted in the deaths of 13 strikers and over 60 wounded, with property damage over $340,000 (about $9 million today). The strike was the effort of the American Railways Union headed by socialist Eugene Debs. The strike would be a battle between socialism and capitalism. Paternalism, philanthropy, charity, the church, and government all offered a challenge to the idea of socialism as the answer for the poor immigrant laborers. Socialists, on the other hand, feared paternal capitalism as economic slavery. In good economic times, paternal capitalism seemed hard to beat. Unions also saw paternal capitalism as a real threat. The Panic of 1893, however, spiraled industrial America into a great depression.

The Panic had started, like most, as a financial crisis in the financial and banking firms, but it soon spread to the heartland. Before the Panic of 1893 ended, a quarter of America's railroads would fail, and steel prices would crash. In 1893 alone, 15,000 businesses failed, along with 158 banks. Most of America's steel mills were idle. Millions of workers were laid off. The railroad industry all but collapsed. The market for luxury Pullman cars was hit even harder than most. For unemployed workers in America's industrial slums, it was a time of social questioning. In the winter of 1892–93, Jacob Sechler Coxey of Massillon, Ohio, formed the idea of a massive march on Washington to highlight the rising unemployment. The march crossed Ohio, and as the army reached Pittsburgh on April 3, it swelled to 300,000 in the city. Hobo towns lined the great railroads leading into the major cities, and the streets were filled with beggars. Immigrants in tent cities struggled to stay warm and eat. The rich suburbs lived in constant fear of looting or attack. Capitalists such as Andrew Carnegie would be forced to spend hundreds of thousands in relief aid for the unemployed, but nothing could tamp down the social unrest that had been building for decades. For many, the socialist call for violence seemed the only answer for change.

Pullman had seen orders for his rail cars plummet as a result of the Panic of 1893. The trouble for Pullman City started in May of 1894 with a layoff of 3,000 of Pullman's 5,800 employees at the Chicago plant. In an effort to save jobs, Pullman cut the wages of the remaining employed by 25 percent. The real mistake was Pullman's hardheadedness in not reducing rents in Pullman City. Whatever Pullman's reasoning, it certainly appeared greedy and far from paternal. Members of the American Railway

Union asked that the rents in the Pullman worker town be reduced. Pullman ended up firing the union representatives, which brought the union president, Eugene V. Debs, into the disagreement. Pullman then locked out the employees. Just before the strike started, Pullman arranged for several of his luxury cars to pack up his family, servants, a stable of six horses, and grooms and move to his summer home on the New Jersey shore. Things escalated quickly to a strike, as Pullman announced a regular dividend to its stockholders. Debs set up his headquarters in Pullman City. The strike slowly started to spread along related railways, as three-quarters of the rails moving in and out of Chicago closed. The union called for a nationwide boycott of Pullman cars. Railroad workers across the nation refused to switch Pullman cars, which effectively shut down railroad operations across the nation. The General Managers Association managed the combination of rail lines and companies. The Association had strong ties in the Grover Cleveland administration as well as with J.P. Morgan.

With the depression of 1893 reaching a peak, the situation was volatile. President Grover Cleveland got involved with hiring 3,600 special deputies and sending 6,000 troops to Pullman City. The troops had the full protection of the United States government. The newspapers supported Cleveland initially, but this position was short-lived. Pullman used scabs and strikebreakers at the factory, which caused even more violence. Federal involvement inspired more rioting by the workers as the unemployed joined in. On July 7, the strike erupted into shootings and deaths as troops clashed with workers in Chicago. The strike started to spread across the country along the railroads. Cleveland was forced to get an injunction against the strikers because the strike interfered with delivery of the U.S. Mail. It was the first time the federal government had used an injunction to stop a strike. However, the strikers stood their ground.

Chicago began to attract socialists and anarchists to "help" out. Ray Baker, second in command of Coxey's army, showed up in Chicago. The country seemed split between fear and outrage. Pullman refused arbitration, and New York and other large cities supported him, characterizing the strike as an attack on society. As famous socialists and anarchists such as Emma Goldman joined the effort, many feared a rebellion in our large cities. Goldman was an anarchist, socialist, Russian immigrant, and revolutionary. She would later inspire Leon Czolgosz, President McKinley's future assassin. Earlier, she had been the girlfriend of the attempted assassin of Henry Clay Frick during the Homestead Strike. The timing was poor for the strikers, as an anarchist had just assassinated the president of France. Republican industrialist Mark Hanna, however, supported the workers, calling Pullman a "damn idiot." Hanna would be one of those to expose Pullman's utopia in Senate proceedings. Other paternal capitalists such as Andrew Carnegie and John Rockefeller were "appalled" at the extent of Pullman's profit making on his "worker city." In truth, Carnegie and Rockefeller had always opposed such worker benefits. After his own violent Homestead Strike, Carnegie, in particular, was happy to see Pullman falter. The strike was reaching levels of the Railroad Strike of 1877 within a month. Mayors from over fifty cities asked Pullman to accept arbitration.

Samuel Gompers, one of the most influential labor leaders of the time, tried to mediate a settlement. He sent a telegram to President Cleveland only to have it rejected. Cleveland commented, if it takes the entire army and navy of the United States to deliver a postal card in Chicago, that card will be delivered. Cleveland sent 14,000 federal troops in, and the nation's anger now turned towards him. Cleveland's use of federal troops was considered anti-workingman, when even capitalists had condemned Pullman for his hardheaded approach on rents.

The strike ended with the heavy federal crackdown, but the courts took over to exact revenge for the upheaval. The result of the "Debs Strike" would change the landscape of American politics. Eugene Debs was sentenced to six months in prison for disobeying the injunction and would later form the American Socialist Party. The Sherman Anti-Trust Act was used to support the conviction, and the Supreme Court upheld its use against labor. In addition, the Supreme Court upheld the use of a federal injunction because of interruptions to the U.S. Mail. The Supreme Court of Illinois in 1897 forced Pullman Company to divest itself of the City of Pullman. The U.S. Senate launched investigations that resulted in condemning Pullman's use of paternalism to profit. Thanks to the oratory of Debs and some exposed abuses of Pullman, the public sided with the workers. The Senate Committee believed that had Pullman reduced the rents with the wage cuts, the strike could have been avoided. The Committee also found that Pullman's rents were 20 to 30 percent higher than similar accommodations in Chicago. The Committee, however, ignored the cost of sanitary and safety measures implemented by Pullman. This overhead severely restricted the popularity of such rental agreements for workers by other capitalists.

The socialists gained back much of what they had lost in the Haymarket Riot. Socialists would oust Samuel Gompers as president of the American Federation of Labor for his middle-of-the-road approach. Eugene Debs would run for president a number of times, getting as high as six percent of the vote in 1912. President Cleveland, a Democrat, lost the support of his party in 1896 and would be forced to run as a third-party candidate. The Democratic majority lay in ruins, and the elections of 1894 and 1896 would sweep in a Republican majority. In general, the Federal government and companies gained enormous power to stop national strikes, which would not be adjusted until the passing of the Wagner Act of 1935. For his part, Eugene Debs made the Socialist Party part of the American scene for years to come. In 1919, Debs was imprisoned again for two years for anti-government strikes during World War I.

Pullman would come back to Chicago but live in fear of assassination. The Pullman Company survived for many years, with its second president being Robert Todd Lincoln, the son of Abraham Lincoln. George Pullman would die in 1898 as a brokenhearted innovator. His utopian experiment had not only failed but widened the struggle between labor and capital. He was despised in Chicago and in many railroad towns. Fearing his body might be dug up and mutilated by his enemies or former workers, Pullman arranged for special precautions to be taken. The coffin was lead-lined and sealed in tar and asphalt. This entombed coffin was then placed in a block of reinforced concrete and steel railroad rails and covered by a massive structure of railroad ties. One Chicago doctor, who had attended the deathbeds of many Chicago capitalists such as Pullman, reported that "he had never seen a very rich man who died happy. There was always family trouble or woman trouble, or some other trouble."[12] Some would argue that this very unhappiness was at the root of philanthropy. Still, it is only recently, as we move from the memory of the Pullman Strike, that Pullman City can be fairly evaluated.[13] The 1890s, however, had cast suspicion on paternalists.

Eleven

The Greatest Paternalist of Them All

George Westinghouse was an American businessman who combined humanitarianism and business at a high level. He exemplified the nineteenth-century version of American Puritanism in business. He had the humility of a monk, but the drive of a capitalist. He cared little for publicity or headlines, and he didn't like his name on anything other than the company. He gave more credit than he needed to his engineers and managers. He believed the best philanthropy was giving back to his employees in the form of wages and benefits. He was often critical of the public philanthropy of capitalists such as Carnegie, who accumulated profits at the expense of the workers. His public charity was always behind the scenes and he played down his legacy. He did enjoy the good life but respected the needs of others. He had great power, but rarely used it. Westinghouse was doing what he loved. He did not see himself as a social reformer or as one touched by destiny to help the world. He simply lived as a capitalist within his Christian framework.

Westinghouse was of Puritan roots, and his family and social behavior demonstrated the same moral consistency. Westinghouse demonstrated tolerance that few managers were capable of with some very difficult people. He helped his employees with house ownership, pension, health expenses, and social needs. He gave directly to their education instead of building schools for the general public. When he did give to schools and educational institutions, he preferred to donate equipment and generators versus money. He avoided the direct cash payment where possible, believing it was better to pay his employees well and create jobs. Other great capitalists such as Andrew Carnegie and J.P. Morgan saw him not only as foolish, but as a dangerous example of paternalism, and eventually the banking trust of J.P. Morgan would break him. It would be Westinghouse in the nineteenth century who met the high bar of Robert Owen.

George Westinghouse was born on October 6, 1846; the Westinghouse family already had three daughters and three sons. The family roots had gone back several generations as New England farmers. The Puritanism of his mother was the family's guiding influence in general. Westinghouse's dominant view on business was the "Holland Puritanism" of his mother. She gave Westinghouse a unique view of capitalism that would be the hallmark of his character and businesses. Puritan ethics were typically adapted to business in nineteenth-century New England. For example, the Westminster Larger Catechism, in which Westinghouse received training, extended the following application of the 8th Commandment, Thou shalt not steal: "The duties required in the 8th Commandment include the following: maintaining truth and faithfulness and justice in contracts and commerce, between man and man; rendering to everyone his due; restitution of goods unlawfully detained from the right owners thereof; ... avoiding unnecessary lawsuits, the care to preserve and respect the property and rights of others just as we care for our own."[1]

The catechism training Westinghouse received from his mother defined his whole life and produced strong ethics in situations that turned to the unethical. It was the reason behind his refusal to join the banking trusts of the day as well as his fierce defense of patent and intellectual property rights. Westinghouse belonged to the famous Pittsburgh East Side Presbyterian, but he was not known as a regular churchgoer.

George Westinghouse, Sr., imparted an array of mechanical skills to his son, but just as important were some necessary inventing skills. Westinghouse, Sr., had a number of inventions to his name and was a contributor to *Scientific American* in its early days. He was quoted in 1850 in *Scientific American* in relation to a patent battle concerning water wheels. Westinghouse, Sr., showed the history of such a design was over 30 years old. He loved to work on engineering drawings and got young George initially trained. He often took young George to visit various manufacturers. The shop of Westinghouse, Sr., had the current journals of mechanics and manufacturers available for young George to read. Young Westinghouse became an expert on steam engines. He could design and draw the parts, machine them, and assemble them by the age of 12.

Young Westinghouse learned engineering at his father's machine shop. He started with freehand sketches to put his original ideas to paper. He would rework these simple drawings as the idea itself evolved. This straightforward approach came from observing machinists in his father's factory. The next step for Westinghouse was to move to detailed engineering prints with dimensions. Westinghouse could easily be given the title of father of drafting. His future companies would have more draftsmen employed than any other U.S. employer. Later in life, he would promote drafting as a discipline in colleges as well as in grade schools. Finally, modeling of the project was used for initial testing. His friend William Ratcliffe had taught him the importance of modeling, a technique he would spend a lifetime perfecting. Of course, none of these techniques were new, but no one had put them together in such a formal approach to design. More than anyone, George Westinghouse, Jr., defined the discipline of modern engineering and design, and the roots of that approach are clearly seen in his youthful projects.

At the age of 18, Westinghouse entered the Union Navy during the Civil War. He was assigned to the *Muscoota*, a steam-powered ship; and the engine room would supply valuable mechanical experience to young Westinghouse. He continued to build models of his rotary steam engine and successfully applied them to small wooden boat models. His position as assistant engineer allowed free time to sketch and model engines. His passion was tinkering with steam engines.

After the war, he returned to New York and entered Union College of Schenectady in the fall of 1865. Union College at the time was a very prestigious school, having been the college of William Seward, Lincoln's Secretary of State. Other nineteenth-century graduates and students included Chester Arthur, former U.S. president; Charles Steinmetz, famous electrical engineer; and Edward Bellamy, author of *Looking Backward*. George, Jr., seems to have struggled through the fall semester in the "scientific department." He then returned to his father's shop, followed by another semester or two at the college. Little is known of his academic record, but observers again noted his love of drawing. The old Westinghouse shop was, at the time, building steam engines for farm equipment and various railroad parts.

After his return to his father's firm, George, Jr., became involved with customers and suppliers in the East. He commonly traveled by train to make these supplier and customer calls. He had the drive, like his father, to branch off on his own, and was well aware of the growth potential in railroad-related products. The invention that launched his industrial career was the railroad "car replacer." The portable re-rail frog, or car replacer, was a portable or permanent track device, which enabled derailed railroad cars to be put back on the tracks. Crowbars and muscle were the more common method of re-railing a car in the 1860s. Westinghouse, like any traveler of the time, was familiar with both methods. Accidents and derailing were common experiences. A rail traveler could expect to experience hours of delay, with time to get out of the car to watch the muscular job to re-rail. Westinghouse wanted to invent, and the car replacer offered that opportunity.

At twenty years old, Westinghouse would have to bring all his sales ability to apply and to promote his new device. He was able to convince two Schenectady businessmen and friends of his father to contribute $5,000 each to form a partnership. The company incorporated as Rawls, Wall, and Westinghouse in 1866; and the three partners would share the profits equally. George would remain working part-time for his father and live at home. Westinghouse would pioneer steel in the railroad equipment, making his rail frogs out of crucible steel.

The sales burden fell on young George to promote his new product, but first he needed a steel foundry to produce his frog on a production basis. Tests around the world had hailed the superior strength and wear resistance of steel over cast iron and wrought iron, but there were few large steel foundries. Crucible steel took weeks of heating and processing into small batches, now that the Bessemer process offered high production and lower-priced steel for Westinghouse. Westinghouse realized that using steel meant a tougher, longer-lived car replacer. Westinghouse was able to contract the new Bessemer steel mill at Troy to build his frogs and replacers. The cast steel frog/replacer was one of the first steel castings ever made in the world. Westinghouse read, studied, and experimented his way to a successful casting method.

This type of intensive study preceded all of Westinghouse's endeavors. Research included public libraries, trade journals at his father's plant, and the stories of local railroaders. Westinghouse had a true love of inventing and engineering. In this case, his study of casting methods gave him metallurgical expertise, which he used throughout his career, building some of the world's greatest foundries by the end of his career. His initial research led him to the Pittsburgh foundry of Cook & Anderson. They felt they could produce the steel frog at a lower cost and were willing to work with Westinghouse. This would bring Westinghouse and his new wife to the industrial city of Pittsburgh.

After setting up a small factory in Pittsburgh, Westinghouse started his work on the revolutionary compressed air railroad brake. The railroad hand brake system of the 1860s required coordination and muscle power. The locomotive engineer would start throttling down the engine as he signaled the brakemen with the whistle. A brakeman was assigned between every two cars on the train. Ideally, the engineer had throttled to a coast as it approached the stop. The brakemen would begin applying friction brakes on each car by the turning of a hand wheel known as the horizontal wheel on a vertical post at the end of each car that multiplied the force of his muscles. The needed strength of the brakemen was the source of the term "Armstrong system." The hand wheel pushed brake shoes on each car against the wheels. The hand wheel used a chain to transfer the power to the brake shoes. After the brakes were applied to one car, the brakemen jumped to the other car to apply the brakes. Poor coordination between the brakemen could cause "locking" and serious jolting to the passengers. Luggage was often thrown wildly inside the passenger cars. Many times brakemen were killed or injured in this difficult task. The danger to the brakemen was unbelievable. Jolting or locking often threw the brakeman off on his way across the car roof to the next car. The average life of a brakeman on the job was estimated at seven years. The brakeman had to race from car to car, often on roofs slippery with ice, snow, and rain. Even on the best days, the swaying, bobbing, and jolting of the cars often caused a loss of footing. The statistics of the time estimated 1,000 brakemen were killed each year with another 5,000 injured.[2]

The invention of the Westinghouse air brake would virtually eliminate deaths and injuries related to railroad braking. This first Westinghouse brake was known as the straight-air brake. It was simple and primitive. A steam pump on the locomotive, using the same steam that drove the engine, generated the compressed air. The compressed air was contained in a reservoir located on the locomotive as well. A pipe using flexible couplings was used to connect the individual brake cylinders on each car. These flexible couplings were three-ply rubber, which was available and could handle compressed air.

One of Westinghouse's biggest supporters in Washington of his railroad projects was William McKinley, then head of the Ways and Means Committee of Congress. McKinley and Westinghouse often talked on railroad safety issues. They would share a passion for industrial safety throughout their careers. They immediately became friends. Westinghouse discussed his new worker community he was developing at Wilmerding to support his air brake operation. McKinley had been a president of the YMCA in Canton, Ohio, and noted its value in communities. Westinghouse would support the YMCA in his factory neighbors.

Maybe more importantly, Westinghouse and McKinley shared government support of business while rejecting trusts, and each had a strong belief in "lunch pail" Republicanism. Another bond shared was their pride in being veterans of the Grand Army of the Republic. Both men would point to their military service as the highlight of their careers. It was a friendship that would grow over the years. Westinghouse was never active in politics, but he was a Republican, going back to his abolitionist roots, and became a strong personal supporter of President William McKinley. McKinley, a devout Presbyterian, shared many of Westinghouse's core beliefs. Westinghouse was even a presidential elector and fundraiser for the McKinley election. As president, McKinley was a house guest at all of Westinghouse's mansions. During the McKinley administration, Westinghouse was a personal advisor to the President and purchased a third mansion in Washington, D.C., known as Blaine Mansion (DuPont Circle). Both men shared the view of paternal capitalism in America. McKinley used the paternalism of Westinghouse to support his policies of protecting American industry with tariffs.

Twelve

Westinghouse's Paternalism

In July 1869, the same year H.J. Heinz opened his first plant in Pittsburgh, Westinghouse Air Brake was formed with a board of directors from the enthusiastic railroad executives. The board consisted of a twenty-two-year-old Westinghouse and railroad executives Robert Pitcairn, W. Card, Andrew Cassatt, Edward Williams, G. Whitcomb, and Ralph Baggaley. The capitalization was $500,000. Cassatt, Pitcairn, and Williams were Pennsylvania Railroad executives, and Card and Whitcomb were from the Panhandle Railroad. John Caldwell, a friend of Westinghouse's partner Ralph Baggaley, was elected treasurer of the new company. By the end of 1869, the nation was aware of the new Westinghouse brake and its potential to improve railroad safety. Within a decade, the Westinghouse air brake was on trains throughout the world.

Westinghouse ran his company like his father's small New York machine shop. His primitive 15-man operation in 1870 on the north side of Pittsburgh had started the practice of closing the shop from Saturday noon to Monday morning; such a practice was unheard of and opposed by fellow industrialists such as Andrew Carnegie. Westinghouse knew his employees well and often would take them to lunch or bring them home for dinner. He initiated a Thanksgiving dinner at his home for his employees. As the company grew, the ritual for Westinghouse's employees and families moved to the best Pittsburgh hotels. When the company got too large for such a dinner, he became the first to start the practice of giving holiday turkeys to his employees. He built parks and baseball fields for his employ-

Westinghouse Air Brake, north side of Pittsburgh, 1880 (Library of Congress).

ees. The generosity and big heart of Westinghouse was well-known throughout the Pittsburgh district. As the company grew, Westinghouse developed employee-driven managers to run his factory.

Westinghouse expanded his production and volume using the crafts model of production. The method focused on the skills of machinists and mechanics. He trained his unskilled labor to eventually move into the skilled jobs, and his skilled workers to become managers. The use of scientific job layout would allow Westinghouse to compete even with later developed assembly-line methods. Unlike the assembly line, the Westinghouse method focused on employee skills and the human element. This type of mass-production craft was perfected by Westinghouse and would be used by the Germans during World War II. The method also had many of the attributes of lean manufacturing of today, which is bringing the human element back to the mass assembly lines in the auto industries.

Westinghouse's plant productivity did boom through good management, good engineering, and a caring approach to his employees. His employee-driven methods were as revolutionary as his air brake. In 1871, his Pittsburgh company produced 18 sets of car brakes and 4 sets of locomotive brakes per day using 105 people. In 1874, Westinghouse brakes were on 20 percent of the nation's trains. All of these were the straight air brake. Production of the automatic brake started in 1874 and replaced the straight air design. The automatic brake system had compressed air reservoirs on each car to allow each car to function independently, thus improving safety. In addition, the "triple valve" allowed a fail-safe condition that applied the brakes when anything disengaged the overall connections. In 1876, Westinghouse had 37 percent of the existing trains, or 2,645 locomotives and 8,500 passenger cars. By 1879, Westinghouse had installed his system, mainly automatic brakes, on 3,600 locomotives and 13,000 cars. With the booming sales of the automatic brake, Westinghouse was in need of good mechanics and machinists. Straight hourly wages for such skilled employees were around two dollars and fifty cents per hour. Westinghouse devised a piece-rate system based on units or work done. It was one of America's first assembly incentive systems.

By 1880 he could meet the world demand, producing over 100 sets of brakes a day. By then Westinghouse had instituted another revolutionary employee benefit, the paid vacation. He developed a company-funded pension and disability program for his employees, sixty years before most American industries had even started consideration for such programs. Employment had grown to over a thousand, but Westinghouse was manufacturing a wide array of equipment as well. By 1890, at his new plant in Wilmerding east of Pittsburgh, he was producing over 1,000 sets of brakes per day as well as assorted railroad equipment, using 6,000 employees. Still, Westinghouse loved to walk the factory and talk to his employees. An employee with an idea would often be invited to his home for dinner and drinks.

Even as the company grew, employees had access to Westinghouse. He never micromanaged, but when an employee had a serious problem or complaint, he might overrule a manager. While he had an inherent belief that treating employees right paid off, his motives went much deeper than that. Westinghouse was a deeply moral person and had a genuine concern for people, and this belief is clearly traceable to his New England Puritan upbringing. Certainly his highly profitable company allowed extremes of employee compensation that maybe others could not. Westinghouse's first biographer, Francis Leupp, reports a telling story of Westinghouse's heart and genuine concern.[1] In the early days of the air brake pension program, a number of loyal employees had reached the age of seventy but were a few days short of the required twenty years of service needed for a pension. When Westinghouse heard of the situation, he forced the board of directors to adjust the plan to meet the requirements for a pension. This was far from an isolated case of Westinghouse's concern for his employees. Westinghouse, many times, overruled his managers in keeping employees through bad times. He even supplied free coal to struggling employee families to heat their homes. Westinghouse's approach was instinctual, going back to his family and Puritan roots.

While the productivity gains were record-setting, they were the ancillary benefit of his employee-driven approach to running a company. His company became a magnet for young dreamers, mechanics, skilled tradesmen, and unskilled laborers looking to improve themselves. Throughout his career, Westinghouse would daily bring employees to his mansion for dinner and conversation. Many of these technical discussions went into the early morning over beer and a game of billiards. His love of engineering and people superseded managing and making money. Westinghouse loved to take his daily walks in the factory just to talk about the product and potential improvements. He left the financial concerns to his partners and accountants. His only interest was having enough money to pursue endless personal engineering projects. He always had time to play with and discuss his engineering models and small steam engine toys. Westinghouse was constantly working on new ideas and building models. He counted on his employees to run the daily operations. He put profits into better pay and benefits for his employees and money for his new projects. His wealth came out of his innovation and passion to create. Money was a tool for him, not an end goal.

One of those projects would bring him to the electrical business. Westinghouse's favorite operation was his "innovation" and research building in Pittsburgh's Garrison Alley. This was his personal lab and workshop, but he also encouraged his employees to bring their ideas to the workshop. It would be here that he would create many more companies such as Westinghouse Electric, Union Switch & Signal, and Westinghouse Machine. He moved quickly from steam engines to electrical generators to railroad electrical devices.

In 1880, he started Westinghouse Machine Company to build a type of high-speed steam engine. These engines would drive electrical generating dynamos for arc lighting; and by 1882, Westinghouse Machine was producing four engines a day. This product seemed to fit well with his small research and development operation at Garrison Alley, which was pursuing electrical switching controls for railroads. The actual manufacturing plant for Westinghouse Machine was the original air brake plant at Liberty Avenue, as air brake production had moved to Robinson Street on Pittsburgh's North Side (then called the city of Allegheny). His new air brake plant would be world-class. Westinghouse had molding machines imported from Scotland when he couldn't find the automation he wanted domestically. His lathes were some of the first gear and cam-driven lathes in the area. Westinghouse studied tooling with a passion, allowing him to always be on the cutting edge. His Garrison Alley operation was a world-class research center rivaling Edison's Menlo Park; and in 1886, it evolved into Westinghouse Electric and Union Switch & Signal.

In 1884, Westinghouse spun off a new company, also known as Westinghouse Machine, which produced steam-powered electrical generators. He took the opportunity to experiment with human engineering as well. Westinghouse pioneered mutual insurance and disability insurance plans. Westinghouse Machine formed the Westinghouse Machine Company Mutual Aid Society. The company funded this separate organization in large part. Records of the initial plan could not be found; but by 1900, there are some statistics. Membership was voluntary for the employee, requiring fifty cents a month. In the case of disability due to sickness, the worker was entitled to $5 a week for 6 months, and $7 a week for disability due to injury. The death benefit was $100 from natural causes and $150 from accidental death. Workers contributed according to the class in which they belonged, there being five, the class was determined by the wages received. Based on wages varying from $35 to $95 or more per month, the contribution ranged from 50 cents to $1.50 per week. The company contributed one-third of the injury benefit and one-third of the accidental death benefit.[2] Pittsburgh's largest employer, Carnegie Steel, offered no such benefits.

Westinghouse had few excesses in his life. He did have a mansion on Pittsburgh's East Side with many famous and rich neighbors, but he was not known for partying. He had a membership in Pittsburgh's Duquesne Club, which from 1873 was the private men's club in Pittsburgh for some of America's greatest capitalists. His partner, Ralph Baggaley, was one of the Duquesne Club's earliest members and an officer. For Westinghouse, membership in the club meant little; he preferred to eat dinner at home and would have nightly business dinners there as well. For lunches, he preferred hearty basic meals and often ate at the Allegheny Valley Railway Company diner car known as "Coach No. 2."

The Westinghouse nightly dinners were known throughout the region. Westinghouse preferred to invite his business associates to dinner with their wives instead of attending the all-men's meetings at places like the Duquesne Club or University Club. The dinners had many famous guests, such as Henry Clay Frick, Prince Albert of Belgium, Nicola Tesla, Lord Kelvin, as well as great scientists, European princes, generals from all over the world, and several American presidents; but he often included his employees. At times, he would mix these great guests with the train crew who would be waiting late to take them home. The train station was a short walk, but Westinghouse built a tunnel from the house to the station so he could come and go with little publicity. He took the train to his plants and office every day. For longer trips, he had his personal Pullman coupled and waiting at the end of the tunnel. He always avoided the press, except in the rare instances of new a product that he wanted to promote.

Westinghouse's Pullman car featured a dining room, kitchen, sleeping quarters and office. The special car was named Glen Eyre and was always ready for a business trip. His journey would start from the tunnel at his mansion that went directly to the train station. He often loaned out his car to help others.

His Pullman car, specially built for his comfort, included a drafting desk and engineering office. He had a drawing board in his Pullman, for Westinghouse found relaxation in drawing and outlining mechanical devices. He was a large man, giving the appearance of a walrus with his Victorian mustache and long coat; he required specially designed chairs in his Pullman. He had designed his train car to be a home, and indeed, he spent many hours in that car. Still, he commuted ten miles from Pittsburgh to his Turtle Creek plants in public cars. He often sat with his younger employees on the daily commute. Westinghouse was a truly modern commuter, taking the train every day from his Pittsburgh home to his plants around the area and his downtown office.

In 1886, Westinghouse built his Union Switch and Signal factory in the borough of Swissvale. Swissvale was a rural suburb just a few miles from his Pittsburgh mansion. It was at this plant that he experimented with paternalism on a community level. Westinghouse's approach to employee housing was much different from that of others. He had experimented with low cost employee houses in Swissvale. Westinghouse, unlike the neighboring mining and steel companies, did not rent these homes, but offered the workers home ownership. These Swissvale homes were six-room homes costing around $1,200 to $2,000. The mortgages were adjusted to employee income and allowed for payments over fifteen years. The houses were also covered by a type of mutual insurance that protected the owner in times of unemployment, disability, and death.

In January of 1886, Westinghouse Electric was formed out of the experimental branch of Union Switch and Signal Company. When Union

Train wreck in 1888 due to lack of signals (courtesy Carnegie Library of Pitts-burgh).

Switch and Signal moved to Swissvale, Garrison Alley became headquarters for Westinghouse Electric. The corporate charter included the mission statement, which was "to manufacture and promote the use of alternating current system equipment." The corporation was formed with a million dollars of capitalization. This would launch the "war of currents," pitting Westinghouse Electric's alternating current system against Edison's and General Electric's direct current systems. Ultimately, Westinghouse would win this industrial war because he recruited and held the world's best engineers. Many had left the autocratic and impersonal organization of Edison. Westinghouse showed that paternalism could be used to motivate innovation in organizations. The success of Westinghouse Electric was as much a triumph of paternalism as technology. From manager to laborer, Westinghouse was a fatherly figure. He often generally outlined a project or need and let the scientist work on it with no interference. Today we see a similar methodology in companies like Google and Gen-Tech.

The great Nikola Tesla would leave Edison to join the innovative atmosphere of Westinghouse. Edison, while brilliant, found it hard to

Westinghouse Electric, east Pittsburgh, 1893 (Library of Congress).

credit those who worked for him. Nikola Tesla was a brilliant, eccentric, independent, and theoretical genius, all things Edison despised. In addition, Edison was autocratic in believing the work of those under him belonged to the organization. Edison put his name on all patents, a practice that upset his workers. Tesla had made a name for himself in European circles. He also had demonstrated electrical skills that would be applied. In the early 1880s, he was one of the young scientists interested in AC current. Tesla invented an AC electric motor in 1882 but had no practical AC power source to promote its use. He moved to Paris to take a job with French Edison Company in 1883. Edison had been interested in Tesla's work on electrical motors, and he hoped to adapt his work to DC motor applications.

When Tesla came to America in 1884, he clashed immediately with Edison, who would have nothing to do with AC current, and had a growing dislike for Tesla personally. Tesla's ability to deal with extreme abstractions, such as the different phases of alternating cycles, further upset Edison. Edison never could come to terms with the theoretical complexity of AC current, and engineers like Tesla threatened him.

Tesla would find the ideal manager of innovation in Westinghouse. Tesla said, "He is one of those few men who conscientiously respect intellectual property, and who acquire their right to use the inventions of others by fair and equitable means."[3] This practice allowed Westinghouse to pool the creativity of many inventors into mega-inventions. Westinghouse never micromanaged, and he respected the work of individuals. Any invention in the Westinghouse organization carried only the inventor's name.

The war of the currents was a gigantic clash of two involving America's greatest inventors and Wall Street, headed by J.P. Morgan in the 1880s and 1890s. It pitted Thomas Edison's based direct current (DC) against George Westinghouse's alternating current (AC) to supply American energy. Thomas Edison took an early lead, based on his direct current lighting systems and the invention of the incandescent light bulb. Edison's first home lighting system was for New York bank magnate J.P. Morgan. J.P. had helped finance Edison initially, and Morgan lined up New York customers for his Pearl Station generating plant. On September 4, 1882, Thomas Edison watched his system light lower New York from J.P. Morgan's office. By the end of 1882, the Pearl Station was lighting 3,400 lamps for 231 customers but covering little more than a city block. Edison was also constructing a central power station in Detroit. The direct current (DC) system had huge technological and cost problems. The direct current system had a drop in voltage as the distance increased. DC power required double the amount of copper wire, and even then, its transmission distance was very limited. To correct this, thick copper wires were required at the generator, tapering off to the end of the line. The cost of copper inhibited the Edison direct current system. He designed a central feeder station concept to overcome the voltage drop and reduce copper usage. While much lower in cost, it would still be more costly than alternating current systems. By the late 1880s, J.P. Morgan was in control of Edison General Electric and the DC system.

The battle of the 1880s was not only between DC and AC current but arc lighting and the incandescent lighting of Edison. Arc and incandescent lighting actually were two separate markets by 1892. Both were growth markets. Arc lighting was created by the electrical arc between two carbon electrodes, much like arc welding today. Arc lights were great for outdoor applications such as streetlights because of their simplicity, power, and brightness. Arc lighting also offered much more candlepower than gaslights and could light railroad yards, factories, and parks. Arc lighting was an extremely profitable business, which had prompted Westinghouse to form his Pittsburgh lighting company in 1880 and would be a growth market into the twentieth century. In 1881, there were 6,000 arc lights in service; by 1886, there were 140,000 in service; by 1895, there were 300,000 arcs in service; and by 1902, there were 386,000 in service. Technically, arc lights could be run by either DC or AC current, but they tended to be DC. Westinghouse had developed a fully functional AC arc lighting system in 1886.

Edison's incandescent lighting and power generation system used direct current. DC had serious transmission problems requiring excessive amounts of copper and a power station every mile. For this reason, Edison's DC systems were favored in densely populated areas such as New York. DC held only one but important advantage: that of a superior commercial electric motor. The DC motor favored DC usage use in streetcar systems such as those of Thomson-Houston. Westinghouse, however, would develop an AC motor with the help of Nikola Tesla. Incandescent lighting could operate on either AC or DC with certain modifications. Edison held most of the patents relating to DC, while Westinghouse owned those for AC. Edison did hold a key patent of incandescent light bulbs, which Westinghouse needed to grow his AC system.

On Thanksgiving of 1886, Buffalo, New York, was lighted by the Westinghouse AC system. Westinghouse had now entered Morgan and Edison territory. J.P. Morgan realized that AC was the best-cost system. In 1888, J.P. Morgan was the largest stockholder of Edison Electric, but Edison had enough stock to block Morgan. Edison Electric remained the largest and most integrated producer of power and electrical lighting systems. Edison controlled enough stock and had friendly stockholders to block Morgan from imposing management or forcing Edison to consider AC, so the war continued. The status of electrical power generation at the end of 1887 told the story. Edison had 121 central power (DC) plants throughout the United States, but primarily in densely populated areas that lowered DC distribution costs. In about a year of market operation, Westinghouse had 68 AC central plants operating or under construction.

Westinghouse saw men like Morgan, however, as exploiters of capitalism, not as drivers. The idea of trusts bothered Westinghouse deeply, and he saw trust formation on a par with socialism as a threat to capitalism. Westinghouse's advertising even suggested that customers needed to support Westinghouse Electric against the "electrical trust." In one advertisement, Westinghouse Electric declared: " We invite the cooperation and support of all users of Electrical Apparatus who desire to have the benefits of competition."[4] Morgan tried to pressure Westinghouse by cutting off capital and loans, but Westinghouse resisted. Morgan tried to buy off the Chicago's World Fair selection committee to freeze out Westinghouse's bid for AC lighting. Westinghouse unveiled the plot and won the bid. Then Morgan sued Westinghouse over the use of the Edison bulb to light the fair. Westinghouse used his own design, and when Morgan stopped suppliers from manufacturing bulbs for him, Westinghouse built his own bulb plant. Westinghouse would have to hire hundreds of men to replace thousands of light bulbs daily because of their poor quality.

Morgan tried a marketing attack on the danger of AC. A horse and cow were electrocuted for the press. At one point, Edison was searching for a circus elephant to electrocute. Edison challenged Westinghouse to an electrical duel running the two currents through their bodies. Edison supported the use of electrocution for the death penalty in New York, so he could advertise the danger of AC. In August 1890, convicted murderer William Kemmler was electrocuted. The system bungled the job, turning it into a cruel spectacle. Morgan supporters promoted the term "Westinghoused" for electrical execution. The market was turning against DC despite the negative ad campaign of Edison because of the economic advantages of AC power. Westinghouse was winning contracts with industry, in particular the steel and aluminum industries. The market was moving toward AC power, but at a great financial cost to Westinghouse.

Morgan made one last run by blocking financial aid to Westinghouse's fair bid. Westinghouse got the support of rival banker August Belmont. Belmont was a pure moneyman, lacking the colossal trust dreams of bankers like Morgan. The building of the great Niagara AC power plant would mark the end of the war of the currents. Years later, Morgan would turn Westinghouse's debt against Westinghouse Electric and take the company down.

Westinghouse Electric's greatest achievement was the AC power plant at Niagara Falls in 1899. The AC Niagara plant would change the world by bringing cheap electricity. It made power available in quantities that allowed for the development of the aluminum industry and the electrochemical industry. In 1899, the Niagara Falls plant was the world's biggest engineering project ever attempted by man. It required almost ten years to complete and it transformed electric theory of laboratories in the Electrical Age. It was the product of the world's greatest geniuses. When Edison invented electric lighting in 1877, no one ever dreamed of transmitting electricity more than a few hundred yards. Prior to Niagara Falls, it took a major DC power plant on every city block to light homes. With Niagara's AC power station, the whole city of New York, 500 miles away, could be lighted, as well as Buffalo, New York.

Westinghouse was the conductor of this great technical orchestra. He developed men to power his technical conquests. He showed humility in this corporate success, crediting all involved. The simple plaque at Niagara Falls, hung in 1899, credited thirteen patents, none of which were his. He credited nine patents of Nikola Tesla, his associate and friend; several of his research directors like Albert Schmidt; and two patents of his competitors. Sometimes simple statements tell us more than volumes of testimonials. The plaque listed the names and patent numbers that made the great engineering feat possible under the name of Westinghouse Electric. This reflected a great respect for individual contributions and a respect for intellectual property rights.

Samuel Gompers, founder of the American Federation of Labor, said of Westinghouse, "If all employers of men treated their employees with the same consideration he does, the AFL would go out of existence." Tesla would further describe the character of Westinghouse: "Though past forty then, Westinghouse still had the enthusiasm of youth. Always smiling, affable, and polite, he stood in marked contrast to the rough and ready men I met. Not one word which would have been objectionable, not a gesture which might have offended—one could imagine him as moving in the atmosphere of court, so perfect was his bearing in manner and speech."[5] It was a true symbiotic relationship between Westinghouse and his employees.[6]

Thirteen

Trusts and Corruption

Westinghouse had the respect of employees, capitalists, and politicians. In 1905, he was asked to serve as a public servant in a securities and insurance fraud issue. A national scandal had broken out in the Equitable Life Assurance Society, which was a national life insurance stock company, one of the largest in the country with $400 million in assets and 6 million policyholders. Its board of directors was a collection of America's greatest capitalists including Westinghouse's Pittsburgh neighbor, Henry Clay Frick. The Equitable scandal would rock Wall Street and Washington and put fear into millions of small policyholders. The great scandal commanded 115 front-page articles in the *New York Times* and 122 in *The World* in a single year.[1] The scandal would tarnish New York's highest society and disturb the normalcy of business in J.P. Morgan's national strategy of trusts. A national select committee was formed to address the scandal. The elected men who were beyond reproach had to quickly rebuild public confidence. It was a troika of former President Grover Cleveland; Morgan O'Brien, a presiding appellate judge and former Supreme Court justice; and George Westinghouse.

It would all start on the evening of January 31, 1905, with one of New York's greatest balls of the Gilded Age. It was given by James Hyde, president of Equitable, at the Sherry Hotel, which had several floors converted into a Versailles-type palace. The Sherry Hotel, at the time, was the most exclusive in New York, with a museum-quality art collection, and was the temporary home of Henry Clay Frick since 1902. The ball included many of the Equitable directors such as Astor, Frick, Vanderbilt, Belmont, Gould, Cassatt, and Winthrop. The ball itself made headlines, but its rumored cost of $200,000 ($4 million in today's dollars) shocked the sensibilities of many. Rumors started that Equitable had footed the bill. The gossip and rumors would start a panic that opened the company up to a charge of misuse of funds. While the link to the ball was never proven, monies had been used to pay fake consultants and directors, buy political favors, and commit numerous types of fraud. Frick, who had no personal stock ties, was selected as chairman of an internal committee to correct the issue, which was causing a panic on the stock market. Frick could not get reform and resigned from the board. August Belmont and Andrew Cassatt also resigned. Many believed that J.P. Morgan and his rival insurance company, New York Life, were waiting to take over by forming an insurance trust. A congressional investigation opened up many political ties as the scandal spun out of control. The stock drop had taken Equitable to the edge of bankruptcy; and the politicians, both nationally and in the state of New York, needed a way out.

The troika of Westinghouse, Cleveland, and O'Brien was given unrestricted authority to reorganize the company. They set out to bring in new and competent managers. Within a year, they reformed the company and headed off what had been called the "Rich Men's Panic." Westinghouse was showered with praise as J.P. Morgan fumed at Westinghouse's success. Another interesting note of the scandal was it made enemies of Morgan, Frick, and Belmont, which would be a future problem for Westinghouse.

Westinghouse already had too many enemies in New York and the banking industry because he had been an opponent of banking trusts, which were taking control of industries. He had beaten back Morgan in the 1880s in the formation of a national electrical trust. Bankers and capitalists alike lined up against Westinghouse. Even in his home town, Westinghouse had strong opposition from financiers Andrew Mellon and Henry Clay Frick. Neighbor and industrialist Andrew Carnegie opposed his views on corporate trusts. In the end, Westinghouse would even be sold out by the great trust-buster, President Teddy Roosevelt.

The beginning of the twentieth century saw the decline of socialism, but capitalism would become its own worst enemy. The great paternalists were gone or retired. Others such as George Westinghouse would be crushed by the big New York banks. Company presidents no longer came from plant operations but from the banks or law schools. United States Steel, formed in 1901, became the model of manufacturing in America. Bankers took control of companies and had no ties to the actual human element of manufacturing. Morgan had been forming controlling corporate trusts since the 1870s. He had price control in mining, steel, electrical, and other products through his many trusts. His huge combinations and mergers meant the loss of jobs, reduced competition, and the end of local philanthropy. Morgan viewed employee-oriented and paternal companies as inefficient. George Westinghouse was his nemesis.

The formation of United States Steel brought together the nation's wealthiest capitalists in J.P. Morgan, John D. Rockefeller, Andrew Carnegie, and a long list of other millionaires. It required the tacit approval of two United States presidents, William McKinley and Theodore Roosevelt. Its mastermind was New York banking magnate J.P. Morgan, who saw bigger as better. The amazing formation of United States Steel created a company that produced more steel than all the steel made in Great Britain and Germany combined, and nearly a quarter of the world's production, with a capacity of 7,000,000 tons annually. It represented about two-thirds of the total United States production. It was the first billion-dollar corporation in history, and it marked the first time the phrase "billion dollar" entered the average American's lexicon. The company's $1.4 billion capitalization was four times the federal budget of $350 million in 1900 and a full seven percent of the GNP.

It had over 160,000 employees and was the world's largest employer. United States Steel would control around 70 percent of the American steel industry and 30 percent of the world's industry. United States Steel was headquartered in New York, far from the steel plants, breaking the symbiotic relationship of cities like Pittsburgh and Chicago. As management became more removed, so did the workers' loyalty. They no longer looked at the company as a benevolent employer of the community. The same was true for J.P. Morgan's electrical trust known as General Electric. Rubber had its own trust in United States Rubber.

The old lions such as George Westinghouse had earlier opposed the formation of these trusts, only to be crushed by New York bankers in the 1907 Panic. J.P. Morgan was the new face of New York capitalism. No single American businessman ever had the power of Morgan over the economy. His strength was undeniable. In 1907, Morgan had control over 40 percent of all capital related to industrial, commercial, and financial industries. Morgan's 1901 formation of United States Steel was the largest capitalization until the late 1980s. He often rationalized that his approach of capitalism maximized shareholder profit. Morgan's power for years went unchecked; refusal to place a Morgan man on the corporate board usually resulted in capital starvation and receivership. Westinghouse held Morgan off longer than anyone (from 1880 to 1907). Ultimately, it took two major panics, an army of allied bankers, and the president of the United States to bring down Westinghouse.

The battle over trusts had begun in the 1880s. Morgan's great electrical supplier had only one competitor in Westinghouse Electric. In the 1890s, Westinghouse realized that the crisis had opened the door to more control of his company by bankers. Still, it was worth it to win the lighting contract for the Chicago Columbian Exposition of 1893, several years earlier. The event led to the use of Westinghouse's AC current throughout the country versus Edison's DC current. Westinghouse had triumphed over the Morgan backed Edison Electric, but he had made many enemies in the process, including the dean of the New York bankers, J.P. Morgan. Westinghouse had further provoked the anger of the New York bankers by his refusal to involve Westinghouse Electric in trusts and combines. Westinghouse opposed any type of trust as an obstruction of free competition. Even worse, Westinghouse was a supporter of Teddy Roosevelt's trust-busting policies. Westinghouse had even become outspoken on the topic, further enraging the New York financial barons. J.P. Morgan and other New York bankers had been unsuccessful at pulling Westinghouse into industrial combines and alliances. Westinghouse, in particular, had rebuffed Morgan in 1890 in an offer to control competition in the electrical industry by price and output agreements. Westinghouse wanted independence. What he was opposed to would be revealed in the 1912 congressional Pujo Committee hearings. The findings of the Pujo Committee were unbelievable. The officers of the five largest New York banks held 341 directorships in 112 major corporations. Morgan related officers were on 72 company boards. Westinghouse Electric had been the notable exception to New York bankers' control of American industry.

Westinghouse was an extremely profitable company in 1907. The problem was that Westinghouse had borrowed heavily to finance plant expansion. It was this debt structure and high interest payments that concerned the bankers and offered them a way to take down Westinghouse. Still, in May of 1907, Westinghouse had some leverage. First-quarter profit had been $2.8 million, but because of his dividend rate used to maintain investment, almost $2.5 million went to cover dividends. The high dividend rate allowed Westinghouse to raise capital quickly for his big projects. Westinghouse had depended on bank credit as well and had many corporate bond offerings. He was also considering another stock offering to raise capital, but the word was out in financial circles that Westinghouse could not be expected to hold a ten percent dividend rate. In general, Westinghouse had little interest in financial maneuvering. J.P. Morgan represented a new style of banker. Morgan was interested in building companies that could generate profits and interest for his banks. He had successfully done that in 1901 with the formation of United States Steel and General Electric in 1892. Westinghouse wanted to invent and build things. The banking barons of New York had little interest in Westinghouse's engineering projects; their interests were in profits. Morgan's modus operandi was to take control of successful companies with strong operations, then put in a financial organization that would send the profits to the banks.

Morgan found it difficult to understand men like Westinghouse. Morgan had broken Edison, but Westinghouse held out. Morgan believed little in paternalism or competition. Morgan had been an early backer of Thomas Edison. Morgan's Madison Avenue home was the first New York home to use Edison's incandescent bulb system in 1880. Morgan was, however, never a satisfied customer, investor, or business partner of Edison. And after a slow but methodical process, Morgan took over Edison's General Electric by 1892, leaving Edison as a figurehead only and eventually totally removing him. For Morgan, the battle with Westinghouse was personal and philosophical. Westinghouse's paternal capitalism had forced Morgan to develop his own employee benefit programs to stay competitive to top talent.

What Morgan couldn't understand was Edison's and Westinghouse's paternal management styles. Morgan also lacked a trust in Westinghouse because of Westinghouse's application of "costly" Christian principles in the workplace. A Christian himself, Morgan tended to separate his Christianity from his businesses. Westinghouse's implementation of the half-day Saturday holiday seemed frivolous and costly to Morgan. His use of corporate money to fund employee pension plans represented a dangerous precedent. Similarly, Westinghouse's establishment of a "Relief Department" to help disabled workers seemed to be out of place to Morgan. After all, if Westinghouse Electric was struggling, how could such huge sums of money be designated for employee programs? No other major corporation had any of these unnecessary expenses. Another enigma was the Westinghouse belief in competition and avoidance of trusts, which could have made his companies more profitable. The idea that some social view could get into the way of business was incomprehensible to Morgan. He could understand the love of engineering; he had seen that in Thomas Edison. But mixing socialism, Christianity, and capitalism seemed too foreign for him. To Morgan, this was not the mark of a successful capitalist, but of a socialist or communal manufacturer such as Robert Owen in Scotland.

Morgan saw paternalism as a top-down form of socialism. Morgan opposed the socialist and Marxist movements in Europe as a misguided and dangerous attack on capitalism. He believed the socialists would never make inroads with the American unions because of the violence seen in Europe. He feared the possible top-down road to socialism from paternalists such as Westinghouse. Morgan also believed that large trusts were good for the economy because they reduced the waste of millions of dollars in patent lawsuits. In 1896, an amazing 300 lawsuits were in litigation covering all fields of electrical applications.[2] Both Morgan and Westinghouse believed this litigation to be wasteful, although for different reasons. Westinghouse, because of his Puritan roots, believed court was the wrong place to settle differences. Morgan saw litigation as a classical failure of unrestricted capitalistic competition and wasteful for the end consumer, who paid part of the cost in the product.

As early as 1887, Morgan had tried to bring Westinghouse into his electrical trust with Edison Electric. Morgan attempted to play Westinghouse against Edison. His overture to Westinghouse came through a lawyer by the name of Doctor Otto Moses, whom Westinghouse had used in patent reviews. The Associated Press ran articles of unknown origin about a possible trust. Westinghouse suspected that Edison was also being manipulated, and wrote a letter directly to Thomas Edison on June 7, 1888: "Dr. Moses came to Pittsburgh some weeks ago with reference to a scheme for the consolidation of all electric light companies in some form of trust. I refused to have anything to do with it, and told him that I saw no reason at all for our combining with a lot of people who had nothing to give."[3] Morgan was able to take over Edison Electric and some smaller competitors. Eventually, Morgan would force Edison out of his own company.

Even Thomas Edison, in 1890, opposed the giant trust of Westinghouse and Edison Electric during the war of the currents. Edison told Morgan that he would have nothing to do with a Westinghouse merger or any other: "You may see things differently from what I do; you may see things through a telescope, while I see the subject through a microscope; still I am sure that if you enter into the slightest connection with him [Westinghouse], it will be at the general Company's expense. We must all expect competition; if not from one person, then from another; but no one can ever convince me that a competitor whose system gives an average efficiency of only 47 per cent can ever prove a permanent competitor for large installations in cities against a system giving 79 to 80 per cent efficiency. But if for other reasons I am incorrect, then it is very clear my usefulness is gone."[4]

Westinghouse also rebuffed any trust talk in a letter to the editor of the newspaper that carried the story. Westinghouse argued that monopolistic control was unethical. Morgan's first attempt to win over the ethical Westinghouse would launch a twenty-year effort by Morgan to bring Westinghouse Electric into the trust. It would not only be a philosophical fight, but a personal one. Westinghouse had rebuffed and held Morgan off at every attempt to force him to merge.

The Panic of 1907 would give Morgan an opportunity to put an end to the Westinghouse competition. In New York on October 23, 1907, J.P. Morgan returned to his office to find Henry Clay Frick, his partner and neighbor of George Westinghouse, waiting for him. The panic had hit the streets, with bank depositors pulling their money, since in those days there was no protection of bank savings. Some creative individuals earned as much as ten dollars a day to wait in bank lines as depositors tried to salvage other parts of their lives. The drawdown on bank reverses caused banks to call in loans from big and small companies. In Boston, retailers had "panic prices" to help generate cash. Morgan held day and night meetings in his library as he moved to take control of the panic. He even forced the banks to issue scrip in lieu of cash to keep the banking system floating.

Women on assembly line at Westinghouse Electric, 1888 (Library of Congress).

In the absence of any government regulation, the public looked to Morgan as their savior. It was an image promoted by the *New York Times*, as Morgan controlled most of their debt. Even Teddy Roosevelt had no choice but to ally with Morgan. Morgan saw an opportunity to build his trusts in return for acting as the "federal Reserve."

Morgan had no interest in saving Westinghouse, who had refused to join his trusts. Besides, J.P. Morgan was alienated from his biggest rival, General Electric. This was the overall strategic approach of Morgan, who awaited only the opportunity to act. Morgan was now ready to close the trap on the only major industrialist who had ever successfully rebuffed him. The meeting with Frick and others on the situation went all through the night, which was typical of Morgan's "library meetings." The Morgan meeting moved to stabilize the nation's banks, while also picking some industrial plums as part of the harvest. Frick and the United States Steel Company moved to purchase Tennessee Coal and Iron to further the great steel trust. Westinghouse was left for another consortium of New York bankers to devour with Morgan's encouragement, but Morgan was pulling the strings.

Morgan's ruse was pulled off by forcing Teddy Roosevelt to allow these takeovers in return for Morgan's saving of the big banks. The Senate committee investigating the panic for years concluded Morgan had taken advantage of the situation. Teddy Roosevelt testified in 1909, no longer as president, that he had given tacit approval to Morgan and Frick to proceed for the good of the country.[5]

In Pittsburgh, Westinghouse knew the banks could not be stopped from calling in his loans. The Pittsburgh banks were unable to help since they all looked to New York for saving cash, and New York banks were failing every hour. Andrew Mellon, the lead Pittsburgh banker, remembered being rebuffed by Westinghouse in the Panic of 1893, and held the Pittsburgh bankers back as well. Andrew Mellon was also Henry Clay Frick's closest friend. In fact, that day the Pittsburgh Stock Exchange closed for three months due to a lack of capital liquidity. Still, as always, Westinghouse had employees and stockholders on his mind. This would affect them far more than himself. Westinghouse Air Brake and Union Switch & Signal Company were safe. However, Westinghouse Electric, Westinghouse Machine, and Nernst Lamp Company would be lost. This night he would pass on his neighborhood dinner at his mansion. These nightly dinners had become legendary throughout Pittsburgh, but this day Westinghouse wanted to be alone. October 23, 1907, would be the beginning of the end for one of America's greatest and kindest industrialists.

Westinghouse Electric was an extremely profitable company; in fact, in 1907 it would report record profits. The problem was that Westinghouse had borrowed heavily to finance new projects and development work. It was this debt structure and high interest payments that concerned the bankers. The panic allowed banker J.P. Morgan the opportunity to destroy the only competition with the Morgan-controlled General Electric. Westinghouse was just one of the casualties of the credit market panic. Today's control of such markets by the Federal Reserve would have never affected a profitable company like Westinghouse Electric. But, in 1907, there were no controls except for the leading bankers. It was J.P. Morgan who pooled $25 million from the government, $10 million from John Rockefeller, and $25 million from New York banks to stabilize the market. He took charge and advantage of the financial crisis. By the end of the month, J.P. Morgan was being hailed as the nation's savior. An ode to honor Morgan ran in the *New York Times* on October 27. Morgan, however, was a major benefactor of the crisis. He had knocked out most of his competition in the steel industry during the month-long panic. United States Steel (a Morgan-backed company) took over its major competition. Westinghouse Electric, General Electric's major competitor (GE was also a Morgan company), was taken over by Morgan. Just as important, Westinghouse would be forced out of Westinghouse Electric.

In late October of 1907, Westinghouse was on a train to New York once again, this time to discuss receivership with the bankers, which would strip him of Westinghouse Electric. It was the same type of banker deal that stripped Edison of General Electric. Westinghouse accepted the deal to protect the jobs of his workers. The train trip would be the most difficult of his career. It had only been a few weeks ago that he had signed the order for thousands of turkeys to be distributed to air brake employees in Wilmerding for Thanksgiving. The tradition went back to 1870, when in the early years he had invited all his workers to Thanksgiving dinner at a Pittsburgh hotel. As he opened the morning paper, the train rolled by his huge complex of Westinghouse Electric and Machine companies in Wilmerding and East Pittsburgh. He could see the great clock tower of his utopian city of Wilmerding. The front page of the paper discussed Westinghouse's poor financial management. The attack had been set up by Morgan to put the blame on Westinghouse. Westinghouse had always enjoyed the support of the local press, and it hurt deeply to have it turn on him. Still, his employees were quick to support him.

Morgan controlled the newspapers, which put the blame on Westinghouse's management skills. The hardest and most unfair criticism of

Westinghouse was made by a jealous Morgan associate, Andrew Carnegie. Carnegie had always been a critic of Westinghouse's paternal approach. Carnegie's remaining investments and friends were protected from the Panic by the hand of Morgan. Feeling a bit superior and lacking details, he was his usual gregarious self on the deck of the ship. Carnegie quotes made the newspapers, and the following quote was typical:

> I feel very, very sorry that George Westinghouse should have trouble and I want to see him out of the woods. Fine fellow, George, George is—splendid fellow. And a great genius. But he is a poor businessman. A genius and a businessman are seldom found in one individual. Now Westinghouse is of too much value to the world, in originating ideas and developing them, to have one whit of energy wasted in business work and worries. You see, all of his business activity would never get him individually a noticeable success, whereas his genius, at play, would keep home an outstanding figure in the world. He should have a good business man, so that he never would have to bother about business details.[6]

Carnegie was just plain wrong. Westinghouse had done things Carnegie had never done as a businessman. Westinghouse started over thirty companies from scratch and built them into multi-million-dollar international companies in twenty different countries.

The personal struggle of Westinghouse after his loss of Westinghouse Electric is not well documented; but as we have seen, his behavior changed. Like Edison after the banking takeover of General Electric, Westinghouse was to have a name-only position as head of the company. He could do nothing. As a puppet president of Westinghouse Electric, he avoided the labs and factories where he had previously been a daily visitor. His wife Marguerite played an even larger role in supporting her husband, but this setback ran deep in a man who "had never been defeated." It was a type of depression that few men know. He had come to the heights only to lose what he cherished most in Westinghouse Electric. Close associates, like Benjamin Lamme, reported that Westinghouse, once a daily visitor to East Pittsburgh, was rarely seen after the takeover. He was never the same, and the depression seemed to lead to many physical symptoms. Westinghouse had always hated to go to doctors or hospitals, but his ailments increased after 1907, requiring him to rest at his summer home in New York. With Marguerite's help and a real concern for the stockholders (many of whom were friends, employees, and family), Westinghouse stayed on as president of Westinghouse Electric and Manufacturing Company for several years. He had to live with the reality that he was no longer in control, and the daily overview bank controlled management. To function in such a situation would be difficult for any person. These were difficult years for him, but he tried to involve himself in engineering projects to help ease his depression.

The real disappointment for Westinghouse had to be Pittsburgh itself. Banker Andrew Mellon had exacted his revenge on Westinghouse for not bringing him into the operation in the 1880s. Still, Westinghouse was a major employer and exporter for the Pittsburgh economy, and as Pittsburgh's greatest banker, Andrew Mellon should have helped. In fact, after the fall of Westinghouse, Mellon Bank started a purchasing plan of Westinghouse Electric stock to gain a board membership in the 1920s. Neighbor Henry Clay Frick proved most disappointing, having powerful ties to both Morgan and Mellon. Frick's home had been wired by Westinghouse himself. The local Pittsburgh press attacked as if owned by Morgan. Pittsburgh business associates, like Carnegie and Schwab, spouted the Morgan line of Westinghouse's supposed mismanagement. The most hurtful aspect was that the city seemed to believe it, with the exception of the surrounding burgs of Wilmerding, Swissvale, East Pittsburgh, and Turtle Creek, who knew better. It was in these burgs where Westinghouse's treatment of his employees and charity were legendary.

Westinghouse lacked the flashy and self-promoting giving of Andrew Carnegie. Westinghouse's philanthropy was, true to his Puritan roots, for the greater glory. It would, however, be a mistake to suggest that he did not give liberally to the less fortunate. His giving was generous to individuals but always undocumented by his own request. Mrs. Westinghouse also followed the same credo and gave liberally as well. The approach was very consistent with his New England Puritan background that molded his whole life. It was also the creed of the Irish Catholic immigrants who were heavily employed by him. For Westinghouse and his wife, giving wasn't giving unless it was done at least quietly, if not anonymously. He avoided the practice of having his name tied to any donation. His friend and partner, Ralph Baggaley, reported on the other unknown part of Westinghouse's charity:

> It is a matter of history, of course, how Mr. Westinghouse carried out this idea. Thereafter his apparent ambition to build up large concerns had a different aspect in my eyes, as I understood the ethical impulse underlying it. While he disclaimed belief in the efficacy of benevolent giving, and shrank from acknowledgement of his kindness, those of us who were closely connected with him knew of many instances where he was supporting whole families and doing other deeds of helpfulness in an unostentatious way. Mrs. Westinghouse was very sympathetic and loved to

relieve distress, and Mr. Westinghouse made her a regular allowance for gratification of her desires in this respect. The amount was stated to me, and it was large.[7]

Westinghouse's charity and giving lacked the fanfare of industrialists such as Carnegie. Charity, philanthropy, and capitalism would merge in Westinghouse's great monument—the town of Wilmerding.

Fourteen

Wilmerding, America's New Lanark

The famous October 1907 train trip by Westinghouse to see the New York bankers took the same route through the industrial Pittsburgh district that Westinghouse had often taken. Westinghouse was on the famous *Pittsburgher* train that went direct from his Pittsburgh East Side home to New York's financial district. It would take him through the area's greatest industrial burgs. Westinghouse's greatest worker legacy was his utopian industrial city of Wilmerding. At Wilmerding, the train would slow for any potential switching signals. For almost a decade, George Westinghouse had taken a twenty-mile train trip every morning from his Pittsburgh home to the industrial Turtle Creek Valley and Wilmerding, which was the home of many Westinghouse factories such as Westinghouse Air Brake and Westinghouse Electric. Pittsburgh was often seen as Andrew Carnegie's industrial utopia; Westinghouse's view from the train was much different. The steel towns were reminiscent of England's industrial ghettos. Carnegie had given the area its libraries, museums, and concert halls. He represented the best and the worst of paternalism.

Westinghouse and his East Side neighbors such as Andrew Carnegie, H.J. Heinz, Andrew Mellon, and Henry Clay Frick made the trip weekly to the New York banking district. At the time it connected the world's greatest industrial center to the world's banking center. The trip would bring these great industrialists face to face with the downside of industrialization. This trip was different for Westinghouse. It was to discuss receivership of Westinghouse Electric with the bankers during the Panic of 1907.

155

The trip to New York in October 1907 would bring back many memories for Westinghouse. It also gave a contrast between Carnegie's and Morgan's capitalism and Westinghouse's capitalism. The view from the train allowed Westinghouse to see many of Carnegie's donated libraries along the way. Across the river from the Pennsylvania Railroad rails, one could see (when one's view was not blocked by smoky smog) the massive Carnegie Homestead steel mill, known for its labor unrest and 1893 strike massacre. Westinghouse would pass through Carnegie's steel town of Braddock. It is here that the train moved through the worker slums of Carnegie's great mill, the Edgar Thomson Works. It was the dark and dirty row apartments of Braddock that, for many, were the daily face of capitalism not often seen by the general public. These steel workers were more interested in feeding their families than trips to the museum. The next stop of the train would be that of Wilmerding in the Turtle Creek Valley. Exiting the Edgar Thomson Tunnel came with a brightening of the skies as Westinghouse approached Wilmerding station. Wilmerding had made Westinghouse famous for his paternalism throughout America and Europe. Westinghouse had first seen this land in 1870 when it was a mere flag switching stop for trains.

Leaving Braddock and coming out of the Turtle Creek Tunnel offered a stark contrast. From the train in 1907, Wilmerding looked like a great castle surrounded by well-planned rows of houses. The streets were cleaned regularly. There were beautiful parks and gardens. The town was a true "company" town in that managers, engineers, professionals, and workers lived there in harmony. The town lacked the slums of Carnegie's Braddock and Homestead. It also lacked a Carnegie Library, yet it was a hub of opportunity for its worker citizens. Training in manual skilled trades was available to all. This had been Westinghouse's model town that rivaled the famous industrial community of New Lanark, Scotland.

The town of Wilmerding was Westinghouse's design. Wilmerding had become an international model for industrial towns. In its early years, reporters from all over the world flooded it to see a new relationship with industry and community. It was hailed by reformers and socialists as the ideal model for industrial towns. It was despised by the bankers and the industrialists of the time, such as J.P. Morgan and Andrew Carnegie, as misguided capitalism. It stood in contrast to the many surrounding steel towns of Braddock, Homestead, Duquesne, and McKeesport. Flowers, birds, insects, and hardwood trees prospered, while neighboring towns favored only the hearty sumac trees and rock pigeons. Houses were well built and surrounded by beautiful lawns, parks, and gardens, versus the slag dumps in the neighboring steel towns. Social, educational, and recreational services and opportunities abounded. A truly symbiotic relationship between company and town existed that was unknown in the Victorian industrial world. This relationship reflected the kindness and humility of the town's founder, George Westinghouse. Yet Wilmerding was no socialist experiment for Westinghouse, but a pragmatic example of capitalism. Westinghouse put it best: "I believe in competition; it is the essence of a free economy. I think employers should compete in improving the lot of their workers as well as in making of more and better goods at a cheaper price. It strikes me as common sense that when men are happy and comfortable they produce more and help make a better profit for the company."[1]

Westinghouse's philanthropy was employee-focused. He believed providing a good job with benefits was the foundation of philanthropy. He built no libraries or museums with his profits, but poured the money back into worker communities. He built no colleges but offered free college to many employees. A young employee and sister of his lead electrical engineer, Benjamin Lamme, also took the train to Wilmerding in years past. Westinghouse would often sit with Bertha Lamme on their train commute from Wilmerding to the Pittsburgh suburbs, encouraging her. Eventually Westinghouse would help her obtain an electrical engineering degree to become America's first woman electrical engineer. He often trained workers in science and then paid for their college education. His ideal industrial city would focus on education and training.

Wilmerding did not exist until 1890 except as a rest stop on several intersecting Indian trails. The Wilmerding location was part of the Turtle Creek Valley, which was a major tributary to the Monongahela River, about 15 miles from Pittsburgh. The beautiful valley had attracted civilization for centuries, the earliest being the Monongahela people around 1000 A.D. From 1500 to 1670, the valley remained unoccupied except for hunting parties from the Iroquois of upper New York. Then in a short period, it was claimed by the nations of France, England, the United States, the Shawnee, the Delaware, the Iroquois, and the Susquehannock. In the early days of colonization it was the road for British armies, such as General Braddock's, to march west, and for Forbes's successful march to take Fort Duquesne and establish Pittsburgh. An early visitor would be a young George Washington, who spent the night at Frazier's post on his way to explore the French forts of the area in 1752. Earlier travelers through the area, such as General Lafayette, Charles Dickens, and Stephen Foster, had noted the beauty of the countryside. The valley allowed for a transition from the Allegheny Mountains to the flood plains of the Monongahela River, and then on to Pittsburgh. In 1884, following the natural contours favored by the Native Americans, the Pennsylvania Railroad was built through the area with a small wooden station at the future site of Wilmerding.

The inn at Turtle Creek was a relay station on the Pittsburgh and Philadelphia stagecoach line in the early 1800s. The creek and hills of Turtle Creek presented a dangerous passage in the early 1800s. A stagecoach traveler in 1810 described the hills as "awful," and the creek swift and deep enough to drown horses. The Pennsylvania railroad opened for business with its tracks going from Pittsburgh to Turtle Creek in 1851. The deep valley and hills prevented the 15 miles of track from reaching Pittsburgh. The Pittsburgh and Connellsville Railroad had extended to Turtle Creek (Port Perry), at which point travelers switched to the stagecoach to make daily rail connections to Pittsburgh. The area's role as part of a transportation network continues to this day. Railroad building started in the 1870s (including tunnels), allowing branches of the old stagecoach route to be converted to rail. Carnegie would build the railroad tunnel to make the route direct to Pittsburgh.

It was a switching flag stop on the Pennsylvania railroad where George Westinghouse first saw this scenic valley. Interestingly, this little station at Wilmerding was the Pennsylvania Railroad's first "Flag Top" station, where Westinghouse's switch and block signaling were used. In the 1880s, Turtle Creek Valley remained a rural setting as its neighbors, Braddock and East McKeesport, boomed as steelmaking towns. Turtle Creek Valley was described as farmland with only a few log houses in sight until Westinghouse built his factories in 1900.

Neighboring Braddock, however, had become the site of Andrew Carnegie's first steel mill in 1875. By 1880, it was the largest and most productive steel mill in the world. The town of Braddock, less than two miles away, had taken its place with Liverpool, Birmingham, Manchester, Coalbrookdale, Essen, and Sheffield as one of the world's top industrial forges. These mill towns were hailed as economic engines by industrialists and loathed by artists and writers such as Charles Dickens. These sulfur-cloaked steel towns of Braddock and Homestead in 1890 were much closer to the satanic visions of poet Robert Blake. The sun rose at 10:00 a.m. and set at 2:00 p.m. due to the thick smoke of the steel mills. An afternoon thunderstorm could make things as dark as night. The streets were muddy or dusty depending on the weather. Spring flooding annually destroyed the streets.

Homestead and Braddock offered examples of company towns left to grow on their own. Andrew Carnegie's first steel mill, Edgar Thomson Works, had been located in nearby Braddock since 1875. The immigrant laborers lived in poor rented one-room apartments with often as many as twelve to a single room. Whole families lived in single rooms with no running water. Toilets were in communal outside courtyards. Wild pigs and chickens that roamed free in the streets were a source of food. Saloons and bars outnumbered grocery stores and retail clothing outlets. Drinking helped the workers avoid the reality of the conditions but took a huge chunk of potential productivity away from the company. Industrial accidents were a daily experience, leaving a significant part of the population disabled and unemployable. Ethnic political machines and gangs ran the towns. For Westinghouse, such conditions were deplorable; he wanted something different for his employees.

From the very origins of Westinghouse's manufacturing enterprise, he had demonstrated the size of his heart. He was a paternalist from the days of his work at his father's New England machine shop and his mother's religious training. He believed the treatment of his workers was directly linked to his and the company's success. Unlike his industrialist neighbor, Andrew Carnegie, Westinghouse's concern for the employees seemed more based on his love of his fellow man than any potential productivity gain. Still, Westinghouse was every bit the capitalist. In fact, bankers would point to his generosity as the root cause of the "failure" of Westinghouse Electric in 1907. The steel mill slums had inspired Westinghouse to have something better for his employees.

On trips to England to study railroad signals, Westinghouse observed firsthand the industrial slums Dickens described in his novels, which so resembled Carnegie's Braddock. He had read Jules Verne's *The Begum's Millions*, the story of a dark and dismal steel town that hauntingly resembled the Pittsburgh area. Verne's story contrasted the German worker community of the Krupps to more utopian ideas in France. Westinghouse had studied the paternal chocolate factories of Germany as well. He would learn much from the paternal capitalism of the Stollwerck brothers. The factory had a lunchroom, coffee house, and store for its employees. The lunchroom had music for the employees. There was a "social" manager to help employees with a variety of problems such as family issues or financial concerns. There were large employee picnics and dinners. The exceptional treatment of the women in the workplace was another principle stressed by the Stollwerck brothers. The factory was particularly interested in the health of its employees, making doctors available to them. Small hospitals were also associated with German factories. Employees were given help with housing as well. The Stollwerck brothers' factory was a version of German paternalism that was more feudal than capitalistic.

Westinghouse had also followed, with interest, the earlier writings of Robert Owen, who had designed the model industrial community in New Lanark, Scotland. Both Carnegie and Westinghouse would visit New Lanark, but only Westinghouse saw its potential. For Westinghouse, Owen offered true paternal capitalism. Wilmerding was clearly modeled on the principles of Owen's New Lanark. Wilmerding emulated the systems of worker housing, education, community education, and employee benefits.

From 1821 to 1840, Owen's success caused a great deal of interest, but few tried to emulate him except on a piecemeal basis. When Westinghouse visited Europe in the 1870s, he studied New Lanark, but there was a closer example a few miles downriver from Pittsburgh. Old Economy, Pennsylvania, had become the final settlement of the Harmonists. The Harmonists were German separatist immigrants who had established communal manufacturing centers in the mode of Robert Owen. In fact, Robert Owen was so impressed that he purchased their community in New Harmony, Indiana. Many of the Harmonists returned to Pennsylvania to establish another manufacturing community near today's Ambridge, Pennsylvania. Westinghouse had visited and studied Old Economy. Old Economy was a communal manufacturing village that was fully integrated into the surrounding capitalistic society. Westinghouse saw Old Economy, like New Lanark, as a perfect blend of capitalism, community, and socialism. He had known Old Economy well through his dealings with railroads. The Old Economy community became so profitable, it was a major investor in the Pennsylvania Railroad. In addition, the goods being shipped helped the railroad prosper and built the roots of what remains even today an industrial valley of the Ohio River.

The success of Old Economy was restricted by its unusual religious views, which included celibacy and a belief in the Second Coming (a common theme among these successful communes). It was only Old Economy's religious rules of celibacy that doomed its future. Westinghouse had noted the religious or social restrictions in the failure of most of the utopian manufacturing communes. Westinghouse was a strong supporter of the application of Christian principles, but he never forced any religious views on his workers. Wilmerding centered on the YMCA supported by Westinghouse, but the churches were those built by the workers. Most reflected the European Catholic and Greek churches of the workers. All of these churches preached a resistance to any type of socialism, as did Westinghouse. Yet Wilmerding would meet the social goals of the nineteenth-century socialists, and attracted them, since they were unwelcome elsewhere.

Westinghouse viewed business and workplace fairness as integrated, not motivational. Furthermore, the Westinghouse approach was a quite simple application of Christian principles without fanfare or expectations of productivity gains. Westinghouse further believed that paternalism should not demand any form of imposed social, religious, or political requirements on the workers. This didn't restrict him from offering guidance such as building a YMCA. Westinghouse's dream represented a new model, one compatible with a pluralistic, democratic society, open to all. Wilmerding was not a company town, but had residents who did not work for Westinghouse. It represented a new type of employee-driven paternal capitalism. Wilmerding, for many, was a compromise between capitalism and socialism. Critics of Westinghouse's Wilmerding noted it leaned closer to socialism than capitalism with his views of a worker community. Westinghouse had found common ground with the goals of socialism; and in fact, many socialists flocked to Wilmerding, which demonstrated the true political freedom of Wilmerding. In 1904, the *Pittsburgh Sunday Leader* credited Wilmerding with being "the leading center of socialism of the peaceful, sane variety." From 1902 to 1912, the Socialist Party ranked second in Wilmerding behind the Republican Party with the Democrats running third. None of this was in any way related to Westinghouse's beliefs, which opposed socialism.

Socialists were attracted to the political openness of Wilmerding, not to any paternal system of Westinghouse. In Wilmerding, local politics were free of company agents, union bullies, machine politics, and corrupt politicians. Local leaders tended to be citizen representatives versus career politicians. In this, Wilmerding was unique in the western Pennsylvania area. Socialists actually held positions in Wilmerding, while socialists could never win a vote in nearby Braddock or Homestead.

Westinghouse believed a well-designed working community was an extension of capitalism, not socialism. His idea integrated an employee community into American society, not as a separatist organization but a seamless attachment and integration. Like industrialist philosopher Robert Owen, Westinghouse saw employee living conditions and corporate productivity as interlinked. He differed from Owen on the matter of creating a separate entity for workers. He tried to avoid the infrastructure of a company, but clearly there was a symbiotic relationship between the town and the company. Most "company" towns in Pennsylvania's mining and steel industries were industrial ghettos formed out of necessity to supply an immigrant workforce.

Westinghouse had been appalled at the development of the Pittsburgh area and its mill towns. European immigrants had flooded the area starting in the 1870s. No type of urban planning existed, and the immigrants formed slums around the great steel mills of the district. The rapid development left these slums devoid of basic comforts such as running water, private toilets, sewage management, and reasonable living space. Eight to twenty family members and friends crowded into rented rooms. Alcoholism and disease were common in these slums, which resulted in absenteeism as high as ten percent. Furthermore, the twelve-hour day took its toll on family life. The unstructured development fostered a type of racism, which favored clustering of the various nationalities and religions. As early immigrants, such as the Irish and Germans, improved their lot, they became fearful of the newer immigrants such as the Slavs, Italians, Hungarians, and blacks. This created a caste system based on nationalities. Ethnic lodges and machine politicians often controlled who got the best work. Schools were lacking in most steel towns and illiteracy was widespread. Churches were left to supply education where they could.

It was this dismal setting of greater Pittsburgh that changed Westinghouse's view of industry and community. The steel workers lived in poorly built rented wooden houses with shared cooking and toilet areas. A single, unheated room would hold 8 to 10 people. Sewage flowed in the streets. Cholera was common. The neighborhoods were part poor farm and part urban in nature. Pigs and chickens were raised for food, and liquor home-distilled for relief. Saloons were open twenty-four hours to accommodate the mill hours and workers' thirst. Employees worked 12-hour days, seven days a week; and if that wasn't bad enough, they rotated shifts every two weeks, using a twenty-hour-long turn to make the change. The mill created the social schedule for weddings, holidays, and birthdays; even funerals were planned around the mill's pace. Funerals, for example, were in the home; and the women would cook two large meals every twelve hours to accommodate workers coming off their shifts to pay their respects. Sadly, funerals were common events, with fatal industrial accidents being a weekly occurrence. These accidents occurred at a pace that is hard to comprehend by today's standards. A one-year study of Pittsburgh's Allegheny County in 1907 recorded 526 fatal accidents. One of over forty steel mills in the Pittsburgh area recorded a record of 80 deaths in a single year. Workers lacked any type of insurance for death and disability. The death or disability of the primary wage earners devastated families. Westinghouse had not grown up in such an industrial setting, and its existence appalled him.

Westinghouse had a new view of philanthropy and community. He wanted to build all facets of community to support his workforce. Westinghouse had, from the beginning, been taught by his father; this relationship and financial success did not corrupt it. After 1886, Westinghouse's many industries advanced from linear to exponential growth with thousands of new employees being added. Westinghouse had first located his factories on Pittsburgh's north side. The physical location on the north side of Pittsburgh needed added capacity to keep up with air brake demand from around the world. Like the Carnegie mills of Pittsburgh, Westinghouse's factories were a magnet for immigrants from Austria, Ireland, Germany, Poland, and Italy. Slavs and Hungarians were also coming in larger numbers to take the unskilled jobs. Blacks and Mexicans represented the smallest influx, but by the 1890s, they were replacing Slavs, Italians, and Hungarians in the lowest industrial jobs. Westinghouse's goal was to help make solid constructive citizens of these immigrants. Westinghouse wanted a planned community to help his workers perform well at work and become owners in the region.

By 1888, Westinghouse was planning a move for Westinghouse Air Brake from Pittsburgh to a new location. He hired architects to help locate a site that could support both the works and a planned community. Westinghouse's business associate, Robert Pitcairn, recommended the Turtle Creek Valley. Pitcairn was an executive of the Pennsylvania Railroad and a board member of Westinghouse Electric Company. Today the town of Pitcairn neighbors the town of Wilmerding. The Turtle Creek Valley offered water, railroad connections, a river port, and availability. The factory and the community would be integrated. The factory was designed to be a safe environment with good lighting and ventilation. A clean and well-planned community would be built into the surrounding hills. Of particular interest to Westinghouse was the use of parks and greens to achieve a campus-like atmosphere. The planned employee houses were to have an emphasis on lawns and trees. Westinghouse had actually started to offer low-cost "cottages" to his workers at Union Switch and Signal in Swissvale around 1886. It had been a real success and he hoped to expand employee housing in Wilmerding with higher quality.

Westinghouse's layout plan seemed related to ideas of Dr. Benjamin Ward Richardson in the mid–1800s. Dr. Richardson was known for his studies of the impact of industrial environment on tuberculosis, alcoholism, and nicotine addiction. Jules Verne made Richardson's ideas on the planning and design of worker communities famous in 1879 with the publication of *The Begum's Millions*. Richardson's design details were very close to those in Wilmerding. For example, Richardson called for " every house to be on a lot planted with trees, lawn, and flowers," and "houses thirty meters from the street."[2] He emphasized flowers whenever possible, and described ventilation requirements, plumbing, and drainage requirements. Westinghouse set similar requirements on construction. He planned citywide parks and gardens using expert gardeners to maintain them. The city's environment and maintenance used Owen's outline of the 1820s in New Lanark. Westinghouse broke with Owen on the social management of Wilmerding.

It was never Westinghouse's plan to control his workers' lives, but rather to inspire and create a culture as well as behavior. He offered prizes, rewards, and awards to assure the beauty of the workers' homes. He set an example with the gardens surrounding the town's Westinghouse headquarters building known as the "castle." He created a culture of beauty that lasted over a hundred years, the remnants of which can be seen even today. He encouraged religious events and employed social reformers to help contain problems such as alcoholism. He, however, put no penalties on workers to maintain a specific lifestyle. Such social restrictions had caused problems in earlier manufacturing communes from New Lanark to Pullman City.

The center and heart of Wilmerding was Westinghouse Air Brake, and he built the town to complement the factory. The factory in 1890 became known as the largest machine shop in the world. Unlike the famed industrial factories of the time, Westinghouse planned a safe and comfortable workplace. He paid special attention to restrooms, lunchrooms, and rest areas. Artesian wells were dug to supply safe drinking water for the employees. The cleanliness of the plant was emphasized and was maintained to strict standards. Lighting was also state of the art throughout the plant. A number of these features were directly related to experiences at his father's New England manufacturing plant.

Westinghouse was one of the earliest industrialists to hire women. The labor shortage in Pittsburgh required him to use women. Westinghouse used the early model of his neighbor, H.J. Heinz, for women workers in Victorian times. Women employees had special lunchrooms with tablecloths. He offered health benefits such as a company doctor available for all family members. Westinghouse also teamed up with the local YMCA to offer training in sewing and cooking for these young women employees. He built a community club as well for women. Like Lowell and Heinz, women had a short career at Westinghouse, moving on to form families later in life.

Westinghouse Air Brake headquarters was a beautiful castle, modeled after one in Scotland. The original central house, however, was a wooden frame house that served as a community club with a library, bowling alley, and swimming pool. The castle also functioned as a training center. It was very similar in scope to Carnegie's first library in Braddock, a few miles away with its bowling alleys and swimming pool built about the same time. One big difference was that the Westinghouse employees had time to enjoy it, while Carnegie's steelworkers were working 12-hour shifts with a day off every few weeks.

Later in the 1890s, Westinghouse created a partnership with the Young Men's Christian Association, another idea he had discussed earlier with his friend and the organization's president, William McKinley. From 1896, the YMCA shared the "castle" with headquarters for Westinghouse Air Brake. For years, the main role of the Wilmerding YMCA was to integrate foreigners into American society. This was unique among most capitalists. Neighboring steelworkers were left on their own to pursue citizenship and language skills. New immigrants in Wilmerding were sent notices of meetings for citizenship, which were conducted by lawyers. Beginning emphasis was on English classes, in which the association worked with the public schools. In addition, the association worked with the Daughters of the American Revolution to present extensive American history programs prepared in seven languages. This cooperative networking was fundamental to the character of the town. In the summer months, the park was used for educational moving pictures. A stereopticon was used as a projection camera. Various languages were used interchangeably in the lectures, which covered the prevention of infectious diseases, prevention of tuberculosis, and American history. This foreign program became the model for the whole United States. The YMCA shared facilities of the castle with Westinghouse Air Brake management until 1907. In 1907, Westinghouse completed the "Welfare Building" for use by the YMCA, and shortly after he built a building for the women (YWCA). These had world-class swimming pools and gymnasiums. The Wilmerding YWCA became the second largest in Pennsylvania by 1910. It was available to all in Turtle Creek Valley.

At the Wilmerding castle, further educational opportunities were offered. These included basic math, electricity, grammar, typewriting, and machine design, among others. One specific course focused on the construction and operation of the air brake. Machining and technical training were essential to Air Brake because the available immigrant workforce consisted mainly of unskilled European peasants. Westinghouse needed to teach them English even prior to technical training, so a full array of

English, writing, and language courses were offered for all employees. Boy apprentices were paid an hourly rate as they attended night school courses. The night school became known as the Casino Night School. Graduates of the school tended to have a fast track in the company, and most of the plant management were graduates. In 1904, it was reported that 160 students were taking evening courses from nine instructors. Besides the courses, there was a wide variety of special lectures and talks. Westinghouse managers and engineers were expected to be instructors and lecturers. Even his plant managers spent time in the training rooms. Educational opportunities were almost unlimited, with college scholarships available as well.

Recreation was a big part of services offered to employees. Many clubs were organized, including squads for chess and checkers. The physical programs offered would rival today's health clubs. Special classes were offered in tennis, wrestling, and fencing, all favorites of George Westinghouse. In addition, the association hired a prominent expert in "physical culture institution," C.H. Burkhardt. Burkhardt built and developed an outstanding track and field program for the town. Services were also held on Sundays and evening Bible schools were offered. These services were a bit problematic for the Roman Catholics fearful of Protestant indoctrination, but Westinghouse never required any type of religion. The town welcomed all denominations.

It is interesting that even today the "castle" dominates the town of Wilmerding, representing the symbiotic relationship of the company and community, while nearby steel towns such as Braddock and Homestead were dominated by the mill superintendent's house or the Carnegie Library, symbols of company power. Unlike Pullman City, Saltaire, New Lanark, and even the religious villages of Old Economy, Zoar, and Harmony, Wilmerding avoided an imposed class structure in housing and amenities. The town was also open to outsiders, preventing a dominant company culture. In addition, employees were not required to live in Wilmerding.

Westinghouse's approach to employee housing was much different from that of others, including his earlier experiments. He had experimented with low cost employee houses at his Swissvale factory a decade before. They were called "bungalows" by the locals because of their wood siding and medium price. Westinghouse wanted to build a better house for his Wilmerding project. He focused on true ownership by the employee versus renting, which was used at New Lanark, Saltaire, Lowell, and Pullman City. More importantly, Westinghouse had learned much from the failure of Pullman City.

Pullman City and other company towns preferred renting over ownership. Initially, in the 1890s, Westinghouse Air Brake purchased the land and built individual houses. The houses were then sold to the employees at cost. The mortgages were adjusted to employee income and allowed for payments over fifteen years. The houses were also covered by a type of mutual insurance that protected the owner in times of unemployment, disability, and death. This stood in stark contrast to the company mining towns and Pullman City, in which, when a death occurred, the company quickly foreclosed on the house. Furthermore, Air Brake's maintenance department would help repair utilities and appliances, as well as some major repairs. In general, the company assured that all houses were maintained in a state of excellent repair. The housing plan was altered by 1902 as reported in the *Wilmerding News*:

> The purchaser of any property is required to pay about one-fifth of the purchase money in cash upon delivery of deed. He then executes a purchase-money mortgage, payable in five years, with interest payable quarterly at the rate of 5 per cent per annum. While no requirement is made, it is expected that the purchaser shall reduce the principal of the mortgage quarterly by such payments on account, as he may be able to make. This plan enables him, during hard times, to keep the transaction in good shape by merely paying the interest, while on the other hand, when good wages are earned, he can discharge such a part of the principal of his mortgage as he may desire. It was much different than that of the nearby coal mining towns, where housing was supplied as long as they were employed. Westinghouse believed ownership was key to maintaining a community.[3]

This type of mutual investment by the company and the employee was characteristic of Westinghouse. He believed in this type of giving versus the giving of Carnegie, Pullman, Frick, and others. This philosophy made for a very different type of "company town." In bad times, when a worker might be laid off for a period, Westinghouse always stood as a lender or a backer of last resort for any of his employees. He could not and would not act as a typical banker of the times with coldness. His heart was too big and too Christian. He understood what Owen had seen as the biggest of problems for workers in a capitalistic society: fear of unemployment or inability to work. Workers and their families feared loss of income.

Westinghouse was known to help employees with all kinds of financial problems. He proved that capitalism could be compassionate in the time of the "robber barons." Westinghouse was not a communist, which many capitalists of the time believed, partly because the town of Wilmerding seemed to attract many socialists. Westinghouse's approach was unique, but he had no socialist or communist leanings, only a passion for the employees who made him a success. He differed from communal manufacturers, such as Robert Owen, in that there was a mutual investment of employees and company. The main difference was that Westinghouse's model was adaptable to heavy industrialization, but few of his industrial counterparts embraced his approach.

Westinghouse also avoided the pitfalls of many paternal communities by not requiring any social behavior. Westinghouse tried only to set an example. He also tried to keep his social programs and civic efforts as separate as possible, but he was always ready to intervene to fill needs or assure living quality. Westinghouse wanted to have all social classes represented in Wilmerding. One such example was the Tonnaleuka Club. Wilmerding had a growing population of professional young men in the engineering and technical trades. The local private hotel failed to supply comfortable living quarters for these men. In 1901, Westinghouse purchased the Glen Hotel building on Marguerite Avenue in Wilmerding. Westinghouse reworked the building by expanding and adding living rooms and dining rooms. In addition, there were smoking rooms, a billiard room, a bowling alley, and a library. A club was formed so that about 30 young men could enjoy this higher class of temporary living; additionally, an associate-type membership was developed for others to enjoy the excellent recreation rooms and fellowship. The club, in particular, catered to single professionals moving to Wilmerding. The success of the Tonnaleuka Club in Wilmerding was duplicated a few years later by the East Pittsburgh Club, which serviced employees of Westinghouse Electric in Turtle Creek and East Pittsburgh.

Carnegie had been known for his excellent treatment of his managers, but even here it was pure capitalism. Westinghouse's approach crossed all class lines. Andrew Carnegie, in particular, saw Westinghouse's views as too close to socialism, yet they shared a similar belief system. Fundamental to both men's views was the idea that there was a need to help those who help themselves. Both men believed in competition and capitalism, and neither believed in unions. Westinghouse was a paternal capitalist, but in a different vein than Andrew Carnegie. Carnegie believed that he and certain others were destined to be public trustees of capital. Carnegie was more patriarchal than paternal. The patriarchal approach was the favored approach of the day.

Carnegie and other capitalists pointed to the growing population of socialists at Wilmerding as proof of Westinghouse's socialist leanings. Carnegie would point to the lack of socialists in the neighboring steel mill towns. However, the lack of socialists in these mill ghettos was not due to the popularity of capitalism among Carnegie's immigrant workers, but their religious opposition of socialism. European socialism of the time hated the church as much as capitalism, seeing the church as compliant with capitalism in oppressing the worker. The priests of the immigrant Catholic churches of the mill towns preached against the godless nature of socialism. Socialism preached dependence on a political system instead of God. The immigrants trusted the priests and the church, which had been on their side during strikes and hard times. The church was their only safety net. In the end, the immigrants rejected socialism as an economic solution.

Westinghouse was more like the father who taught his sons by buying them tools and training them how to use them. He was a follower of fellow New Englander Ralph Emerson in his insistence on self-reliance. Westinghouse gave freely, demanding nothing in return. This is where he differed from similar programs developed later by Henry Ford, who would demand a certain type of moral code from his employees in return. Westinghouse and Ford both, however, believed in manufacturing assets over capital assets, whereas Carnegie believed in the primacy of capital in manufacturing. This emphasis on manufacturing assets naturally extended to the employee. The other characteristic of Westinghouse employee programs was the planning for bad times. It was a personal philosophy of Westinghouse, which he had applied to all of his companies, with the notable exception of Westinghouse Electric, which he leveraged to support major engineering projects.

Westinghouse separated his personal and religious beliefs from his employee benefits. The town of Wilmerding was formed as a separate political entity, but Westinghouse often allowed company resources to be used for the enhancement of the community. The company employees often maintained the parks and streets, although the borough did pay reduced rates for the company services. The borough was legally incorporated in the state of Pennsylvania, and its political functioning was similar to that of neighboring boroughs. The town did tax houses at a rate of ten mills to support the schools. This tax rate was about average for Pittsburgh-area boroughs; but the schools were superior, with Westinghouse hiring the best teachers. The borough taxed businesses as well to help support schools. It also, on a very limited basis, floated bond offerings. Schools were part of the public school system of Pennsylvania. The borough paid for street paving and street lighting, but again the company would help, when necessary, to maintain the beauty of the town. Wilmerding was always uniquely a Westinghouse Air Brake town with over 85 percent of the residents being Westinghouse employees. The balance was a mix of small businessmen, service providers, and a few thinkers who were attracted to the system. Westinghouse wanted it to be an open community.

Another unique feature of the borough of Wilmerding was its economic and social mix. While still predominantly a "mill town," it had a large segment of college graduates working as managers, engineers, designers, department heads, scientists, and administrators. Westinghouse was almost the only exception in that he lived in the Homewood section of Pittsburgh and took the train to Wilmerding each day. Wilmerding offered a refreshing oasis in the smoky and dirty boroughs of the steel companies the train traveled through on the way. Westinghouse remained at a distance to stay clear of local politics or any idea of him as the town's master. Politically, the majority party of Wilmerding was Republican, as was Westinghouse himself. Republicans dominated the mill towns of Pittsburgh until the New Deal of the 1930s, when the Democratic Party took over. The Democratic Party ranked only third in Wilmerding with the Socialists ranking second (by ballots cast); but it was this minority of socialists that distinguished the borough from nearby mill towns. The Socialist Party probably got more press than it deserved, primarily because some elected borough leaders were Socialists. It is doubtful that registered Socialists ever exceeded 3 percent of the population; yet in the political-machine-controlled neighboring borough, it would be impossible for a socialist to run for office, let alone win. The Socialist Party's presence in Wilmerding had nothing to do with George Westinghouse. A staunch Republican, Westinghouse had no sympathy, yet alone empathy for the socialists. Westinghouse maintained a hands-off policy concerning the workers' political preferences.

In 1905, the population of Wilmerding was about 5,000. The town, however, was part of a Westinghouse-dominated Turtle Creek Valley consisting of East Pittsburgh, Turtle Creek, Pitcairn, and East McKeesport. In particular, East Pittsburgh was a Westinghouse Electric town. The valley population was 30,000 in 1905. Politically, efforts to combine these communities into a "Westinghouse Valley" failed due to strong resistance from the town of Wilmerding, which maintained a superior position in services, educational resources, civic pride, and beauty. The first movement to combine Turtle Creek, East Pittsburgh, and Wilmerding in 1900 seemed logical since they were home to solely Westinghouse employees. The idea was to call the combination Westinghouse or Westinghouse City, but Westinghouse was opposed to this.

Wilmerding, Pennsylvania, 1911 (Library of Congress).

The free political nature of the town allowed for a responsive local government free of corruption. The politicians were not connected to political machines common in neighboring towns. These machines preyed on new immigrants rather than integrating them into society. In these surrounding towns, the political machine was a complex mix of ethnic bosses, political bosses, and mill bosses. Wilmerding offered a rare application of true democracy.

The borough of Wilmerding fostered superior services and utilities for its residents. The five-man police force was actually larger than those of boroughs of equivalent size. The volunteer fire department was considered one of the best in the valley. The volunteers were paid by the hour when called out by the borough. Westinghouse donated fire trucks. Wilmerding had not only paved streets but also paved sidewalks before most of the Pittsburgh-area towns. As noted, all houses had running water (a rarity in some boroughs) supplied by the Pennsylvania Water Company, an independent utility of the community. Because of complaints regarding service and high electrical rates of the Monongahela Light, Heat & Power Company, the town formed its own independent illuminating company.

In 1904, with the use of local capital, the United Electric Light Company was formed to supply electricity. As noted, the Pennsylvania Railroad connected Wilmerding to Pittsburgh from the beginning. By 1893, electric streetcars connected Wilmerding to the major towns of Braddock and McKeesport. The nearby towns did offer more merchants. Wilmerding residents used the streetcars to shop for the harder-to-find items in Braddock and McKeesport.

Another distinction of Wilmerding among the mill towns of Pittsburgh was its cultural and social diversity. The racial and nationality mixture of Wilmerding was similar to that of nearby mill towns. Westinghouse had shown no bias whatsoever in his hiring practices. In 1904, seven Christian churches including Roman Catholic, Methodist Episcopal, Presbyterian, United Presbyterian, Episcopalian, Lutheran, and United Brethren were represented in Wilmerding. The Roman Catholic was the largest denomination. What was different was the lack of taverns and bars so dominant in the other mill towns, as well as the absence of gambling. This was due to the town's culture versus any legal or religiously imposed morals. Alcoholism, which plagued nearby mill towns as a means of escape, found less fertile soil in Wilmerding. Clearly, the impact of the YMCA and the churches had elevated the community. Just as important was the example of Westinghouse, whose behavior inspired a corporate and community culture. Wilmerding had often been described as a "Midwestern college town." It offered a clean and very wholesome environment in a time of industrial plight.

Westinghouse's Air Brake factory in Wilmerding was as revolutionary as the town. The factory would be one of the safest plants built, with ventilation systems, sanitary restrooms, and state-of-the-art lighting. Westinghouse developed an employee committee system to take ownership of safety to the employees. The plant had its own fire chief and safety chief. These chiefs had the authority to shut down operations, if necessary, to assure safety. The safety chief had a committee of eight employees. Each committeeman oversaw a section of the plant, but there were also planned audits of other areas. Committeemen held weekly meetings and discussed areas needing improvement. Safety committeemen received extra pay for the work required.

Westinghouse's work with safety as motivational would also be confirmed by Congress in 1911. The great management consultant, Fredrick Taylor, had been asked to study the high death rate in American heavy industry. Congress believed that the pushing of production and productivity was being done at the expense of worker safety. Taylor's study concluded what Westinghouse already knew: the safest factories were the most productive. Employees responded to true paternal concern.

Just as innovative were the plant design, layout, and operation. Westinghouse's automation augured the assembly lines of the 1910s. Westinghouse had spent a year at the start of his career studying metallurgy and the casting process. He had pioneered and improved the steel casting process. Air Brake would, in 1890, open the world's most automated foundry to cast brake parts. The foundry, while associated with Air Brake, would make castings for Westinghouse Electric and Manufacturing and Westinghouse Machine Company. The new foundry used conveyors to move the molds for casting throughout the foundry. He employed the earliest known machinery to make the sand molds, which normally was a highly labor-intensive operation. Conveyors then moved the molds to be filled with hot metal from furnaces known as cupolas. The conveyer then moved the mold to a shakeout area to remove the castings. The sand was then recycled by conveyor back to the molding area. The conveyors were balanced to achieve a continuous operation twenty years before Henry Ford applied the principle to auto manufacture. In addition, he built specialized equipment for scraping and cleaning the casting. The foundry would host a stream of visiting engineers and executives daily from all over the world. Westinghouse used his methods and employee systems to build world-class electrical factories in neighboring East Pittsburgh.

Fifteen

Capitalism with a Heart— Westinghouse's Vision

The legacy of Westinghouse remains today. He changed industry, technology, and Pittsburgh forever. This was a man loved by his family, employees, and city. He truly was the father of paternal capitalism.

Between 1895 and 1904, the East Pittsburgh, Wilmerding, and Turtle Creek corridor became a massive Westinghouse manufacturing complex, including Westinghouse Electric, Westinghouse Machine Company, and the nearby Trafford City Foundry (Trafford was three miles away) that supplied both great organizations. This part of the Turtle Creek Valley was the engineering Mecca of the world with hundreds of engineers visiting daily. No greater manufacturing valley had ever existed for heavy industry. In its peak, "Westinghouse Valley" would have over 30,000 employees. The valley boasted world-class foundries of iron, steel, and brass as well as electrical equipment factories. The automation was the best in the world, foreshadowing the great assembly lines of Ford. The management system was one of the first in the country to fully implement the scientific management concepts of Fredrick Taylor. His factories were the world's most productive. Westinghouse was correct when he questioned his critics in the press in 1907 as he passed thorough on the train to turn Westinghouse Electric over to bankers. This manufacturing complex of the Turtle Creek Valley rivaled anything in the world. Certainly it deserved to be one of the seven wonders of the industrial world, which would include the Rhine Valley of Krupp in Germany and the Monongahela Valley of Carnegie.

The real innovations of Westinghouse were in the evolution of employee benefit systems from his original air brake plant in 1867. Westinghouse companies were self-insurers for mutual benefits using the company financial resources as collateral. The company and the program were independent, except that the company bore the expense of administration. Participation in the program was voluntary; the disability benefits covered about three-fourths of the Westinghouse employees. The rates for the life and disability insurance offered were lower than those of private insurance companies of the time such as Prudential and Home Guards. The interest paid on benefit investment, four percent, was unique. The weekly payment still represented a significant portion of the weekly wage, but most employees invested. Unlike private insurance, Westinghouse did not charge higher fees for those working dangerous jobs. Of course, Westinghouse plants were safety oriented and had a significantly lower accident rate than the steel mills of the area. In addition, Westinghouse plants had doctors and nurses available to employees daily at the plant. Employees who were disabled, to a lesser degree, were often given light work assignments to keep them employed.

The plans in 1904 were detailed as follows:

> To insure a certain income to the employees who might become unfitted for work through illness or injury and in the event of death to pay the beneficiary a stipulated sum. Any employee under 50 years of age is entitled to membership, subject to successful physical examination, but membership is not compulsory. Members contribute according to the class in which they belong, there being five, the class being determined by the wages received, varying from $35 to $95 or over per month, the contribution ranging from 50 cents to $1.50 [per week]. A member may receive benefits for 39 consecutive weeks, in event of disability extending so long a period. The air brake company is the custodian of the funds, but being such does not benefit the company pecuniarily, as it pays four per cent interest on monthly balances to the credit of the relief fund. The company goes further and guarantees payment of all benefits, and if the money received from the monthly contributions be insufficient to meet the requirements the company makes good such deficit.[1]

By 1913, two years before the Workmen's Compensation Act in Pennsylvania, Westinghouse started to fully fund a workmen's compensation program. The fund was totally maintained by Air Brake Company with no payments by the worker, and all workers were covered. Again, Westinghouse pioneered the way for what would become state law. Even with the law, Air Brake payments were much more generous, and payment began immediately, while the state allowed for a ten-day waiting period. The Westinghouse model was the basis for the design of the state system.

Similarly, Westinghouse had one of the first pension plans for his employees and continued to improve on it. There is much evidence that Westinghouse had an informal pension plan in the 1890s based on approval of company officers. The 1906 pension plan of the company required no employee payment and was based solely on years of service; it was not at the discretion of management. This program allowed an employee to retire at sixty to sixty-five years of age, depending on circumstances, after at least twenty years of service. Even more amazing was that the pension benefits continued to his dependents after death. The fund was maintained in a separate account that insured the funds, even if Air Brake were to go out of business, an idea far ahead of its time. It would be the first major pension plan in American heavy industry. Pensions did exist at Carnegie Steel in the area, but were based on a demonstration of need after "long and creditable service." The Carnegie Steel plan, known as the Carnegie Relief Fund, was actually a gift of Andrew Carnegie in his retirement to his old company; and it was a trust of four million dollars to be administered by Carnegie Steel.

A few years later, Westinghouse pioneered an employee stock program. This experiment was clearly visionary, but consistent with Westinghouse's idea of employee ownership. The plan allowed employees to buy stock, but was not a matching program. This was a time when the mechanics of the stock market and capital requirements limited the ability of the worker to buy a small amount of stock. The plan allowed for small installments and gave a small bonus after five years. The money would be taken directly out of the paycheck, or the local savings and loans were brought into the purchasing program. This type of automatic plan was at least fifty years ahead of its time.

Westinghouse followed Cooper in the development of an extensive apprentice program for the electrical trades. The Westinghouse system was a powerful application of his father's New England machine shop management in the new industrial revolution. Westinghouse pioneered the electrical apprentice program in the United States. Both in machine apprenticeships and electrical apprenticeships, few companies approached the numbers of Westinghouse Electric and Air Brake. He created an ordinary apprentice program for non-engineering grads and an engineering program for graduates. Preference to enter these programs was always given to employees and their family members. Westinghouse was soon generating more apprentices than he needed; but the demand was high in the Pittsburgh area, and he expanded it to all members of the community.

Westinghouse's style of capitalism required a deep respect for individuals. He detested legal suits, which were inconsistent with his Puritan roots, yet a lot of his business career was spent in courtrooms. Respect for intellectual rights was part of the dignity of man as well as the core of his view of capitalism. He had never forgotten his first partners' efforts to steal his invention of the railroad frog and car replacer. Without an absolute respect for intellectual rights, capitalism loses its ability to innovate. Certainly, Westinghouse today would be on the forefront of free trade, but he would never deal with a country, like China, that shows no respect for American patent law. He had fought capitalist giants, such as Morgan and Vanderbilt, over this very point. Even more importantly, he didn't believe that corporations had rights over individual innovation. To Westinghouse, the individual owned all rights to and rewards from any invention. Bankers stood in shock as Westinghouse paid huge sums for marginal inventions of his employees. It was typical of the period to take ownership of individual innovation. He never tried to infringe on a patent, even when lawyers suggested the possibility. Westinghouse stood tall in the Victorian era, which trampled on individual rights for more profits and industrial "efficiency." Such respect for intellectual rights gained him the loyalty of Nikola Tesla.

Yet Westinghouse understood well the inefficiencies of competition in the marketplace. Patent battles had been costly to all in the electrical industry, running into the billions. The huge costs of these legal battles were factored into product costs and prices. These legal battles not only cost huge sums, but slowed progress or wasted time in legal solutions. The waste of legal costs in patent battles was something that both J.P. Morgan and Westinghouse agreed on. Westinghouse called for a bigger role of the engineering societies in limiting these battles and settling them in the technical arena.

Westinghouse did propose a novel cooperative board of engineers and lawyers to make decisions without the legal court costs between Westinghouse Electric and General Electric. The arrangement was announced on March 13, 1896. The two companies agreed to share patents and royalties under the management of a board, which became known as the Board of Patent Control. The board consisted of four members, two from each company, and a fifth member to act as an arbitrator. The arrangement was a pure application of the teaching of the Westminster Larger Catechism, which Westinghouse had studied all his life, to avoid unnecessary lawsuits. The government (McKinley administration) showed little interest in exploring its legality. Since General Electric and Westinghouse controlled the market, this today would be monopolistic behavior. Pressure did mount to a point, and in 1911, both companies allowed the agreement to expire.

Westinghouse's Wilmerding was an inspiration for many capitalists and politicians. President McKinley toured and often directed other Americans to visit Wilmerding, hoping to promote this type of paternal capitalism. Pennsylvania chocolate baron Milton Hershey designed his "Chocolate Town" (Hershey, PA) in 1904 after Westinghouse's Wilmerding. Hershey built his town around his factory with rows of modern homes. These homes had indoor plumbing and electricity. Hershey's town did come with some restrictions, such as no saloons. Hershey, a student of the Rochdale Society of Equitable Pioneers, tried to set up a cooperative department store, but the residents rejected it. Hershey did build a power plant, parks, and a library. He installed an electric trolley system to connect his town to others.

At the time, like Wilmerding, Hershey's town won much praise. Edward Woolley, editor of *McClure's*, noted: "I found numerous families of plain factory workmen living in trim little houses, some of them which had a cost of $5,000 or more. These were the same class of people who in most industrial cities live in disreputable tenements or tumble down shanties, surrounded by hideous litter and filth."[2] Hershey and Westinghouse would become friends and exchange ideas.

In February of 1914, while fishing, Westinghouse fell into the water, which led to a serious cold. For weeks, his doctor slept in the adjoining chambers, as Westinghouse struggled through each night. He was confined to a wheelchair for the period as well. In March arrangements were made for Westinghouse, in New York, to be looked at by specialists. His wife Marguerite made arrangements for a suite of rooms at the Manhattan Hotel Langham overlooking Central Park.

It was here on March 12, 1914, that he passed peacefully. Marguerite followed him in death in June. The funeral was at Fifth Avenue Presbyterian Church in New York. Floral arrangements came in from kings, princes, and presidents. The funeral was attended by most of Pittsburgh's, New York's, and Washington's social elites, and eight longtime employees carried the casket. Delegates from all the nations' engineering societies were present. George Westinghouse III, a Yale graduate, and his wife, who would ultimately be the sole heir, had married in 1909. The many factories and plants in Europe and America were idled for a few hours to honor their founder. It is estimated that over 100,000 men halted work to honor Westinghouse. In Wilmerding, the plant was shut down for two days as many took the train to New York for the funeral. Westinghouse was buried at Woodlawn Cemetery; but in 1915, both he and Marguerite were moved to a grave in Arlington Cemetery. They had taken many walks together in Arlington while at Blaine House. The simple inscription on the stone was *Acting Third Assistant, U.S. Navy.* The scenes in death reflected the humility of his way of life.

At his death, Westinghouse owned or controlled over 15,000 patents, and 314 were his. He had formed over 60 companies and created millions of jobs worldwide. He had over 50,000 employees working directly for him at his death. He had created the town of Wilmerding and developed many others including East Pittsburgh and Turtle Creek. He had honorary doctorates from Union College and Kaniglicke Technische Hockschale in Germany. Westinghouse held the Legion of Honor from France, the Order of Leopold of Belgium, and the Royal Crown of Italy. He had won Germany's highest engineering award, the Grashof Medal, and America's Edison Medal. Other awards included the John Fritz Medal of the American

Women's lunch room at Westinghouse Electric, 1905 (courtesy Carnegie Library of Pittsburgh).

Association for the Advancement of Science and the Franklin Institute's Scott Medal.

His real tribute would come over a decade later. The Westinghouse Memorial was dedicated on October 6, 1930, but its funding had come from years of small donations. The memorial was the result of voluntary donations of over sixty thousand employees of the many companies he founded. It was meant to be a reflection of the man they knew. Today it is a quiet spot surrounded by key roads for that section of Pittsburgh; but any visitor can feel the spirit of a great man. As one approaches the memorial, a pond is encountered which forces one to look first at a distance of 20 yards or so. What appears is a bronze statue of a youth who looks on to three panels of granite and bronze. The dedication reads:

> George Westinghouse accomplished much of first importance to mankind through his ingenuity, persistence, courage, integrity, and leadership. By the invention of the air brake and automatic signaling devices. He led the world in the development of applications for the promotion of speed, safety, and economy of transportation. By his early vision of the value of the alternating current electric system he brought about a revolution in the transmission of electric power. His achievements were great, his energy and enthusiasm boundless, and his character beyond reproach; a shining mark for the encouragement of American youth.

It would have been unlikely that Carnegie's employees would have ever erected a memorial or made such a statement of greatness. While Westinghouse may have a lesser place in the pantheon of American industrialists, his place in the hearts of his employees was unequaled. It may explain why the truly enduring memorial to Westinghouse in the Pittsburgh area was the happiness of those who worked for his companies, such as my mother. This imprint that he left on his organizations has to be part of his story.

Sixteen

A Government Policy for Philanthropy and Paternalism

The success of Heinz in food, Carnegie in steel, Libbey in glass, and Pullman in railroads was the direct result of an average protective tariff of 40 percent. The government's protection of these industries created jobs and encouraged philanthropy. The mutual arrangement of industry, community, and government had been started by Abraham Lincoln. Lincoln is most often remembered for freeing the slaves, but many consider his contributions to business on an equal par. Lincoln, a former Whig, actually ran on a strong economic policy of American protectionism and the advance of industry. Lincoln had been the first national candidate since Henry Clay in the 1830s to have the united support of labor and manufacturers. That alliance would include the manufacturing districts of Illinois, Pennsylvania, Ohio, Kentucky, and Virginia that carried Lincoln to the presidency. It was no surprise that the Republican Party would be born at an 1856 convention in Pittsburgh at the heart of Whig country. Lincoln carried industrial Pittsburgh's Allegheny County by a record 10,000 votes. He called the concentration of votes in this manufacturing area "the State of Allegheny."

Lincoln's winning margins were similar in the iron districts of Ohio, where Iron Whigs and protectionist Democrats had found a new home in the Republican Party. In western Virginia, support of the Pig Iron Aristocrats (iron manufacturers, as they were known) for the protectionist Lincoln split the state and laid the ground work for the creation of West Virginia. These Pig Iron Aristocrats had forged an alliance with iron labor as well. A strong pig iron industry was necessary for both management profits and labor employment. Industry growth took priority over unionism and profits. These districts knew the recessions caused by free trade policies, believing the still lingering Panic of 1857 was a result of Democrats' passing lower tariffs. As a result of war and protectionism, the pig iron industry would see great advances in technology. The Pig Iron Aristocrats were rewarded for their votes with the 1862 tariff act, which was the highest ever on pig iron at 32 percent. As the Pig Iron Aristocrats responded with massive investments in industry and philanthropy, Congress moved the tariff rate to 47 percent in 1864. The pig iron industry grew an amazing 65 percent during the Civil War. By the end of the war, the Pig Iron Aristocrats were a genuine national political force with the wealth and ability to employ tens of thousands and to pour money into local communities. The American pig iron industry was the world's greatest.

Lincoln used tariffs to raise money for the national improvements, which was a basic use of tariffs as proposed by the Federalists earlier. Lincoln's economic advisor, Henry C. Carey, was a huge supporter of Clay's American System. Carey became a key political force in forming the Pennsylvania Society for the Encouragement of Manufacture as well as the American Industry League. Carey was a prolific writer in support of tariffs throughout his career. Carey was the most influential economist of the 1850s, 1860s, and 1870s. He was for easy money and strong tariff support, ideas supported by Henry Clay and President James Garfield, and in the 1890s by President William McKinley. Carey understood the nature of the money supply as a stimulus and supported the printing of greenback dollars. He correctly identified the "enemy" as the eastern banking monopolists who favored importing and trade. Carey argued that these bankers were actually hostile to American industrial enterprise. In fact, the public often saw big bankers and business as one and the same. Carey also predicted the bankers' takeover of the railroad industry to control trade. The fact was that big bankers made money on the sheer volume of trade and cared little whether it was from imports or exports.

Carey was the major influence on Lincoln's tariff policy that would become the policy of the Republican Party for many decades. Carey's disciples in the Congress such as Congressmen "Pig Iron" Kelley, James Garfield, William McKinley, and Thaddeus Stevens, carried the protectionist banner in the time period between Henry Clay (1820s) and Herbert Hoover. These men also demanded congressional oversight to assure profits gained from tariff protection were invested back into the industry, creating employment and community building.

Congress passed the highest tariffs ever, along with an increase in tariffs across the board, during the Republican supremacy of the late 1800s. At the time the government's main source of income was tariffs, not income taxes. Almost all industries benefited, but iron, glass, textile, forgings, tinplate, and mining boomed. The protectionist representatives wrote the tariff bill, assuring iron received the highest level of protection. This political alliance would assure Republican protectionist policies for the next seventy years. Lincoln's protectionism and policy of American economic growth would peak in 1890 with the McKinley Tariff Bill. It would be William McKinley who brought protectionism and tariff management to a science.

President William McKinley (1843–1901) had been born into a Scotch-Irish industrial middle class family. McKinley's father, William, Sr., was born in New Lisbon, Ohio, in 1807. The McKinleys produced cannon balls for the War of 1812. William Sr. moved to nearby Niles in the 1830s. The president's parents, Nancy Allison and William McKinley, Sr., married in Niles, Ohio. William Sr., was a manager and part owner of an iron furnace and rolling mill. The family and the region depended on tariffs to keep their furnaces profitable. The iron furnace would close during recessionary times.

The loss of his father's furnace operation during the recession of 1857 forced his father to find work in Michigan. A flood of cheap British iron and banking credit problems created a pullback in the Mahoning Valley of Ohio. McKinley's father reinvested in the iron industry but had to travel weekly to Michigan. The middle-class McKinley family experienced firsthand the struggle of economic hard times and mill closings. There is no question this influenced the young McKinley's views on economic policy. His belief in a full dinner pail was rooted in the economic cycle's impact on his own family. They knew firsthand the worries for feeding a family when a mill closes, and the strain on the breadwinner to find work. Few presidents in our history have had this type of personal experience with economic downturns.

McKinley had come from a middle-class industrial family, and he carried this perspective throughout his life. He passionately believed in labor as the barometer of the health of our nation. He represented the populist segment of the Republican Party, which opposed the eastern blue-bloods of the party. He was opposed by big Republican bankers but supported by Republican industrialists. His homes were middle-class cottages and he lived a simple life. His blueblood vice-president, Teddy Roosevelt, made fun of his style of living as beneath a president. McKinley worked his way from private to major in the Civil War, where most upper-class family members started, through battlefield promotions. He was a pioneer in the civil rights for blacks and women. In summary, his life was more representative of an ironworker than a captain of industry. He borrowed money for his presidential inauguration suit.

The Tariff Bill of 1890 was the career signature of William McKinley, and it would give him national support and a local defeat. What at first was called his Waterloo would actually forge the sword of victory. The Fifty-first Congress of 1888 formed with what was believed to be a mandate for tariff reform. The Republicans controlled the White House and both branches of the legislature. Providence seemed to favor McKinley, and his power was peaking. The tariff issue, now preeminent, was what McKinley had studied his whole life. Although not a personal friend of McKinley, the new president, Benjamin Harrison, was for high tariffs. McKinley drew on old friends such as former President Rutherford B. Hayes for advice. McKinley showed true brilliance in his compromises and teamwork, not only in the House, but also with the Senate and White House. He was dealing with a mix in both parties. The tariff bill included many innovations that helped American farmers and manufacturers. It was an extremely well-prepared bill on industry and product statistics. The bill completed the evolutionary steps of American tariffs from revenue generating to protective to industry development. No bill before had been directed at policy to build industries such as tinplate and sugar. There would be a small increase initially in prices, but prices would actually decrease long-term as industry invested in research and development because of stable prices. This was a pleasant surprise that long-term market stability actually improved investment. Philanthropy blossomed throughout the nation. The excess profits also help paternalism flourish.

McKinley believed that fair wages, industrial growth, better work conditions, and mobility to the middle class were the answers to labor unrest. In his defense of the Ohio coal miners, he had learned how poor working conditions could lead to labor discontent. He had often talked to his friend, George Westinghouse, on the importance of being fair as an employer. He was, of course, well aware that greed was the Achilles' heel of capitalism. He opposed the paternal capitalism of Andrew Carnegie, preferring better wages to community welfare and philanthropy.

McKinley's Bill of 1890 was the best researched ever and used science and statistics to apply the tariff rates. First, McKinley argued that the revenue tariff approach was the real problem, not protective tariffs, since revenue tariffs were much higher than those required for simple protection of industry. Protective tariffs would still allow for imports. His statistics were convincing: "Before 1820 nearly all our imports were dutiable;

scarcely any were free; while in 1824 the proportion of free imports was less than 6 percent; in 1830, about 7 percent.... The percent of free imports from 1873 to 1883 was about 30 percent, and under the tariff revision of 1883 it averaged 33 percent."[1]

McKinley argued that protective tariffs had not restricted exports or created trade wars, and again the numbers supported him: "We sell to Europe $449,000,000 worth of products and buy $208,000,000 worth. We sell to North America to the value of $9,645,000 and buy $5,182,000. We sell South America $13,810,000 and buy $9,088,000." McKinley was not alone in his evaluation. Bismarck in 1882 had hailed the protective tariffs of America: "Because it is my deliberate judgment that the prosperity of America is mainly due to its system of protective laws." The McKinley tariffs were focused on building America, not restricting trade. They were applied in a manner that did not produce trade wars. Still, McKinley was clear that his tariffs were nationalistic: "The free-trader wants the world to enjoy with our citizens equal benefits of trade in the United States. The Republican protectionist would give the first chances to our people, and would so levy duties upon the products of other nations as to discriminate in favor of our own."[2] McKinley's extensive study had truly brought scientific management into tariff rates, but Congress preferred politics to science. A tariff commission was also established to monitor the impact of the tariffs. This regulatory committee helped the opposition assure fairness, and companies invested in jobs and the community, not filling their pockets. It was a successful relationship between government and industry. It required worker support at the ballot box; thus, paternalism was part of the equation.

Statistics for the 1890 to 1900 decade support the conclusion that prices came down, profits rose, capital investment went up, and wages held or slightly increased (real wages clearly rose). Average annual manufacturing income went from $425.00 a year and $1.44 a day in 1890 to $432.00 a year and $1.50 a day in 1900. The average day in manufacturing remained around ten hours a day. Heavily protected industries such as steel fared slightly better with wages. The cost of living index fell during the decade from 91 to 84, or about 8 percent. The clothing cost of living dropped even more, from 134 to 108, or 19 percent. Food stayed about the same, but the cost of protected sugar dropped around 25 percent. The bottom line is that the real wage index (adjusted for cost of living) rose from $1.58 a day to $1.77 a day in 1900, or about a 12 percent increase.[3] Steel production went from 1.3 million tons in 1880 to 11.2 million tons in 1900 to 28.3 million tons in 1910. In 1898 the American steel industry surpassed

Britain in pig iron production. The U.S. gross national product grew from an estimated $11 billion in 1880 to $18.7 billion in 1890 to $35.3 billion in 1910. The American glass industry was another struggling industry in 1880. Due to tariffs, by 1910 the glass industry had increased its output five to tenfold. During the peak tariff years of 1896 to 1901 under President McKinley, steel production increased 111 percent; electrical equipment production increased 271 percent; and farm equipment increased 149 percent. During the same period, wages rose 10 percent and employment increased 20 percent.

Consumerism, coupled with protected industries, allowed for the rise in the middle class. Consumer driven industries such as textile makers employed 112,900 in 1890 and 324,000 in 1900. The leather industry employed 6,000 in 1890 and 13,200 in 1900. Even more dramatic, foundries and machine shops employed 15,500 in 1889 and 145,400 in 1899. The depth of this economic boom is nothing short of amazing. The consumer market of America was the greatest in the world. The upward spiral of factories and consumers built a middle class that was rich compared to most countries.

McKinley was a paternalist in his own right. He had supported the eight-hour day from his earliest days, and in 1890 promoted a federal bill for the eight-hour day for government workers. McKinley had often talked with Samuel Gompers on the expansion of the eight-hour day to industry and had it included in the 1900 platform. He had promoted, throughout his career, safety acts for miners, railroad employees, and streetcar workers. Both at the federal and the state levels, he promoted bills for the formation of unions. In Ohio, he passed arbitration bills to assure the fair treatment of labor and the right to impartial tribunes. As governor, he used his own funds to help hungry striking miners. He correctly envisioned the American union/management system as an option to violence and socialism. He would not allow violence and used overwhelming force when necessary; but he often rebuked owners publicly. He hoped for an age of cooperation, realizing that laws would be needed to address abuses.

McKinley used labor leaders as White House consultants and often assigned them to committee investigations. When he signed the Erdman Act, he assigned labor leaders to arbitration boards. Former AFL chief Samuel Gompers and former chief of the railway union, Frank Sargent, were assigned to his Industrial Commission to study trusts and tariffs. M.M. Garland, who had been president of the Amalgamated Iron and Steel Workers during the Homestead Strike, was assigned as a duty commissioner. Terence Powdery, former head of the Knights of Labor, was made General Commissioner of Immigration. McKinley also gave many lower-level government jobs to midlevel labor leaders. McKinley's "Full Dinner Pail" policy required the cooperation of labor and capital, and he did his best to maintain the balance in government.

Not surprisingly, McKinley was one of our most popular presidents. He formed an unusual political voting bloc of labor and management. While the union leaders opposed the Republicans and McKinley, workers broke ranks to vote for McKinley. His assassination by a radical socialist in 1901 was a blow to workers. Pennsylvania Railroad Board of Directors supplied a special funeral train for McKinley's body, accompanied by his Cabinet and family, to cross the nation from Washington to McKinley's home of Canton, Ohio. In darkness, the train passed through Pennsylvania coalfields, where thousands of miners came out of the shafts with their lanterns to pay tribute to a friend. The train passed Westinghouse's factories in Wilmerding and East Pittsburgh. Thousands of women employees lined the tunnels and bridges in the area. The crowds in Washington were almost unmanageable as thousands pressed to the Capitol to view the body. As the train with McKinley's body passed by the steel mills of Braddock and Homestead, work was stopped for ten minutes as steelworkers lined the tracks holding their dinner pails high as a tribute to the "Napoleon of Protectionism." What reporters noted was the large proportion of women in the crowds at a time when women, without the vote, often paid little attention to presidents. McKinley was, however, the first president to support women's suffrage. In 1872, when the Equal Rights Party nominated Ohio-born Victoria Woodhull for president, McKinley calmed local outcries by having a reception for her at his Canton home. As governor, he helped get the right for women to vote in school board elections. McKinley was a handsome man who had the aura of future president John F. Kennedy.

The train passed George Westinghouse's home in Pittsburgh. McKinley was a close personal friend of George Westinghouse. At Pittsburgh's Second Avenue, the train passed the exact location where the railroad air brake had been tested successfully, saving the life of a peddler. McKinley had passed legislation over the years that had made air brakes mandatory on American trains. Also in the crowd at the Pittsburgh station was M.M. Garland. Garland, like Samuel Gompers, had come to realize that prosperity meant union membership as well as corporate profits. Union membership quadrupled during the McKinley administration as industry rapidly expanded.

As the train drew closer to McKinley's boyhood home in northeast

Ohio, the crowds were large even in these rural areas. Many trains were halted to allow the funeral train to pass through America's highest concentrations of tracks in industrial northeast Ohio. The Mahoning Valley had been the bastion of support for protective tariffs since the days of Henry Clay. Here glassworkers joined steelworkers to honor the slain president. The train moved past some of the coal Ohio mining districts where the young lawyer McKinley had helped miners with their struggle for better working conditions. It was a sunny autumn day, and the crowds grew as the train approached Canton. Flags increased as veterans of the Civil War amassed along the tracks to honor "the major." At Canton, over 100,000 flooded the streets of this industrial town.

United States Steel called for a holiday to allow steelworkers to travel by rail to Canton. McKinley's full Cabinet, most of Congress, all of the Supreme Court, and swarms of politicians descended on the small city of Canton. In addition to America's aristocracy, hundreds of steelworkers and miners came to Canton. Thousands camped in the streets of Canton. The whole country honored McKinley on burial day. Chicago factories declared a holiday, as did those in other industrial towns. New York City closed completely for the day. A national tribute of pausing the nation's work for five minutes occurred as the body was laid to rest. Every train, factory, steel mill, mine, and activity stopped for five minutes. The nation's entire telegraph was shut down for five minutes. Foreign capitals also paused to praise the American president. London, in particular, hailed the president who, two years earlier, had led American industry in overtaking that of Great Britain. London was filled with pictures of McKinley, and Westminster Abbey held a special service. In many ways, McKinley represented the American version of Queen Victoria, who had died in early 1901. Like Victoria in 1840s Britain, McKinley had ushered in America's industrial empire in the 1890s.

Manufacturing was the base of American economic philosophy of the 1890s. The success would be emulated around the world. Otto von Bismarck, Chancellor of Germany in the 1870s and 1880s, built up industry around his nationalistic capitalism. In effect, Bismarck developed a national community for manufacturing. He moved Germany from national free trade to the type of managed trade that had led to America's success. Bismarck believed that working people were happier and better off, but he worried about the abuses of capitalism. Protectionism required worker support, and paternalism was the key to that support. Abuses did come into the American system by the 1900s; the death of McKinley, in many ways, was the start of the decline of true paternalism.

Seventeen

Corporate Paternalism

With the decline of paternal capitalists came the rise of unions, internationalism, the bureaucratic bigness of corporations, scientific management, and the expansion of government. The passage from paternal capitalism was, in many aspects, necessary and evolutionary. Abuses had been common, and even the best paternal companies had their shortcomings. McKinley had shown that government had a major role in paternalism. Paternalism had been personal and dependent on the ethics and views of the company owner. The problem with paternal capitalism was that it was not contractual or embedded in the long-term infrastructure. As the founder moved from the direct management of the company and the second generation took over, often the paternal bond was lost. This was the case with companies like Ford Motors and Firestone. In many cases, the move from private ownership to corporate governance changed the paternal management to a corporate approach to paternalism.

Incorporation cut the heart of companies and often broke the bonds with the community. The necessity to develop community passed as companies became more globalized. The care of society and its enrichment would slowly pass to government. The worker would have union protection, Social Security, unemployment compensation, and Medicare. Another gap was the growing distance of the foreman from the owner. For the worker, the foreman controlled the workplace, not the often remote owner. The foremen and managers would need to be trained in the better treatment of workers. The science of management and its training would move into business schools. Joseph Wharton, and later Oliver Sheldon, would make that bridge between paternal capitalism and paternal corporate management. The workplace would change just as rapidly, and there would be setbacks such as the rise of scientific management from 1911 to 1920.

The great paternal capitalists had built America's educational system, but none of these addressed the "science" of management. As America moved from private ownership and partnerships to corporations, paternal capitalism could no longer be counted on to maintain an ethical balance with the needs of the workers. In the 1890s, colleges were used to train lawyers, doctors, and scientists. There were some "business colleges," like Duff's in Pittsburgh, for the training of accounting clerks, but nothing to address the science of managing. Managers were trained on the job in the image of the owner. Early training of managers often focused on the science of efficiency and productivity. In fact, the rise of scientific management of the 1880s focused on efficiency and productivity with little concern for the worker.

The great industrialist Joseph Wharton had built his steel mills and factories during the Industrial Revolution. Joseph Wharton was born in 1826 into a family of Quakers. His parents, William Wharton and Deborah Fisher Wharton, were both from prominent early American immigrant families of Quaker descent. He had an early love of chemistry. When he was 19, Wharton apprenticed with an accountant for two years and became proficient in business methods and bookkeeping. At 21, he partnered with his older brother Rodman to start a business that manufactured white lead. In 1849, Wharton started another business, manufacturing bricks, using a patented machine which pressed dry clay into forms. There was substantial competition in the brick business, which was affected by cyclical business swings; and Wharton soon decided there was little profit in this enterprise. However, from the endeavor, he gained valuable experience. In 1853, Wharton joined the Pennsylvania and Lehigh Zinc Company near Bethlehem, Pennsylvania, first managing the mining operation and later the zinc oxide works. He had lived the transformation from private ownership to corporate governance. Wharton believed that paternalism did not offer a long term solution for workers and managers. He believed that the economy of the 1890s had become too complex for simple on-the-job training.

Wharton had proved highly successful and took ownership of the zinc works. Hoping to profit from the use of nickel in coins, Wharton, in 1863, sold his interest in zinc and started the manufacture of nickel at Camden, New Jersey, taking over a nickel mine and refining works at Nickel Mines, Pennsylvania. Wharton won wide acclaim for his malleable nickel, the first in the world, and also for nickel magnets; and he received the Gold

Medal at the Paris Exposition of 1878. His factory produced the only nickel in the U.S. and a significant fraction of the world supply, making Wharton one of America's wealthiest capitalists. Through the 1870s, Wharton began to buy into Bethlehem Iron Company, which produced pig iron and steel rails. Gradually he invested more of his own time and energy, eventually taking full ownership, but without involvement in the day-to-day operations. During this experience, he realized that he was dependent on his managers to be paternal in their approach to management.

Wharton was not a hands-on executive, and his Bethlehem Steel had hired the father of scientific management to implement efficiency practices. Fredrick Taylor had some support for his radical management practices at Bethlehem, but the company lacked the paternalism of its founding. Charles Schwab would become president of Bethlehem Steel in 1904. Schwab was famous for his Carnegie Steel–based paternalism. Taylor had been fired as a consultant prior to (and maybe in anticipation of) Schwab's taking over. Scientific management à la Taylor would appear to have many similarities with the "Carnegie way," known as the "drive system." Both systems focused on goalsetting and rewards, but the methodology was much different. Taylor looked at setting goals, then setting corporate procedures to achieve them. Taylor rewarded men for fast work and advocated incentives. The "Carnegie way" was to set the goals and assign them to management, and then to motivate managers and workers to meet them. The Carnegie way was people oriented. The result was a broader approach to management training and education. Managers needed to be trained in people skills as well as scientific methods.

Wharton believed that workers and management needed to be educated to maintain long-term employment. He wrote extensively on economic matters, such as protective tariffs, as well as labor problems. Wharton preached the biggest threat to both the worker and owners was the business cycle. In the 1800s, he was a visionary on the need to protect workers in business downturns. He became focused on methods to manage business cycles. Wharton became a proponent of national capitalism and protectionism as a means to assure social security for the workers. In addition, Wharton believed that managers needed to be trained in the art of management in an arena where many views could be brought into discussion. This would bring a more enlightened approach to managing employees of large corporations.

In the last half of the 19th century, business education for managers typically consisted mainly of training on the job or serving an apprenticeship. Wharton conceived of a school that would teach how to develop and run a business, and to anticipate and deal with the cycles of economic activity. In 1881, Wharton donated $100,000 to the University of Pennsylvania to found a School of Finance and Economy for this purpose. He specified that the Wharton School faculty advocate economic protectionism as he had when lobbying for American businesses in Washington. Wharton, like prior paternalists, believed profitability of the company needed to form the basis of paternal employee practices. The anvil, the school's symbol, reflects Wharton's pioneering work in the metal industry. Wharton envisioned creating a new foundation in order to produce educated leaders of business and government.

At the time of the Wharton School's founding in 1881, the idea of a collegiate business school was a novel concept. Most managers rose through the worker ranks with no training. There were no business professors, textbooks, or model curricula. The Wharton School's rise transformed the study of business from a trade into an academic science and research-intensive endeavor. Wharton created the first business textbooks. Wharton's school produced America's first professional managers. Other schools such as MIT and Harvard would adopt schools of business. Unfortunately, the early focus of business education was on the science of efficiency. In the early 1900s, the focus moved from employees to efficiency, including the instruction at the Wharton School.

The problem with making corporate managers more responsive to workers in the early 1900s was the popularity of the efficiency-oriented scientific management of Frederick Taylor. While early curriculum at schools was employee-focused, the efficiency approach of Frederick Taylor swept the nation. Taylor published his famous book, *The Principles of Scientific Management*, in 1911. The approach focused on making the worker as efficient as a machine. It represented the peak of the industrial efficiency movement of the prior decades. Taylorism, as it became known, was the application of the scientific method to management practices. Scientific management looked to optimize the way tasks were performed by simplifying the jobs so that workers could be trained to perform their specialized sequence of operational tasks in the most efficient way. But it often resulted in the dumbing-down of the worker. Taylor had been working on the approach since the 1880s at companies such as Midvale Steel and Bethlehem Steel. In 1908, Harvard Business School based its first-year curriculum on Taylor's scientific management; but it soon became as popular at most business schools as it was on the factory floor. Henry Ford was an early adopter of scientific management, as was Louis Brandeis in the railroad industry. Modern management writer Peter Drucker ranked

Fredrick Taylor among Darwin and Freud as one of the seminal thinkers of modern times.

Taylorism became the first management fad by 1911; and after America's success in World War I, it spread throughout the world. No single management system has achieved such broad acclaim with the possible exception of Ed Deming's statistical process control of the late 20th century. France and Russia, in particular, mandated the use of Taylorism in industry. Considered the foundation of industrial engineering, Taylorism remained the basic theme of American management until the 1980s, when it came under attack by Japanese-oriented management. Taylorism became linked incorrectly with the basic problems of the factory system.

Frederick Winslow Taylor (1856–1915) started as an apprentice pattern maker at Midvale Steel. He worked at night school to earn a degree in mechanical engineering from Stevens Institute of Technology in Philadelphia. Taylor worked his way from the factory floor into management. In 1890, his joined a consulting firm for "systematizing of shop management." He later joined Bethlehem Steel to implement his system. Frederick Taylor's early work on scientific management was a search for the best methods to do things. He worked with better handling and work techniques for laborers. He perfected his methods, like a scientist doing experiments, to determine the best results. He was best known for his famous shoveling experiment combining the factors of shovel size, physical attributes of the worker, and material density. He ignored the possibility of motivation increasing production.

Taylor would also become known for incorporating time study and inventive programs in his approach. Taylor published his best-known paper, "A Piece-Rate System, being a Step Toward Partial Solution of the Labor Problem" in 1895. Taylor went back into consulting in 1901 and fine-tuned his theories. He eventually became a business professor at Dartmouth College. Taylor became the preacher of the scientific management gospel, which was furthered by Henry L. Gantt (1861–1919), Carl Barth (1860–1939), Frank Gilbreth (1868–1924) and Lillian Gilbreth (1878–1972). Taylor was often brought in to testify and function as a consultant for the United States Congress. In this capacity, he studied and reported on industrial safety and the efficiency, of the railroads.

Frederick Taylor took the approach used in science and adapted it to management. He recommended a manager fully study an operation prior to developing work procedures. Taylor was one of the first to argue that much of the inefficiency in industry was related to poor management. Scientific management centered on four principles detailed in Taylor's book:

1. Replace rule-of-thumb work methods and procedures with methods based on the scientific method.
2. Scientifically select, train, and develop each employee rather than passively leaving them to train themselves.
3. Provide detailed instruction for each worker in the performance of their tasks.
4. Divide work equally between managers and workers, so that the managers apply scientific management principles to planning the work and workers actually perform the tasks.

These basic principles proved particularly well suited to convert unskilled immigrant labor into skilled labor. Scientific management proved especially well suited for the defining and implementing of assembly-line work, but often lost the importance of the human element.

Taylorism and scientific management became the basis for the development of industrial engineering, industrial psychology, and shop scheduling. Taylor argued that factories and companies should have a planning department. Scientific management revolutionized the machining industry with its scientific approach to the speeds and feeds of automated machines. Taylor required the use of a strong cost system and analysis. Its most powerful impact was the use of "SOPs," or Standard Operating Procedures. This came as a break from a crafts-driven system where procedures were passed verbally from a master craftsman to an apprentice. In general, scientific management was a critical step in the transition from the crafts model to that of the Industrial Revolution, but it also reduced the importance of paternalism in the workplace. The scientific management approach made for easy training of new workers. It created process and product consistency. Taylor stressed standardization throughout the operation, including all tools, implements, and methods used in the trades.

Taylorism and Scientific Management has come under heated criticism. Taylor's use of the stopwatch and time study often found resistance from unions and workers. Other management scientists argued it dehumanized work, creating monotony. While Taylorism proved good at breaking down tasks to run assembly lines, it proved a poor technique for overall job design, which requires the analysis of skill variety, task significance, autonomy, and feedback. Old paternal companies opposed the use of Taylorism, preferring employee motivational approaches.

Taylor's scientific approach to management would lead educators to look at psychological and human factors in factories. The research would lead to a new look at the old paternal practices of Owen, Westinghouse, Heinz, and others. Harvard Business School would be the first to hire a psychologist to take a scientific look at paternalistic practices in 1892. Hugo Munsterberg (1863–1916) would become known as the founder of industrial psychology. He had earned a Ph.D. in psychology in Germany. His experimental studies of industry at Harvard would bring many to Harvard to consult with him. Even President Woodrow Wilson was interested in spreading this psychological approach across the nation. The interest was followed at the Wharton Business School as well.

Wharton's promotion of the use of science in the study of management would lead to a new focus on the importance of paternal management and a questioning of Taylor's approach as well. Practitioners and graduates of Harvard and Wharton started their own management experiments at their factories. The first experiments of the 1920s were at the Hawthorne plant of Western Electric, which was the equipment-manufacturing arm of AT&T. These experiments started as an extension of Taylor's scientific approach. The initial experiment was to answer the modest question of the effect of workplace illumination on worker productivity. The study would start with a number of professors from Massachusetts Institute of Technology in the electrical engineering department. Experiments used groups and control groups formed from factory workers to study the effect on operator productivity. A number of variables were studied over a three-year period. The surprising conclusion was that the productivity of all groups with various intervening variables went up regardless of the level of illumination. The output of assemblers was increased an amazing 35 to 50 percent. The lead researcher, Homer Hibarger, believed there were other variables at play and developed another set of experiments. A professor, Clair Turner, was brought in from MIT's public health department. Once again, these experimental groups showed across the board increases in productivity. This would launch a new employee-focused approach to combine with the scientific approach.

Clair Turner attributed these productivity increases to (1) small group identity, (2) positive supervision, (3) increased earnings, (4) the novelty of the project, and (5) the attention given to the workers. The importance of management attention came to be known as the "Hawthorne Effect." George Elton Mayo (1880–1949) was brought in from Harvard to help analyze the results. Mayo started a detailed survey of the workers. The results would be a revolutionary new approach to management. Mayo concluded that emotional factors were more important than physical factors in determining productivity and efficiency. Mayo's interviews further concluded that supervisors had a major impact on worker productivity. In particular, supervisors should be more people-oriented and less aloof.

Mayo argued that a human relations style of leader was needed. This conclusion would go against traditional scientific management thinking.

Mayo took the study and its conclusions further. He suggested a radical new approach based on human relations, psychoanalysis, philosophical rationale, and the psychopathological analysis of industrial life.[1] In reality, he was applying the scientific approach to paternalistic approaches of decades earlier. Mayo argued that managers believed the solution to industrial problems was rooted in logical and rational behavior, which could be found by scientific experiments, when the problems were actually of a social nature. He believed industrial operations had destroyed the needed social connections of the individual and, in turn, lowered morale and productivity. This conclusion was consistent with the emerging progressive view in American thinking as well as that of paternalists such as George Westinghouse, who had intuitively discovered the importance of morale and productivity. Mayo's conclusions would lead to a human relations-oriented program for training managers in American schools. Mayo favored a liberal arts background for managers over technical expertise. However, his findings did inspire the reading of the writings of Robert Owen in management schools. Mayo also favored testing potential supervisors psychologically to assure the right people were selected to manage. This new behavioral school approach to management would develop in the thinking of Oliver Sheldon, Mary Parker Follett, Lillian Gilbreth, Hugo Munsterberg, and Chester Barnard.

In the 1920s, Oliver Sheldon (1894–1951) would propose to train a new breed of educated managers who had the old beliefs in fair treatment and community. His approach would borrow from the early paternalists. Sheldon was a manager of Rowntree Company in England. Founded in 1862, the company developed strong associations with Quaker philanthropy. It was one of the big three confectionery manufacturers in the United Kingdom, alongside Cadbury and Fry. The company was founded by Seebohm Rowntree in 1899. Rowntree introduced employment practices which broke new ground in Great Britain—an eight-hour day, a pension scheme for employees, free medical and dental care on site. He believed that the existence of companies that paid low wages was bad for the nation's economy and its workers.

Benjamin Seebohm Rowntree (1871–1954) carried out a comprehensive survey into the living conditions of the poor in York, during which investigators visited every working-class home. The results of this study were published in 1901 in his book, *Poverty: A Study of Town Life*, which soon became a classic sociological text that significantly influenced research methods in the social sciences and would become the basis for Oliver Sheldon's work. The application of scientific methods, which had not previously been applied to the study of poverty, led Rowntree to develop the concept of the safety net—the minimum weekly sum of money required for a subsistence level of existence. Rowntree tried some novel approaches to downturns in the economy, such as job sharing, lifetime employment, and communal pay cuts to save jobs. The various Rowntree studies would become an important issue of future New Deal politics in the 1930s. Oliver Sheldon learned many of the methods from his work at Rowntree; but Sheldon went further, putting worker treatment ahead of profitability. Sheldon, like Robert Owen, believed worker treatment is the foundation of profitability.

Sheldon believed paternalism should be institutionized, not dependent on the benevolence of the owner. Sheldon was the twentieth century's Robert Owen. Sheldon's concern was that joint stock corporations lacked not only paternalism, but moral values. Furthermore, Sheldon saw the rise of stock corporations as disturbing the economy as a whole. A hundred years ago in 1914, Sheldon noted problems in our capitalistic economy because of the lack of "a national minimum wage, cooperation and profit-sharing, the problem of the unfit, the problem of the unemployment and the lack of efficiency."[2] Sheldon went even further in defining the new role of corporate management in terms of the principles of paternalism. He defined the role of the industrial corporations: " Commodities and services must be furnished at the lowest prices compatible with an adequate standard of quality, and distributed in such a way as to promote the highest ends of community ... it must be governed by certain principles inherent in the motive of service to the community."[3]

Sheldon advocated a human-relations style of management which placed the individual in a human context.[4] He saw the worker as motivated by emotional and psychological needs. In this, he disagreed fundamentally with contemporaries in the early 1900s such as Fredrick Taylor, who saw economic need as being the primary motivator of workers. Sheldon argued that, while basic economic needs must be met, wider personal and community needs were equally important.

Sheldon would also address the shortcomings of paternal capitalism in relationship to trade unionism. A common fault of even the best of the paternal capitalists was their stubborn resistance to the union movement. They failed to realize that it was impossible for them to assure fair treatment in large organizations. Sheldon also noted that unions opposed profit sharing because it threatened the union movement. This standoff remains a problem today in profit-sharing problems. Sheldon argued that employee safety and security were the responsibility of all levels of management. Even the front-line manager should try to supply welfare work in short disruptions of work.

Sheldon also addressed the most difficult fears of the worker such as unemployment. Unemployment had posed a problem for even paternal capitalists. Many of these paternalists supplied fuel and food for the unemployed, but workers still feared the loss of income. Others supplied "welfare" work in downtimes. Sheldon believed "welfare" work had to be part of corporate management. First, managers at all levels were to maintain work as much as possible in bad times. Sheldon believed that unemployment had to be addressed at all levels. He believed it was a problem basic to industry and noted:

It is customary to regard unemployment as if it were detachable from other features of industrial life. In truth, it is but the reverse of the picture of employment. Work and lack of work are two sides of the same coin. Whatever may be our philosophy of the one will apply equally to the other. If we regard work as a fortuitous occurrence in the economic life of the worker, equally shall we regard lack of work as a mischance associated with the present circumstances of production. On the other hand if we regard work as the duty which every citizen owes to the community, we shall regard involuntarily lack of work as a matter of immediate concern to the community. If the community requires work of its citizens, it must ensure that work is available, and if for the moment it cannot provide work, it must maintain until it can."[5] Sheldon saw welfare work as a corporate and community responsibility.

He also proposed a larger solution that would not become a reality until the 1940s. As early as 1905, Sheldon maintained that there should be cooperation between management, the union, and the community to assure worker income in bad times. All three of these would share the responsibility and cost. His own suggestion was much like that of today: "A single man, for instance, receiving half his normal wages and a married man half, 10 percent on behalf of his wife, and 5 percent for each of his dependent children, up to a maximum figure of 75 percent of his normal earnings."[6] Sheldon, like paternalists before, argued that such approaches to unemployment and social security were necessary for productivity.

Sheldon was not alone in understanding the relationship between unemployment and productivity. Early communal manufacturers had offered one solution. Andrew Carnegie had tried to tie wages to the economy in an effort to reduce unemployment while preserving his own profits.

The Homestead Strike of 1892 showed the failure of this type of "economic" solution. In the great depressions of 1873, 1892, and 1907, capitalists did set up welfare programs, but this did little for worker morale. In 1916, Henry Dennison (1877–1952) of Dennison Manufacturing in Massachusetts created one of the first corporate unemployment insurance funds. Dennison would become an advisor to Franklin D. Roosevelt, who implemented a national unemployment insurance fund. The discussion continues to this day with many Japanese companies offering lifetime employment, but with the collapse of the Japanese economy in the 2000s, many of these same employers were forced to drop such plans. It seems clear that such programs require cooperation between government and manufacturers.

Eighteen

Unions, Industrial Democracy and the New Deal

Unemployment and economic downturns remained a core problem in the 1930s. For decades, capitalism and socialism struggled as economic options to meet the needs of society. Paternal capitalism had held off European-style socialism from 1850 to the 1910s. World War I came at a time when paternal capitalism was in decline as a result of economic growth, industrialization, and globalization. Critics called it welfare capitalism. Socialism had also declined as a threat to capitalism in America for political and social reasons. Socialism's propensity for atheism, equating church and government as controlling the worker, also made it unpopular with the religious base of America. It stated that no economic theory could deal with economic downturns and unemployment.

Progressivism had emerged as an American blend of both systems. Still, capitalism offered the best pure economic system in the American democracy. Socialism emerged as a political system with a government structure in progressivism. Progressivism also came with problems such as the growth of government and high tax burdens. The problem of capitalism was that greed often won out over the needs of the worker. Workers could not always count on the paternalism of the owners. Furthermore, for the worker, capitalism offered little safety in economic downturns. Eventually, the government would supply a safety net and necessary regulation. It would be unique to the American workplace and change the nature of paternalism.

Paternalism would be replaced by a new paradigm in society between workers, managers, and the government. This new paradigm would evolve out of the challenges of the Great Depression. This evolution came to a peak in the 1930s as the depression challenged capitalism. Paternalism didn't break down but would be replaced by a fairer system with its own problems and tradeoffs. The sheer size of the emerging twentieth century businesses was itself a problem for paternalism. The first change was the union movement. In many cases, paternalism had been the owner's answer to unionization. Paternalism had many shortcomings from the workers' perspective. Like the old monarchies of Europe, paternalism depended on who was king. Paternal capitalists tended to be first-generation owners, who grew up with the business. As the business grew, it would become more impersonal. Second-generation owners usually moved to upper-class cities and regions. Internationalism would also make the business less responsive to any local community. Also, as companies moved from private ownership to corporations, paternalism was often lost in bureaucracy. Other companies turned over the welfare of workers to government agencies.

It wasn't just management that changed in the 1930s, but workers as well. Abuses increased as the levels of management increased between the foreman and the owner. Workers could no longer count on the "good king" to arbitrate individual problems. Access to the owner was no longer possible for the worker. Foremen were no better off as they became distant from the owners. In addition, as the owners' wealth increased, they often left the working community, losing touch. Workers no longer saw the owners as members of the factory community, and the owners became part of their new living communities. Even the factory managers themselves lived elsewhere. Unionization took root in the once-great paternal industries of steel, rubber, automotive, and others, not so much because of low pay as poor treatment. These industries remained the highest paid, but management took over more control of the workplace and workers no longer had a personal connection with the company. The worker no longer owned the job or had any control of the workplace. Unionization was a means to return ownership of the job to the worker. The Great Depression would force change.

The old lions of paternal capitalism saw unionization as a rejection. They failed to understand the feelings of their workers in the working community. The owners could hardly be "paternal" in cities such as Akron, while living in the distant wealthy neighborhoods of New York and Florida. Community had been at the heart of paternal capitalism starting with owners such as Robert Owen. Harvey Firestone, at his Florida home, didn't see the coldness of his evolving international company. From his mansions on Fifth Avenue or in Scotland, Carnegie no longer could see the smoke, fire, and living conditions of his Pittsburgh mill towns. Even for George Westinghouse, things changed when he moved to Berkshire Hills in New York, no longer taking his daily 15-mile trip with many of his employees to his East Pittsburgh factories. In the 1920s, two of the biggest rubber companies, Goodrich and U.S. Rubber, moved their headquarters to New York. Such moves hurt manufacturing towns such as Akron, Ohio, where the products were made. Similarly, in the 1920s, New York bankers took control of Goodyear, ending decades of symbiotic communal relationships in Akron. Headquarters and the factory were now separated by hundreds of miles. Philanthropic efforts tended to focus on the city where the headquarters was located, such as New York, instead of the factory town. Carnegie Hall and the New York Philharmonic Orchestra meant little to workers in the industrial towns like Detroit, Akron, and Pittsburgh.

Local unions often replaced corporate paternalism and even philanthropy with their own form of paternalism. Unions were really a necessity in the twentieth-century big business environment and an outgrowth of democracy. The unions of the 1930s offered an answer to the pressing problems of struggling workers. These problems were different from the money issues of unions in the nineteenth century. Workers wanted more control of the workplace. Unions grew to protect the workers from the abuses of capitalism; unfortunately, even the paternal capitalists were swept up by the movement. In the unionization movement of the 1930s, industrialists such as Henry Ford, Harvey Firestone, and Bill O'Neil (General Tire) moved away from their paternal practices. Ford's antiunion strategy was very public. His opposition to unionization was not about wages or benefits, because he was paying the highest in the United States. For Ford, as with most industrialists, it was control; and he was unwilling to share decision-making with the union.

World War I would bring the clash of unionism versus corporate paternalism to a head. President Woodrow Wilson was a progressive who wanted to move unionization along in America. The huge government contracts for war materials offered a means for the government to get involved. The government war boards were determined to bring employee representation to heavy American industry under President Wilson. President Woodrow Wilson's progressive view led him to create a special agency for handling labor disputes in the war industries in 1918 if union or employee representation was lacking. Wilson's agency was known as the National War Labor Board (NWLB). The National War Labor Board had limited authority, requiring the president to force compliance. The worry was more in their mission as stated. Priority one was to prevent production disruption caused by strikes and lockouts. However, the NWLB stated their principles as: the right of labor to organize, with no action against organizing efforts by the companies; the right of union shops to exist; the right of the worker to a "living wage." The Wilson administration often used these broad principles to award contracts to unionized companies. Even more disturbing was the government's propensity to support union activity and collective bargaining where it did not exist. The NWLB often strong-armed factories whenever possible. Collective bargaining became an unofficial requirement for government orders under the Wilson administration.

American capitalists, and some government administrators such as future President Herbert Hoover, believed a better option was the use of employee councils and representation teams. In 1919, this seemed a popular compromise for the workers and industrialists at companies such as Goodyear Tire and Rubber, Denison Manufacturing, Colorado Fuel & Iron, Firestone, Midvale Steel, Bethlehem Steel, and many others. Employee representation plans offered a bridge between corporate governance and paternal founders. While many of the plans were progressive and innovative, they could not fully resolve the issue of who controls production and wages.

In 1914, the country was shocked by a bloody strike in Colorado known as the Ludlow Massacre. The Ludlow Massacre was an attack by the Colorado National Guard and Colorado Fuel & Iron Company camp guards on a tent colony of 1,200 striking coal miners of the United Mine Workers and their families at Ludlow, Colorado, on April 20, 1914. Some two dozen people, including women and children, were killed. During the battle, four women and eleven children had been hiding in a pit beneath one tent, where they were trapped when the tent above them was set on fire. Two of the women and all of the children suffocated. The deaths of children and even infants made this a low point in American labor history. A monument erected by the UMWA stands today in Ludlow in remembrance of the deaths. The company guards clearly had a role in the burning of the tents housing families. The chief owner of the mine, John D. Rockefeller, Jr., was widely criticized for the incident. The reason for the initial strike was very complex. The stated reasons in the union demands included increased wages, enforcement of the eight-hour day, independent weight inspectors for paying tonnage bonuses, strict adherence to safety laws, and the right of workers to live in non-company boardinghouses and visit non-company doctors.

The Colorado coal mines, like many of the eastern coal mines, were company towns. The miners were forced to use the company stores and boardinghouse, which were run at a profit. During the strike, the striking workers were evicted from their boardinghouses, forcing families into tents. Public outcry forced a Senate investigation of mining company practices. The novel *King Coal* by Upton Sinclair, loosely based on the origin and aftermath of the Ludlow Massacre, further rallied public support. President Woodrow Wilson believed that he should use his executive power to force unionization in heavy industry during the war. Rockefeller, with ties to the steel industry as well, decided to propose his own solution to the breakdown of paternalism and avoid government takeover.

Ultimately, the UMWA failed to win recognition by the mining companies; however, the strike had a lasting impact both on conditions at the Colorado mines and on labor relations nationally. In particular, employee representation plans were implemented in many industries. John D. Rockefeller, Jr., engaged labor relations expert and future Canadian Prime Minister, W.L. Mackenzie King, to help him develop reforms for the mines and towns, which included paved roads and recreational facilities, as well as worker representation on committees dealing with working conditions, employee complaints, safety, health, and recreation. The Rockefeller plan was accepted by the miners in a vote in 1914, and would be widely accepted in the steel and rubber industries as well. Union critics and social reformers saw these plans as little better than company unions. Rockefeller had his critics in industry as well. Elbert Henry Gary, president of United States Steel, opposed the plan as no better than an employee union. Harvey Firestone and Henry Ford also saw the plan as a step toward unionization. National unions also called them "company unions." The representation plans did grow in popularity as an alternative to the prounion push of the government. By 1924, there were 814 employee representation plans covering over one and a half million workers.

Many industrialists, however, embraced the "Rockefeller Plan" as a compromise or alternative to independent unions. Critics called it a company union, but the model became popular in its own right because of the aggressiveness of President Wilson to unionize industry. President Wilson was a strong supporter of collective bargaining and used his war authority to implement it wherever he could by making government contracts dependent on the fair treatment (unionization) of workers. Companies implemented their own form of the Rockefeller plan to avoid government interference.

In the fall of 1918, Midvale Steel and Bethlehem Steel simultaneously adopted the employee representation plan. Both these companies were major arms suppliers. These steel company plans called for employee representation committees to engage in collective bargaining while maintaining the right of the company to set overall policy. In particular, hiring and layoffs for economic reasons were the right of the company. Still, there were no defined limitations to issues that could be considered by the employee bargaining committee. The employee representatives on the plant committee would be elected on the basis of one per 300 employees throughout Midvale Steel. In addition, there would be a company-wide committee of a representative for every 300 employees. Election and employee selection requirements were defined in the plan. A grievance would go first to management and plant committees, although every effort would be made to settle the grievance between the department management and the representative. It could then be appealed to company-wide committee/management. Finally, the last appeal could be to binding arbitration.

The political victories of the Republicans, the end of the war, and President Wilson's priority of a League of Nations ended the National War Labor Board and its meddling. However, the end of the war brought an even more aggressive union organizing effort by workers. The American Federation of Labor's 1918 conference in Pittsburgh had discussed workers' rights. The conference resolution called for collective bargaining, the eight-hour day, double-time pay for overtime, one day's rest in seven, abolition of the twenty-hour-long shift used to rotate the men, seniority-based wages, and the abolition of company unions and employee representation plans.

Goodyear Rubber put together a unique employee representation plan to address unionization. With its dynamic leader, Paul Litchfield, Goodyear had the strongest anti-union forces with its Industrial Assembly from World War I and its flying squadron of loyalists. Paul Litchfield opposed any form of pay by length of service, wanting a merit-based system. Litchfield had developed Goodyear's Technical University to offer advancement for employees. He put together an Industrial Assembly in 1917 as an employee representation organization to slow the unionization movement of the Wilson administration. The Assembly was able to suggest even wages, but the company reserved veto rights. The plan worked well at Goodyear because it remained extremely paternalistic.

In 1919, the unions felt that with government support, they could challenge big industry on a broad basis using the power of national strikes. An American Federation of Labor conference held in Pittsburgh in May 1919 had discussed and approved a fall national strike. The conference resolution called for the same reforms that had been sought by the 1918 conference.

After Labor Day of 1919, the trouble started with the steel companies well prepared. Union organizers could not rent meeting rooms, and local police and private guards seized literature and ran others out of town. The economic downturn gave the companies the upper hand. The union appealed to Wilson and was counting on his support, but Wilson's political power was slipping. Judge Elbert Gary, president of United States Steel, refused to deal with the union. Charles Schwab at Bethlehem and William Corey at Midvale Steel were counting on their employee representation plans to protect them. On September 22, 1919, when Gary refused to negotiate further, a national walkout started. President Wilson would have a stroke on September 26, 1919, which many believe prevented government intervention. Wilson's advisors held back when he became incapacitated, and the fact that Wilson had been rejected in the midterm elections meant public support was not with him. Furthermore, Wilson was looking for steel money and support for his League of Nations, and he needed big business. The union was completely crushed. The failure of the 1919 Steel Strike slowed the union movement for a decade. The 1920s saw the decline of progressivism as the economy boomed. Only the economic downturn of the 1930s rejuvenated the union movement and government support.

The New Deal politicians of the 1930s were pushing for unionization, and the Committee for Industrial Organization of the unions was ready to challenge America's biggest and the highest paying industries. Unionization of the largest industries was about control of the factory floor, not wages. Arbitrary layoffs, however, created bad blood. Workers wanted more say and help in bad times. This 1930s unionization truly was not about money, since the rubber workers and steel workers were the highest paid in America. The barons who had actually doubled the wages in the rubber industry and gave so much to the community would feel betrayed, but this movement was not personal. The workers didn't want more money or even more hospitals; they wanted the control and freedom for their lives that the barons had. The more radical workers saw the community gifts of the barons as part of their feudal system of control. New Deal supporters in the press referred to paternal capitalism as welfare capitalism. The Depression and President Roosevelt's New Deal would end large-scale paternalism and replace it with unionization.

The progressive politicians would open the door to unionization through legislation. The National Labor Relations Act, or Wagner Act, would be the cornerstone of President Franklin D. Roosevelt's New Deal social legislation. It would end decades of struggle in the steel and related heavy industries to unionize employees. This Act changed the very landscape of labor in the United States in hopes of avoiding widespread social unrest during the Great Depression. The Wagner Act would usher in a wave of unionization in the steel, automotive, rubber, mining, and electrical industries. At the start of the 1930s, less than 10 percent of America's labor force was unionized; after the 1935 passage of the Wagner Act, the decade ended with 35 percent of the labor force unionized. The Act declared that democracy must apply in the workplace. Furthermore, the Act declared the means to this democracy was the right of workers to organize and bargain collectively through employee representatives. The Act established the National Labor Relations Board (NLRB) to implement and oversee the Wagner Act. The NLRB had great authority under the Act.

Unionization in America had had a very difficult path over the years prior to the 1935 passage of the Wagner Act. Progressive liberal Democrats had continued the fight, but even Woodrow Wilson's War Labor Boards, with war powers, could not overcome the industrial owners. The Great Depression brought on more social unrest and union activity. New York, in particular, was a hotbed of unions, socialists, and communists. Progressives and conservatives alike feared the influence of European socialists and communists. Many complained of the use of spies, firing union organizers, and blacklisting by the companies. Even enlightened paternalists such as John D. Rockefeller and Charles Schwab realized that somehow employees needed to be brought into wage and work disputes. Many company representation plans had failed by the 1930s and paternal owners were few.

The union movement was fractured, with John Lewis's Committee for Industrial Organization (CIO) fighting with the American Federation of Labor for the representation rights in the steel and automotive industries. The New Deal Democrats and Progressive Republicans thought it was necessary to take a bold step into labor policy. This resulted in the Wagner Act.

Interestingly, the Act does not apply to government workers and supervisors. Federal workers remain today one area where strikes have been restricted. The National Labor Relations Act was, to some degree, an overreaction, and balance would be achieved only after years of debate and amending. The hoped-for effect of the Act, improving the economy by increasing wages, was never achieved. The first major success came in 1937 with the victory of the CIO union over General Motors, followed by the unionization of United States Steel Company.

The heart of the Wagner Act is Section 7: "Employees shall have the right to form, join, or assist labor organizations, to bargain collectively through representatives of their own choosing, and to engage in other concerted activities for the purpose of collective bargaining or other mutual aid and protection." The key was a secret ballot election of the union under the auspices of the National Labor Relations Board. Since the passage of the Wagner Act, there have been over 360,000 secret ballot elections. The NLRB has five members appointed by the president with Senate oversight. Early on, employers and the AFL, which argued CIO unions were favored, questioned the neutrality of the NLRB. Neutrality had proved difficult over the years. Even President Roosevelt was concerned that the Act went too far. Still, companies had also gone too far in restricting employee representation. The National Labor Relations Act, or Wagner Act, would face 20 years of challenges in Congress. Two major amendments would be the Taft-Hartley Act in 1947 and the Landrum-Griffin Act in 1959. The National Labor Relations Board today remains a type of court for employee complaints.

The Wagner Act had many critics, but in the end, the Supreme Court upheld it in 1937 (*NLRB v. Jones & Laughlin Steel*). The argument over individual choice did continue, and President Roosevelt did try to counterbalance some of the extreme activist supporters to expand the intent of the Act. Still, the Act creates a number of issues to this day. One is the terminology of collective bargaining as a "right." Opponents maintain that fair treatment in the workplace is the right, and collective bargaining is but one method to guarantee it. This argument has once again surfaced today with large government unions. Another issue was the so-called closed shop. Once a union was certified by the National Relations Board election, it basically could not be removed. Furthermore, workers would be required to join the union to keep working at the shop. In 1947, the Taft-Hartley Act limited the application of a true closed shop. It allowed "union shop," which is a form of closed shop. However, under the Taft-Hartley Act, states could pass right-to-work laws to make even union shops illegal. Today we see the spread of right-to-work laws in southern and western states. These right-to-work laws have caused a movement of northern factories south. The Taft-Hartley Act also addressed some abuses of unions, such as secondary boycotts and mass picketing. The Wagner Act did unleash a wave of unionization that took over the steel, rubber, and auto industries. By the end of the 1930s, most of America's big industry was union. Still, more was needed to protect workers from unemployment, and this would require direct government involvement.

The 1930s also brought the Social Security Act and other New Deal legislation. The idea of social security found support across political and class lines. Such a safety net was difficult except for the most profitable companies. President Franklin D. Roosevelt, following up on a campaign pledge, formed the Committee on Economic Security in June 1934. This committee solicited opinions from the grassroots using a national town hall format. The committee proposal passed quickly through Congress. On August 14, 1935, President Roosevelt signed the Social Security Act. The concept of social security can be considered far more evolutionary than revolutionary. The earliest roots go back to the English Poor Law of 1601, which established a legal basis for the responsibility of the state to provide for the welfare of its citizens. The fear of disability and income loss had been addressed by Robert Owen in his communal manufacturing villages. Owen had kept people working even in business declines, but with great difficulty. In colonial America, Scotch-Irish communities taxed citizens for the establishment of poorhouses. In addition, many American fraternal organizations such as the Odd Fellows, Elks, Eagles, and Moose took on the role of helping the less fortunate in society, as did churches. The first federal program in the area of social security was Civil War pensions. In 1862, legislation created pensions for disabled soldiers. By 1890, this was expanded to disabilities of soldiers after their service to be eligible for pension. By 1906, old age of Civil War veterans was enough to qualify for a pension. In Germany in the 1800s, some social security laws were passed.

The severity of the Depression made the Social Security Act very popular at the time. It was designed as social insurance to protect the elderly, not a retirement plan. The plan was to buy insurance through equal employer and employee payroll taxes. In 1937, the payroll taxes were one percent for the employer and one percent for the employee. Payroll deductions were mandated under the Federal Insurance Contribution Act (FICA). Amendments to the Act in 1939 increased family protection to include help for wives and dependent children. The first benefit payment was not paid until 1940. Amendments in 1954 added domestic workers to the base of employees covered. In 1956, the Social Security payroll tax was increased to two percent for employer and two percent for employee. In 1965, an amendment added Medicare and Medicaid under President Lyndon Johnson's "Great Society" program. In 1972, an amendment added cost-of-living adjustments to Social Security benefits.

The real problem facing the worker and his family was not wages or working conditions, but recessions. The recession of 1907–1908 caused a 21 percent cut in the workforce and a 10 percent to 30 percent cut in wage rates. Those lucky enough to stay working were on the job an average of 2 days a week instead of 6 or 7 days. The 1930s brought unemployment rates of 30 percent or more, and most of those working were part time. These downturns created havoc in families and budget. Unemployment insurance was also established by the Social Security Act of 1935. Wage-earners who were laid off or otherwise involuntarily became unemployed (for reasons other than misconduct) would receive a partial replacement of their pay for specified periods. Each state operates its own program. The amount and duration of the weekly unemployment benefits are based on a worker's prior wages and length of employment. Employers pay taxes into a special fund based on the unemployment and benefits-payment experience of their own workforce. The federal government also assesses an unemployment insurance tax of its own on employers. States hope that surplus funds built up during prosperous times can carry them through economic downturns; but they can borrow from the federal government or boost tax rates if their funds run low. States must lengthen the duration of benefits when unemployment rises and remains above a set "trigger" level. The federal government may also permit a further extension of the benefits payment period when unemployment climbs during a recession, paying for the extension out of general federal revenues or levying a special tax on employers.

For the old lions of paternalism, the formation of unions and the New Deal was a slap in the face. They felt rejected by the very men they had helped so much. The more enlightened owners realized that their companies had grown too big for true paternalism. Unemployment insurance and Social Security were hailed by many as a safety net and would soon become part of the fabric of American industrialization.

Nineteen

Visions Come True

The 1940s and 1950s would represent the embodiment of Robert Owen's vision of a worker utopia in America. American industrial workers had the highest standard of living in the world. Steelworkers, rubber workers, glass workers, auto workers, and others now vacationed in Florida and on East Coast beaches. Such vacations had been limited to the capitalists for decades. These workers had the best health and retirement benefits ever seen in the world. Postwar employment was at all-time highs. Many workers now fell under a type of national paternalism. All this had been achieved with cooperation between management, workers, unions, and government. There were, of course, many challenges left to bring more Americans into this worker prosperity. Still, any kid of the 1950s saw America as the world's greatest country.

In the 1950s, the typical manufacturing family had three children and lived in good but modest homes, often in the new suburbs of the period. These were one-income families in most cases. Mothers stayed home except during the occasional strike when they often found employment in retailing. The year to workers and their families was marked with great holidays and celebrations such as Easter, Christmas, Halloween, graduations, first Communions, Memorial Day, the Fourth of July, and the summer trip to the Jersey shore. There was also the once-in-a-lifetime trip to Florida or Disneyland. Kids flooded to baseball games as their fathers worked in the mills and factories. Amusement parks were common for local entertainment. Community and grandparents played a key role in the lives of these kids as their fathers worked long hours in the factories to earn the high wages. There were weekend trips to the great museums, science centers, and libraries endowed by the earlier paternal capitalists. Finally, the workers and their families could appreciate these gifts.

No child of factory workers in the 1950s dreamed of a better world. They had the new toy products coming on to the market weekly. Christmas was special as the kids visited the city's major department store to find a full floor dedicated to toys. These toys included chemistry sets, Erector Sets, and trains, reflecting American industry. Vacation trips to destinations nationwide were made possible by extended five-week vacation benefits for members of industrial unions. Workers' kids could now afford college, and company scholarships were abundant. Communism was universally feared and denounced. Socialism was considered a gateway political system to communism. Most workers were conservatives but voted Democratic. Both parties were somewhat conservative, and at least on American nationalism, could find agreement. The unions and management had their differences, but it was not framed in the class struggles of Europe. Imports were novelties.

The paternalistic alliance of industry, workers, and government had been held together by national capitalism. Since the Civil War, the Republican protective tariffs and national capitalism had made American plants highly profitable. In 1950, American automakers controlled almost 80 percent of the world market. At its 1950s peak, the American steel industry made over 60 percent of the world's steel. American steelworkers were earning $2.92 an hour compared to 75 cents an hour in Germany and 45 cents an hour in Japan. The workers also had full retirement and health benefits. Over 40 percent of the world's tires were made in Akron, Ohio. The American highway system was the world's greatest.

The Federal-Aid Highway Act of 1956 would supply the federal funds for over 42,000 miles of highway. The Act appropriated $25 billion over 12 years for the entire system. It would actually cost $114 billion over 35 years, fueling massive employment. The money for the system came from an established Highway Trust Fund, to be paid for by taxes on gasoline and diesel fuel. The federal government paid for 90 percent of the system, with the balance being paid for by the states. The system made profound changes in American business and life, such as long-distance truck hauling overtaking the railroads, the growth of suburbs, the rise of mega vacation sites, and travel-related options such as motels, station wagons, fast food, and campgrounds.

The workplace had evolved toward the original vision of Owen as well. American management had found a balance of scientific management and paternalistic workplace practices. The approach of American management had become humanistic. In 1946, psychologist Abraham Maslow completed a series of articles on worker motivation. The most famous of the series was "A Theory of Human Motivation" in the *Psychological Review*. The theory would have a latent effect on the science of management, slowly building into a core part of business analysis by the late 1960s. The new field of humanistic psychology approach was considered revolutionary and an alternative to behavioral motivation. Maslow's theory became known as "humanistic psychology." His theory was based on a hierarchy of needs, which were satisfied in the order of human importance. There were five tiers of needs from the bottom up: physiological, safety and security, love and belonging, esteem, and self-actualization. Using Maslow's hierarchy of needs, managers could design better motivational programs, incentive plans, and improve workplace productivity. The theory would truly help the field of industrial psychology advance to the utopian treatment proposed by Robert Owen, and later George Westinghouse.

The decline of employee-driven approaches to pure productivity came with the loss of profitability. American industry had, for over a hundred years, functioned in the protected world of national capitalism. Internationalism and globalization would change all this, putting American workers in competition with subsistence workers in third-world nations.

Twenty

And the Wolf Finally Came— Deindustrialization and Globalization

---

Robert Owen had viewed paternalism and profitability as symbiotic. America's prosperity was based on this relationship prior to World War II. The government had, with a hundred years of protectionism and national capitalism, generated amazing prosperity and profits for industry. The taxes on those profits created the world's best safety net of benefits. Unions had reaped the benefits of this prosperity as well, with generous contracts improving wages and benefits. Globalization and internationalism would put all in competition with the world's lowest paid workers. The government did it for the idealistic goal of world peace, but it would change the American factory floor negatively. It would end paternalistic approaches.

The roots of American globalization go back to April of 1947 in Switzerland. The exact location was Mont Pelerin overlooking Lake Geneva. The meeting was assembled by free-market economist Friedrich von Hayek at the luxurious Hotel du Parc. Of the 36 free-market economists, there were only two reluctant Americans present. The group was committed to the belief that economics was the key to world peace. The majority of participants were Austrian economists interested in starting an international counterrevolution on the level of that of Karl Marx. One plank of their six guiding principles was the "creation of an international order conducive to the safeguarding of peace and liberty and permitting the establishment of harmonious international economic relations."[1]

214

The Mont Pelerin economists were activists looking at economics as a way to change social behavior. They would discuss, for hours, the reasons for the growth of National Socialism in Germany as well as the problems of national capitalism. While they lamented the rise of communism after World War II, they feared more the return of a German-type national socialism. They saw nationalism in any form as a challenge to world peace. They believed free-market economics was the foundation of international peace and saw capitalism as international. Free trade would turn out to be closer to international socialism, redistributing wealth around the world. America would have to pay for this world peace.

The General Agreement on Tariffs and Trade (GATT) was implemented by the western nations after World War II to regulate trade and assure the world economic recovery and peace. Still, no one believed that free trade practices would come fully to the United States; but in less than 30 years, the Mont Pelerin Society dominated American thought. An unintended consequence was the death of costly paternalistic practices. No one in 1947 would have envisioned the future scale of American deindustrialization or the change in the American workplace. The year 1947 in America was highlighted by the consumer demand outstripping supply. America was looking at ways to increase imports to help meet demand. Industrial and labor cities dominated America's top cities in population rankings. Detroit was #5, followed by Pittsburgh (#7), St. Louis (#8), Cleveland (#9), Buffalo (#14), and Cincinnati (#18). These cities had been built on over 100 years of American protectionism. The Mont Pelerin Society would invade traditional economics, creating a beachhead with their view on free trade in late 1947, and would dominate industrial policy by 1980. National capitalists and protectionists sat at the same university lunch tables as creationists by 1980. The only free trade occurred between states such as Michigan and Ohio. The government told industry it had to become competitive with low-price world labor. Workers and their benefits were merely a cost stream to the company.

But even the politicians, who originally accepted this move to "free" trade, knew that it would cause unemployment. The Kennedy administration was first to embrace the use of trade as a peace strategy. However, John F. Kennedy realized that free trade, as envisioned by the Mont Pelerin Society, would cost a lot of American jobs in the long run. The Kennedy administration passed the Trade Adjustment Assistance Act in 1962 as part of a total free-trade package. The bill got little press in a nation that had few imports other than nickel and dime toys; in 1962, prosperity and lack of imports made free trade of little interest to American workers at the time. Free trade at the time seemed a necessity as exports poured out of America in an embarrassment of riches. Even the unions in 1962 supported free trade because international trade was a big source of American jobs.

As Japan and Europe rebuilt, things would soon change. The Trade Adjustment Assistance Act in 1962 called for payments to be made as additions to unemployment compensation. It wasn't until 1974 that any real need surfaced for the Act. Then the program was expanded under the Trade Act of 1974. The program never covered workers' losses to their communities. Kennedy's words in 1962 would ring hollow but true: "When considerations of national policy make it desirable to avoid higher tariffs, those injured by that competition should not be required to bear the full brunt of the impact. Rather, the burden of economic adjustment should be borne in part by the Federal Government."[2]

Free trade would be the core of deindustrialization and decades of welfare benefits to displaced workers. Unemployment benefits were extended by industry. The government poured money into retraining programs for displaced workers. Academics even called it creative destruction as a natural part of the shift from manual to mental work. Blame was passed around to unions, management, banks, Wall Street, one political party or the other, and, of course, imports. Political solutions went to the symptoms. Huge amounts of federal money were injected into retraining. Companies were pictured as cold as they tried to survive.

Politicians, who once stood at the gates of big industry on election days, could no longer be found. The industrial unions no longer had the votes or money. Unions violated their founder Samuel Gompers's principle of one-party support. By the 2000s, workers lacked the support of politicians, unions, government and management. The truth was, as Robert Owen had pointed 200 years earlier, paternalism and worker-driven programs required profitability. Even the government without corporate profitability lacks the tax money to sustain welfare programs.

Paternalism died as American industry became uncompetitive in wages, forcing a coldness in employee relationships. By the 1980s, heavy American industry had imploded. Regional devastation was deep as the industries of major cities collapsed, as did the benefit-dependent services of dentist offices and optometrists. Real estate prices crashed, as did small businesses dependent on the local economies; but as an aggregate, the American economy absorbed the setbacks in the 1980s and 1990s. As with the collapse of guild weavers in the 1700s, labor tried to adjust. The single-family wage earner disappeared, as families required two smaller incomes to maintain their standard of living. Decades of government retraining programs supplied few well-paid jobs but kept workers busy. Politicians argued small businesses were the real drivers of employment, forgetting that big business was the driver behind the creation of small business. Steel, rubber, and glass companies tried to adjust with early buyouts to force retirements, so plants could be downsized. Companies started to merge to reduce costs and other industries sold out to foreign companies. In all cases, wages and benefits were reduced. World competition pushed harder as the American heavy industries were forced into bankruptcies with the burden of huge pensions.

The days of full pensions and fully paid benefits disappeared. Industrial union membership declined. Divided political parties prevented a political solution. Bankruptcies ended generous union contracts. Workers, as in the days of the collapse of guilds and feudal systems, had to adjust their lives. Former giants of American industries faltered. Companies like General Motors had to sell assets, close plants, and restructure. GM's bond ratings declined, making it more difficult to raise cash. Its 650,000 retirees continued to be a problem, while companies like Toyota and Honda had few legacy costs such as retirement and health benefits. Regardless, Toyota and Honda opened American non-union plants with lower wages and minimal employee benefits. Workers' loyalty in union shops disappeared. America was now experiencing what Europe had in the 1700s. Once highly paid workers went to welfare or took low-skilled jobs.

While economics was the major cause of the death of paternalism, there were other factors. The passing of paternal capitalism took away the American workers' most prized benefit of the old system: opportunity. The ability to work your way up from the factory floor disappeared. The closing of that ladder widened the gap between worker and manager. The worker did gain protection with the union but at the cost of wider opportunity. Now managers would be trained in business colleges versus the factory floor. Paternalism would not be forgotten but would become more of an enlightened approach of college.

Paternalism had changed by the 1960s. The new managers of the 1960s were university trained and mobile. Community mattered little in their business decisions. They saw the need for efficiency and productivity in global competition. What they didn't see was the role of the worker or community in that effort. Accounting, robotics, and productivity goals were all that was needed. The lack of heart and even passion was reflected in the low motivation of the workers.

The story of Tom Coyne personalizes the passage of paternal capitalism and the collapse of the great paternal companies of their founders such as Harvey Firestone. Tom Coyne was an operations manager who had worked under Harvey Firestone and set production records; he loved and admired Harvey Firestone. Having worked his way up to management had been the proudest part of his life. He was a "gum-dipped loyalist." He had worked his way up from the factory floor and had been promoted for his drive and loyalty in the 1930s, 1940s, and 1950s. He knew Harvey Firestone personally, and if he had a problem, he could talk directly to him. He and his family lived in Firestone Park, a community for company managers. He had a membership in the country club. He was proud to live in the "Rubber City."

By the 1960s, with the old lions such as Harvey Firestone gone, rubber managers had to have college degrees. The 1960s became an era of depersonalization for American industry. Tom Coyne was a middle manager who had risen through the ranks. Maybe that change in management is best exemplified by Joyce (Coyne) Dyer's description of her father's demotion at Firestone by the human resources department manager: "One day in 1962, my dad was told that because he had only a high-school diploma, he was going to be demoted.... He was not promotable without a college degree. His salary would necessarily also be reduced, you certainly will understand, Tom."[3] It would be a crushing blow to a hard-working company loyalist so proud of his ascent. Tom would never bring himself to tell his family of the demotion. It would be many years and after his death that the family knew the whole truth. Tom Coyne, always proud, ended his career at Firestone as a janitor. Tom remained loyal to the memory of the old company but was crushed by the new.[4] This was the story of millions of American workers by the 2000s.

Deindustrialization and globalization had not only taken the heart out of paternalism, but taken the heart out of a nation. Globalization had divided the nation as in the Civil War. Capitalism, on an international level, may be efficient for profitability, but it has coldness. It reduces wages and destroys the American middle class. It redistributes wealth to the poorer nations, but with great pain to all workers. It also makes an international class of the super wealthy. International capitalism is part socialism and greed. America today awaits an industrial Joan of Arc to return it to the greatness of paternal capitalism.

Chapter Notes

Introduction

1. Paul Litchfield, *Industrial Voyage* (New York: Doubleday, 1954), 252.

2. John White, "Andrew Carnegie and Herbert Spencer: A Special Relationship," *Journal of American Studies* 13, No. 1 (1979): 70.

3. Paul Boyer, ed., *The Oxford Guide to United States History* (New York: Oxford University Press, 2001), 591.

4. Quentin Skrabec, *William McGuffey: Mentor to American Industry* (New York: Algora, 2008), 49.

Chapter One

1. John Winthrop, "A Model of Christian Charity," reprinted in Allan Heimert and Albert Delbanco, editors, *The Puritan in America: A Narrative Anthology* (Cambridge: Harvard University Press, 1985), 91.

2. Lawrence Friedman and Mark McGarvie, *Charity, Philanthropy, and Civility in American History* (New York: Cambridge University Press, 2002), 51.

3. William Bradford, *Of Plymouth Plantation* (New York: Knopf, 2002), 24.

4. Bradford, 93.

5. Friedman and McGarvie, 383.

6. Skrabec, *McGuffey*, 67.

Chapter Two

1. Chessman Herrick, *White Servitude in Pennsylvania: Indentured and Redemp-tion Labor* (New York: University Press, 1969), 28.

2. Henry Dubbs and Henry Stiegel, "Baron Stiegel," *Pennsylvania Magazine of History* 1, No. 1 (1877): 68–69.

3. Howard Harris, ed., *Keystone of Democracy: A History of Pennsylvania Workers* (Harrisburg: Pennsylvania Historical and Museum Commission, 1999), 25.

4. Solon J. Buck and Elizabeth Buck, *The Planting of Civilization in Western Pennsylvania* (Pittsburgh: University of Pittsburgh Press, 1967), 35.

5. Richard Wade, *The Urban Frontier* (Urbana: University of Illinois Press, 1996), 45.

6. Daniel Wren, *History of Management Thought* (New York: John Wiley & Sons, 2005), 106.

7. Joseph Rishel, *Founding Families of Pittsburgh* (Pittsburgh: University of Pittsburgh, 1990), 1–39.

8. Wade, 46.

9. Joseph Ellis, *After the Revolution* (New York: W.W. Norton, 1979), 50–123.

Chapter Three

1. John Barry, *Roger Williams and the Creation of the American Soul* (New York: Penguin Books, 2012), 85.

2. Norman Murray, *The Scottish Hand Loom Weavers, 1790–1850: A Social History* (Edinburgh: John Donald Publishers, 1978), 23.

219

3. Sean Wilentz, *Chants Democratic: New York City and the Rise of the American Working Class 1788–1850* (New York: Oxford University Press, 2004), 62–63.

4. Wilentz, 32–33.

5. Ellen Vincent McClelland, *Duncan Phyfe and English Regency* (New York: William Scott, 1939), 91–130.

6. Harris, 46.

7. Robert Owen, *The Life of Robert Owen* (London: Effingham Wilson, 1857; reissued by Augustus M. Kelley, 1967), 261.

8. Harwood Merrill, ed., *Classics in Management* (New York: American Management Association, 1960), 23.

9. Robert Owen (editor Gregory Claeys), *New View of Society and Other Writings* (New York: Penguin, 1991), 16.

10. Robert Owen, *New View of Society* (New York: E. Bliss and E. White, 1825), 62.

11. Owen (ed. Claeys), 8.

12. B.L. Hutchins, *Robert Owen: Social Reformer* (London: The Fabian Society, 1912), 6–13.

13 Hutchins, 20.

14. Erick Roll, *An Early Experiment in Industrial Organization: Being a History of the Firm of Boulton and Watts* (London: Longmans, Green & Co., 1930), 226.

15. Mark Holloway, *Heavens on Earth: Utopian Communities in America* (New York: Dover, 1966), 101–116.

16. *Zoar: An Experiment in Communalism* (Columbus: The Ohio Historical Society, 1967), 20–44.

Chapter Four

1. Robert Remini, *Henry Clay: Statesman of the Union* (New York: W.W. Norton, 1991), 230.

2. Allan MacDonald, "Lowell: A Commercial Utopia," *New England Quarterly* 10 (1937): 37–62.

3. John F. Kasson, *Civilizing The Machine: Technology and Republican Values in America, 1776–1900* (New York: Grossman, 1976), 67.

4. Charles Dickens, *American Notes* (London: Chapman and Hall, 1850), 40–50.

5. Stephen Yafa, *Cotton: The Biography of a Revolutionary Fiber* (New York: Penguin, 2006), 103.

6. Yafa, 96.

7. Massachusetts House Document No. 50, March 1845.

8. Mary Beaudry, "The Lowell Boot Mills Complex and its Housing: Material Expressions of Corporate Ideology," *Historical Archaeology* 23, No. 1 (1989): 19–30.

9. Anthony Wallace, *Rockdale: The Growth of an American Village in the Early Industrial Revolution* (Lincoln: University of Nebraska Press, 1972), 290–340.

10. John Hamer, "Money and Moral Order in Late Nineteenth and Early Twentieth-Century American Capitalism," *Anthropological Quarterly* 71, No. 3 (July 1998): 139.

11. Wallace, 387–388.

Chapter Five

1. Calvin Colton, *The Rights of Labor* (New York: A.S. Barnes, 1847), 6–8.

2. Bernard Mandel, *Labor, Free and Slave: Workingmen and the Anti-Slavery Movement in the United States* (Urbana: University of Illinois Press, 2007), 60–70.

3. Quentin Skrabec, *The 100 Most Significant Events in American Business: An Encyclopedia* (Santa Barbara: Greenwood, 2013), pp 23–24.

4. Quentin Skrabec, *A Genealogy of Greatness: The Ethnic Shaping of Industrial America* (New York: World Audience, 2008), 64–100.

5. "Bottle Machine as an International Landmark," The American Society of Mechanical Engineers, May 17, 1983.

Chapter Six

1. C. Summer Spalding, *Peter Cooper: A Critical Bibliography of his Life and Works* (New York: The New York Public Library, 1941), 1.

2. Rossiter Raymond, *Peter Cooper* (New York: Houghton Mifflin, 1901), 10–14.

3. Lester, 35.

4. Miriam Gurko, *The Life and Times of Peter Cooper* (New York: Thomas Y. Crowell, 1959), 177.

5. Lester, 37.

6. Nathan Walker, *Peter Cooper* (Scituate, MA: Unitarian Universalist Association, 2005), 1–3.

7. Gurko, 235.

8. Edward C. Mack, *Peter Cooper: Cit-*

izen of New York (New York: Duel, Sloan, and Pearce, 1949), xiv.

9. Mack, 337.

10. Scott Molloy, *Irish Titan, Irish Toilers* (Lebanon: University of New Hampshire Press, 2008), 93–96.

11. Molloy, 145–154.

Chapter Seven

1. Thorstein Veblen, *The Theory of the Leisure Class: An Economic Study of Institutions* (New York: Macmillan, 1899), 12–200.

2. Thomas DiLorenzo, *How Capitalism Saved America* (New York: Three River Press, 2003), 123–124.

3. H.W. Brands, *American Colossus: The Triumph of Capitalism, 1865–1900* (New York: Anchor, 2010), 20–102.

Chapter Eight

1. Joseph H. Appel, *The Business Biography of John Wanamaker: Founder and Builder* (New York: AMS Press, 1930), 59.

2. John Wanamaker, "The John Wanamaker Commercial Institute—A Store School," *Annals of the American Academy of Political and Social Science* 33, No. 1 (1909): 151–154.

3. Herbert Adams Gibbons, *John Wanamaker* (Port Washington, WI: Kennikat Press, 1971), 287.

4. Roger Fischer, "Holy John" Wanamaker: Color Cartoon Centerfold, *Pennsylvania Magazine of History and Biography* 115, No. 4 (October 1991): 451–473.

5. Hamer, 141.

6. Skrabec, *100 Most Significant Events*, 131.

7. Peter Krass, ed., *The Book of Business Wisdom* (New York: John Wiley & Sons, 1997), 19.

8. Quentin R. Skrabec, *H.J. Heinz* (Jefferson, NC: McFarland & Co., 2009), 201–220.

9. June 6, 1915, dedication of the Sarah Heinz House, Senator John Heinz Historical Center, Heinz Papers.

Chapter Nine

1. White, 58.

2. E.C. Kirkland, ed., *Andrew Carnegie:*
The Gospel of Wealth and Other Essays (Cambridge: Oxford Press, 1962), 26–27.

3. Andrew Carnegie, *Triumphant Democracy* (New York: Private, 1886), 32.

4. Gerald Eggert, *Steelmasters and Labor Reform 1886–1923* (Pittsburgh: University of Pittsburgh Press, 1981), 13.

5. Andrew Carnegie, *Gospel of Wealth* (New York: Private, 1901), 15.

6. John Conway, "America's Workmen," *The Catholic World* 56 (January 1893).

7. Abigail Van Slyck, *Free for All: Carnegie Libraries and American Culture* (Chicago: University of Chicago Press, 1995), 21.

8. Ibid., 21.

Chapter Ten

1. Liston Leyendecker, *The Palace Car Prince* (Niwot: University Press of Colorado, 1992), 113.

2. Anthony Arthur and John Broesamle, *Twelve Great Clashes that Shaped Modern America* (New York: Person, 2006), 32.

3. Arthur Pound and Samuel Moore, eds., *They Told Barron: The Notes of Clarence W. Barron* (New York: Harper & Brothers, 1930), 32.

4. W. Ashworth, "British Industrial Villages in the Nineteenth Century," *Economic History Review* 3, No. 3 (1951): 378.

5. Pound and Samuel, 33.

6. Pound and Samuel, 33.

7. "Interview with George Pullman," *New York World*, December 23, 1892.

8. Leyendecker, 165.

9. Leyendecker, 164.

10. Jane Eva Baker, "The Paradox of a Capitalist Utopia: Visionary Ideals and Lived Experience in the Pullman Community," *International Journal of Historical Archaeology* 16 (2012): 655.

11. Lane S. Hart, *Annual Report of the Secretary of Internal Affairs* (Harrisburg: State of Pennsylvania, 1884), 337–338.

12. Pound and Samuel, 272.

13. Baker, 663.

Chapter Eleven

1. *Westminster Larger Catechism*, Presbyterian Church in the U.S., 1861, Question 141.

2. *The Search for Safety* (Pittsburgh: Union Switch and Signal Division of American Standard, 1981).

Chapter Twelve

1. Francis Leupp, *George Westinghouse: His Life and Achievements* (Boston: Little, Brown and Company, 1918), 102–8.
2. Harris, 129.
3. Leupp, 28–90.
4. Westinghouse Electric and Manufacturing Company, Annual Report, May 18, 1892.
5. Nikola Tesla, "Tribute to George Westinghouse," *Electrical World & Engineer* (March 21, 1914).
6. Leupp, 28–90.

Chapter Thirteen

1. Patricia Beard, *After the Ball* (New York: Perennial, 2003), 5.
2. "The End of the Electric Patent War," *Scientific American* (March 21, 1896).
3. Letter, George Westinghouse to Thomas Edison, June 7, 1888, Edison Paper Archives, Rutgers University.
4. R. Conot, *Streak of Luck: The Life Story of Edison* (New York: Bantam, 1980), 283.
5. Pound and Moore, 80–88.
6. Greater Pittsburgh Chamber of Commerce Report, printed by Robert Forsythe Company, 1928.
7. Leupp, 248.

Chapter Fourteen

1. I.E. Levine, *Inventive Wizard: George Westinghouse* (New York: Julian Messner, 1962), 134.
2. "Building Intelligence," *Manufacturer and Builder* (May 1887).

3. *Wilmerding News*, November 23, 1904.

Chapter Fifteen

1. *Wilmerding News*, November 23, 1904.
2. Michael D'Antonio, *Hershey* (New York: Simon & Schuster, 2006), 182.

Chapter Sixteen

1. William McKinley, "The Value of Protection," *The North American Review* 150, No. 403 (June 1890): 747–48.
2. Ibid.
3. Albert Rees, *Real Wages in Manufacturing, 1890–1914* (Princeton University Press, 1961).

Chapter Seventeen

1. Elton Mayo, *The Human Problems of an Industrial Civilization* (New York: Macmillan, 1933), 1–106.
2. Oliver Sheldon, *The Philosophy of Management* (London: Pitman & Sons, 1923), 2.
3. Sheldon, 285.
4. Sheldon, 102–200.
5. Sheldon, 169–170.
6. Sheldon, 173.

Chapter Twenty

1. Mont Pelerin Society, "Statement of Aims," April 6, 1947.
2. Papers of John F. Kennedy 1963, Public Papers of the Presidents of the United States (Washington: Government Printing Office).
3. Joyce Dyer, *Gum-Dipped: A Daughter Remembers Rubber Town* (Akron: University of Akron Press, 2003), 125.
4. Dyer, 25–100.

Bibliography

Adams, G. *The Age of Industrial Violence, 1910–1915: The Activities and Findings of the U.S. Commission on Industrial Relations.* New York: Columbia University Press, 1966.

Appel, Joseph. *The Business Biography of John Wanamaker: Founder and Builder.* New York: AMS Press, 1930.

Arthur, Anthony, and John Broesamle. *Twelve Great Clashes that Shaped Modern America.* New York: Person, 2006.

Ashworth, W. "British Industrial Villages in the Nineteenth Century." *Economic History Review* 3, No. 3 (1951): 378–387.

Baker, Jane Eva. "The Paradox of a Capitalist Utopia: Visionary Ideals and Lived Experience in the Pullman Community." *International Journal of Historical Archaeology* 16 (2012).

Barry, John. *Roger Williams and the Creation of the American Soul.* New York: Penguin Books, 2012.

Beard, Patricia. *After the Ball.* New York: Perennial, 2003.

Beaudry, Mary. "The Lowell Boot Mills Complex and Its Housing: Material Expressions of Corporate Ideology." *Historical Archaeology* 23, No. 1 (1989).

Boyer, Paul, ed. *The Oxford Guide to United States History.* New York: Oxford University Press, 2001.

Bradford, William. *Of Plymouth Plantation.* New York: Knopf, 2002.

Brands, H.W. *American Colossus: The Triumph of Capitalism, 1865–1900.* New York: Anchor, 2010.

Buck, Solon J., and Elizabeth Buck. *The Planting of Civilization in Western Pennsylvania.* Pittsburgh: University of Pittsburgh Press, 1967.

Butler, H.G. *Industrial Relations in the U.S.* Geneva: International Labor Office, 1927.

Carnegie, Andrew. *Gospel of Wealth.* New York: Private, 1901.

_____. *Triumphant Democracy.* New York: Private, 1886.

Colton, Calvin. *The Rights of Labor.* New York: A.S. Barnes, 1847.

Conot, R. *Streak of Luck: The Life Story of Edison.* New York: Bantam Books, 1980.

Conway, John. "America's Workmen." *The Catholic World* 56 (January 1893).

D'Antonio, Michael. *Hershey.* New York: Simon and Schuster, 2006.

Dickens, Charles. *American Notes.* London: Chapman and Hall, 1850.

DiLorenzo, Thomas. *How Capitalism Saved America.* New York: Three River Press, 2003.

Dubbs, Henry, and Henry Stiegel. "Baron Stiegel." *Pennsylvania Magazine of History* 1, No. 1 (1877): 68–69.

Dyer, Joyce. *Gum-Dipped: A Daughter Remembers Rubber Town.* Akron: University of Akron Press, 2003.

Edsforth, Ronald. *The New Deal: America's Response to the Great Depression.* London: Blackwell, 2000.

Eggert, Gerald. *Steelmasters and Labor Reform 1886–1923*. Pittsburgh: University of Pittsburgh Press, 1981.

Ellis, Joseph. *After the Revolution*. New York: W.W. Norton, 1979.

Fischer, Roger. "Holy John" Wanamaker: Color Cartoon Centerfold. *Pennsylvania Magazine of History and Biography* 115, No. 4 (October 1991): 451–473.

Friedman, Lawrence, and Mark McGarvie. *Charity, Philanthropy, and Civility in American History*. New York: Cambridge University Press, 2002.

Gibbons, Herbert Adams. *John Wanamaker*. Port Washington, WI: Kennikat Press, 1971.

Gurko, Miriam. *The Life and Times of Peter Cooper*. New York: Thomas Y. Crowell, 1959.

Hamer, John. "Money and Moral Order in Late Nineteenth and Early Twentieth-Century American Capitalism." *Anthropological Quarterly* 71, No. 3 (July 1998).

Harris, Howard, ed. *Keystone of Democracy: A History of Pennsylvania Workers*. Harrisburg: Pennsylvania Historical and Museum Commission, 1999.

Herrick, Chessman. *White Servitude in Pennsylvania: Indentured and Redemption Labor*. New York: University Press, 1969.

Holloway, Mark. *Heavens on Earth: Utopian Communities in America*. New York: Dover, 1966.

Hutchins, B.L. *Robert Owen: Social Reformer*. London: The Fabian Society, 1912.

Kasson, John. *Civilizing The Machine: Technology and Republican Values in America, 1776–1900*. New York: Grossman, 1976.

Kirkland, E.C., ed. *Andrew Carnegie: The Gospel of Wealth and Other Essays*. Cambridge: Oxford Press, 1962.

Krass, Peter, ed. *The Book of Business Wisdom*. New York: John Wiley & Sons, 1997.

Lester, C. Edward. *The Life and Character of Peter Cooper*. New York: John Alden, 1883.

Leupp, Francis. *George Westinghouse: His Life and Achievements*. Boston: Little, Brown and Company, 1918.

Levine, I.E. *Inventive Wizard: George Westinghouse*. New York: Julian Messner, 1962.

Leyendecker, Liston. *The Palace Car Prince*. Niwot: University Press of Colorado, 1992.

Litchfield, Paul. *Industrial Voyage*. New York: Doubleday, 1954.

MacDonald, Allan. "Lowell: A Commercial Utopia." *New England Quarterly* 10 (1937).

Mack, Edward. *Peter Cooper: Citizen of New York*. New York: Duel, Sloan, and Pearce, 1949.

Mandel, Bernard. *Labor, Free and Slave: Workingmen and the Anti-Slavery Movement in the United States*. Urbana: University of Illinois Press, 2007.

Mayo, Elton. *The Human Problems of an Industrial Civilization*. New York: Macmillan, 1933.

McClelland, Ellen. *Duncan Phyfe and English Regency*, New York: William Scott, 1939.

Merrill, Harwood, ed. *Classics in Management*. New York: American Management Association, 1960.

Molloy, Scott. *Irish Titan, Irish Toilers*. Lebanon: University of New Hampshire Press, 2008.

Murray, Norman. *The Scottish Hand Loom Weavers, 1790–1850: A Social History*. Edinburgh: John Donald Publishers, 1978.

Owen, Robert. *The Life of Robert Owen*. London: Effingham Wilson, 1857; reissued by Augustus M. Kelley, 1967.

_____. *New View of Society*. New York: E. Bliss and E. White, 1825.

_____. *New View of Society and Other Writings*. Gregory Claeys, ed. New York: Penguin, 1991.

Pound, Arthur, and Samuel Moore, eds. *They Told Barron: The Notes of Clarence W. Barron*. New York: Harper & Brothers, 1930.

Raymond, Rossiter. *Peter Cooper*. New York: Houghton Mifflin, 1901.

Rees, Albert. *Real Wages in Manufacturing, 1890–1914*. Princeton: Princeton University Press, 1961.

Remini, Robert. *Henry Clay: Statesman of the Union*. New York: W.W. Norton, 1991.

Rishel, Joseph. *Founding Families of Pittsburgh*. Pittsburgh: University of Pittsburgh, 1990.

Roll, Erick. *An Early Experiment in Industrial Organization: Being a History of* the Firm of Boulton and Watts. London: Longmans, Green & Co., 1930.

Roth, L. "Company Towns in the Western United States." In *The Company Town: Architecture and Society in the Early Industrial Age*, edited by John S. Garner. New York: Oxford University Press, 1992.

Sheldon, Oliver. *The Philosophy of Management*. London: Pitman & Sons, 1923.

Skrabec, Quentin. *A Genealogy of Greatness: The Ethnic Shaping of Industrial America*. New York: World Audience, 2008.

_____. *H.J. Heinz*. Jefferson, NC: McFarland & Co., 2009.

_____. *A Manufacturing Manifesto*. West Conshohocken: Infinity, 2009.

_____. *The 100 Most Significant Events in American Business: : An Encyclopedia*. Santa Barbara: Greenwood, 2013.

_____. *William McGuffey: Mentor to American Industry*. New York: Algora, 2008.

Spalding, C. Summer. *Peter Cooper: A Critical Bibliography of his Life and Works*. New York: The New York Public Library, 1941.

Van Slyck, Abigail. *Free for All: Carnegie Libraries and American Culture*. Chicago: University of Chicago Press, 1995.

Veblen, Thorstein. *The Theory of the Leisure Class: An Economic Study of Institutions*. New York: Macmillan, 1899.

Wade, Richard. *The Urban Frontier*. Urbana: University of Illinois Press, 1996.

Walker, Nathan. *Peter Cooper*. Scituate, MA: Unitarian Universalist Association, 2005.

Wallace, Anthony. *Rockdale: The Growth of an American Village in the Early Industrial Revolution*. Lincoln: University of Nebraska Press, 1972.

Wanamaker, John. "The John Wanamaker Commercial Institute—A Store School." *Annals of the American Academy of Political and Social Science* 33, No. 1 (1909).

Westminster Larger Catechism. Presbyterian Church in the U.S., 1861.

White, John. "Andrew Carnegie and Herbert Spencer: A Special Relationship." *Journal of American Studies* 13, No. 1 (1979).

Wilentz, Sean. *Chants Democratic: New York City and the Rise of the American Working Class 1788–1850*. New York: Oxford University Press, 2004.

Winthrop, John. "A Model of Christian Charity." In *The Puritan in America: A Narrative Anthology*, Alan Heimert and Albert Delbanco, editors. Cambridge: Harvard University Press, 1985.

Wren, Daniel. *History of Management Thought*. New York: John Wiley & Sons, 2005.

Yafa, Stephan. *Cotton: The Biography of a Revolutionary Fiber*. New York: Penguin, 2006.

Zoar: An Experiment in Communalism. Columbus: The Ohio Historical Society, 1967.

Index

Index